Determining the Antiquity of Dog Origins

Canine domestication as a model for the consilience between molecular genetics and archaeology

Michelle J. Raisor

BAR International Series 1367
2005

Published in 2016 by
BAR Publishing, Oxford

BAR International Series 1367

Determining the Antiquity of Dog Origins

© M J Raisor and the Publisher 2005

The author's moral rights under the 1988 UK Copyright,
Designs and Patents Act are hereby expressly asserted.

All rights reserved. No part of this work may be copied, reproduced, stored, sold, distributed, scanned, saved in any form of digital format or transmitted in any form digitally, without the written permission of the Publisher.

ISBN 9781841718095 paperback
ISBN 9781407327983 e-format
DOI https://doi.org/10.30861/9781841718095
A catalogue record for this book is available from the British Library

BAR Publishing is the trading name of British Archaeological Reports (Oxford) Ltd. British Archaeological Reports was first incorporated in 1974 to publish the BAR Series, International and British. In 1992 Hadrian Books Ltd became part of the BAR group. This volume was originally published by Archaeopress in conjunction with British Archaeological Reports (Oxford) Ltd / Hadrian Books Ltd, the Series principal publisher, in 2005. This present volume is published by BAR Publishing, 2016.

BAR

PUBLISHING

BAR titles are available from:
  BAR Publishing
  122 Banbury Rd, Oxford, OX2 7BP, UK
EMAIL info@barpublishing.com
PHONE +44 (0)1865 310431
FAX   +44 (0)1865 316916
  www.barpublishing.com

Table of Contents

I	INTRODUCTION	1
II	BASICS OF MOLECULAR GENETICS	4
	What is DNA?	4
	What is a gene?	4
	What is a mitochondrial DNA?	4
	Mitochondrial inheritance	8
	What is a microsatellite?	9
	Nuclear and mitochondrial size	9
	What is PCR?	9
	Development of the canine genetic map	9
	Organization of the canine genetic map	11
	Microsatellites as genetic markers	13
	Evolutionary relationships of canids	13
	Molecular evolution of canids	15
	Timing of genetic divergence	16
	Phylogenetic tree of the dog and wolf	19
	Ethiopian wolf	26
	Coyote	27
	Red wolf	28
	Jackals	30
	Variability of wild-type dog breeds	31
	Genetic variability of primitive dog breeds	32
	Australian dingo	32
	New Guinea Singing dog	33
	Carolina dogs	35
III	BEHAVIOR OF WOLVES	36
	Reproductive development	36
	Neonatal development	36
	Behavioral development	36
	Facial expressions	40
	Instinctual vs. cognitive processing	41
IV	THE ARCHAEOLOGICAL RECORD	44
	The complicated process of domestication	44
	Morphometric differences in the skeletal remains of dog and wolf	48
	The fossil record of *Canis familiaris*	55
	North America	55
	Meso America and South America	60
	Greenland	60
	Great Britain	60
	Germany	61
	France	62
	Ireland	63
	Sweden and Denmark	63
	Hungary	63
	Iraq	64
	Russia	64
	Armenia	65
	Israel	65
	Africa	66
	Egypt	66
	Kazakhstan	66
	Thailand	67
	Australia	67

	Japan..	67
	Siberia	68
	China..	69
V	DISCUSSION	70
	Problems with mtDNA inheritance..	70
	Potential limitations of DNA sequencing	73
	Some new alternative methods	74
	Limitations of current molecular studies	76
	Contributions of animal behavior studies to the understanding of dog domestication..	79
	Limitations of the archaeological record	82
VI	CONCLUSION	84
	Domestication of the Dog: An Alternative Hypothesis	84
LITERATURE CITED		90
APPENDIX		97

LIST OF FIGURES

1	Over 400 varieties exist today, ranging in size, shape and color............................	5
2	Modern breeds of dogs exhibit many differences in head shapes.	6
3	Mastiff-like breeds were depicted on Egyptian tombs, similar to the mastiff above..	7
4	Canine mitochondrion, complete genome...	8
5	Labrador retrievers have been used to study the genetic inheritance of narcolepsy.	12
6	Four phylogenetic divisions proposed by Wayne and Ostrander (1999) based upon DNA analysis.	17
7	Composite family tree of canids.	18
8	Neighboring-joining tree of wolf and dog haplotypes based on 261 bp of control region sequence.	20
9	Haplotypes found in East Asia, Europe, and Southwest Asia are indicated in separate networks with orange, blue, and green.	22
10	Siberian Husky...	23
11	Hairless breeds of dogs from top left to bottom, Chinese crested, Xoloitzcuintli (Mexican hairless), and Peruvian Inca Orchid.	24
12	Coyote (*Canis latrans*)..	27
13	Red wolf (*Canis rufus*)..	28
14	Australian dingo, *Canis lupus dingo*	32
15	Examples of primitive dogs.	34
16	Wolf pups are born blind and deaf with limited motor ability	37

17	Socialized wolves will become more bold and assertive as they become more confident with their experimenters, sometimes leading to a full blown attack.	40
18	Various behavioral tests have shown that wolves are unable to skillfully interpret human social cues, facial expressions and lack the ability to have face/eye contact with humans.	42
19	After multiple generations, tame foxes began exhibiting changes in coat texture and color such as piebald spotting.	47
20	Elements comprising the canid skull and mandible of a modern wolf, *Canis lupis*.	49
21	The skulls of a 43 kg wolf (left) and a 43 kg dog (right).	51
22	Skull and mandible of a domestic dog, *Canis familiaris*	52
23	Comparison of skulls of present-day wolf, late Paleolithic wolf, and late Paleolithic short-faced wolf.	53
24	A mitochondrial mutation may have led to selective replication of paternally derived DNA (green) in muscle	71
25	Egyptian artists often depicted dogs resembling the present day Pharaoh hound	83

LIST OF TABLES

1	Key citations in the study of canid molecular genetics from oldest to most recent.	11
2	Phylogenetic listing of Carnivora by order, superfamily, family and common name	14
3	Phylogenetic listing of Canidae by family and genus	15
4	Phylogenetic listing of Canis, consisting of 8 species	15
5	Thirteen measurements of the skull and dentition considered to be the most diagnostic	50
6	Earliest reported canid archaeological material worldwide by region.	56

Abstract

Archaeologists have favored a date of 14,000-15,000 years before present (BP) for canine domestication. However, recent studies of mutations in the mitochondrial DNA sequence by molecular geneticists have implied that dogs were domesticated over 100,000 years ago, which has challenged traditional theory. Geneticists have further hypothesized that dogs originated from wolf ancestors based upon the number of substitutions observed in dog and wolf haplotypes. Although both disciplines provide substantial evidence for their theories, the origin of dog domestication remains controversial. Several areas continue to be debatable. First, both geneticists and archaeologists incorrectly use the term domestication to describe events that clearly can not be proven to under human control. Second, the evolutionary development of canines is viewed by molecular biologists as well as archaeologist to be indicators of domestication without any further exploration of other probable causes. Third, the studies in canine genetics are so complex that most archaeologists have difficulty in providing evidence that would be contradictory to molecular theory. Fourth, both fields of study continually ignore innate behavioral characteristics of wolves that would make domestication highly improbable. Fifth, geneticists rely heavily on data gathered from sequencing of mitochondrial DNA, which has been assumed to maternally inherited. However recent human studies have shown that this assumption has now been proven to be incorrect. And finally, not only are morphological traits of fossilized dogs and wolves so similar that making a taxonomic identification improbable, but also the amount of archaeological remains available are too sparse and fragmented for accurate affiliation.

An alternate theory of canine domestication will be proposed utilizing data gathered from the archaeological record and molecular research. I hypothesize that dogs diverged naturally from wolves 100,000 years ago as a result of the natural course of evolution, not human intervention, and had already evolved into a dog prior to being domesticated by humans 14,000-15,000 years ago. Evidence will be presented to clearly show that this hypothesis is a more accurate scenario of canine domestication.

Keywords: Dog Domestication, *Canis familiaris, C. lupus,* dog behavior, wolf behavior, fossil record, molecular genetics

About the author:

Michelle Jeanette Raisor received her Bachelor of Science from Texas A&M University with a major in recreation and parks. She was awarded a Master of Arts in anthropology, also from Texas A&M University, with an emphasis on osteology and paleopathology. While attending graduate school, she worked as a research associate in molecular genetics laboratories in the Departments of Soil and Crop Science, Biochemistry, Forest Science, and Horticulture. She was also a research associate at the College of Veterinary Medicine in the Department of Pathobiology. Ms. Raisor has had a life-long passion for dogs and has trained, bred and owned numerous award-winning dogs. Her permanent address is 1604 Armistead, College Station, Texas 77840.

Introduction

The date of the earliest domestication of the dog is a topic of great interest to both archaeologists and geneticists. At present both fields of study agree that the domesticated dog (*Canis familiaris*) diverged from the ancestral wolf line (*Canis lupus*) at some point in prehistory. However, at the present time, little consensus exists as to the date of this divergence. Archaeologists and paleontologists tend to favor a Terminal Pleistocene date for the first appearance of domestic dogs in prehistory since, worldwide, the earliest candid remains found to date are from an archaeological context in Germany that dates to 14,000 years before present (BP). However, recent molecular studies mapping of the dog genome leads most geneticists to the conclusion that domestication occurred as early as 15,000 to 40,000 years ago or as late as 135,000 years ago, much older than the fossil record indicates. What can account for the magnitude of discrepancy between the archaeological and molecular evidence? Paleontologist have traditionally linked animals based upon anatomical traits and have derived evolutionary roadmaps based upon differences and similarities observed in the fossil record. As new discoveries are uncovered, the evolutionary phylogenetic tree is revised and updated. Such changes are open to human interpretation and bias, largely dependent on a common-sense approach in classifying the morphological traits. Additionally, sampling bias as well as the lack of preservation of archaeological samples further hinder interpretations.

However, molecular biologists are totally reliant upon the analysis of genes to derive such information. As gene sequencing has become more precise, geneticists have focused on mitochondrial DNA (mtDNA) rather than genomic DNA to extrapolate evolutionary antecedents of the mitochondria to a single ancestor. Mitochondrial DNA is much easier to sequence than nuclear DNA, because of the smaller portion of DNA coding for the essential function of the mitochondria. Even among some geneticists this method has come under scrutiny, with them pointing out that information derived from mtDNA studies are analyzed by computer which is fed information by human researchers who decide which information is pertinent or not.

An equally problematic issue is whether or not the early divergence as seen between wolf and dog resulted from selective breeding by man or if it was simply a result of natural selection in response to environmental influences, and if it was natural selection does this qualify as "domestication" as defined by zoologists and archaeologists. As one wildlife ecologist put it, "Everything that anyone publishes about the origin of dog is controversial because even the man on the street feels he is an expert on the dog".

In order to understand the complexities of the origin of the dog, several areas of study will be discussed in-depth.

First, critical to this discussion is a review of the basic skeletal differences that archaeologists use to differentiate wolves from dogs. Because of their similar size and body structure, archaeologists, biologists and zoologists have been able to ascertain where the canine skeletal structure shows distinct changes less resembling a wolf and more closely resembling a dog. These significant differences, especially in the crania, have been used to provide archaeological evidence of dog domestication.

Second, I will review dog fossil remains at archaeological sites worldwide. Since central to the archaeological debate is when did dogs first appear, only the oldest recorded remains will be reviewed. However, archaeological evidence of domesticated dog is quite scant beyond 10,000 yrs BP given that dogs and wolves were still morphologically similar and difficult to differentiate.

Third, issues surrounding the continuing debate of wolf behavior will also be discussed. Many archaeologists, as well as geneticists, hypothesize that early humans raised wolf puppies that were selected over time to be more docile and submissive. However many animal behaviorists expert in wolf behavior have argued that this scenario is unlikely. Since wolf domestication is pivotal to both the molecular and archaeological hypotheses of dog domestication, a lengthy discourse of wolf behavior will address the complexities of socialization, training, patterns of aggression, submission responses, physical development and tamability will be discussed.

The fourth topic to be examined concerns what is domestication and how is it identified in the fossil record. Molecular geneticists have used the term "domesticated dog" to identify the point where mutational differences in the mtDNA indicate that dogs diverged from wolves. However an important question that needs to be examined is whether or not evolutionary divergence of two species can truly be labeled as domestication or is it the result of natural selection brought about by environmental influences. Numerous species of animals such as cow, pig and sheep are known to exhibit similar morphological changes when domesticated. Some of the more obvious changes include shortening of the muzzle, crowding of teeth, reduction of canine length, smaller physical size, and deviation of wild-type color. These changes have been witnessed in dogs, as well. Many of these skeletal modifications can be seen in the fossil record and give archaeologists and approximate date of when such domestication events occur. Since molecular geneticists only focus on mutations in sequencing to determine domestication, whereas archaeologists concentrate on anatomical traits to classify a species as domesticated, conflict has arose between the two fields on which method is more accurate. However, both disciplines may be making a very broad assumption by using the term "domesticated". Domestication implies a specific intent by humans to propagate certain desirable characteristics in a species through selective breeding or culling those animals that are not as desirable. To label a mtDNA sequence or skeletal change as proof of domestication may be erroneous. Theories of domestication will be discussed as well as the association of skeletal changes diagnostic of the early process of domestication of dogs.

Finally, the basics of molecular genetics will be discussed and the scientific terminology employed in this field will be defined according to Russell (1992) Tamarin (1993) Boyer (2002). These terms will be further simplified by relating the complex terminology into terms more familiar to the non-molecular geneticists. Key studies that have utilized mitochondrial DNA sequencing, microsatellites, DNA hybridization, and blood groupings in the reconstruction of phylogenetic relationships and the measurements of variability of dogs and wild canids will be summarized and discussed.

Current molecular research has been based on comparisons between dogs, representing hundreds of purebreeds and crossbreeds, and on wolves from populations throughout North America, Europe, Asia, Africa, Japan and the Arctic. However even among geneticists there appears to be some discrepancy on the timing of the wolf-dog divergence. While Vila, Wayne and colleagues maintain an estimate of 135,000 yrs BP for divergence to occur, Savolainen and fellow researchers make a more conservative estimate of 15,000-40,000 yrs BP. This gap is the result of different researchers analyzing different phylogenetic groups within the dog sequence and estimating the amount of time for divergence to occur by examining the differences in the mtDNA genotypes. However, most geneticists seem to agree that dogs were not derived from a single source, but by at least 4-5 different founding female wolf lines. The same is true for trying to pinpoint the geographic areas where domestication/divergence occurred. Since wolves are highly mobile, the geneticists hint at multiple worldwide locations from which the dog evolved although specific locations can not be identified. Additionally, Vila and colleagues have inferred that given the broad phenotypic diversity of dogs, it has been suggested that domesticated dogs periodically mingled with wolves.

Studies in molecular research rely upon using a selected control region within the mitochondrial DNA. According to Vila et al. (1999a), this control region consisting of 261 base pairs(bp) was used for comparison in dogs, wolves, coyotes, Ethiopian wolves, and golden jackals. The dog and wolf sequence differed by 0-12 substitutions, and dogs always differed from coyotes, jackals, and Ethiopian wolves by at least 20 substitutions. Within the dog sequences it was shown that the dog sequences clustered into 4 clades. Vila et al. concluded that either wolves were domesticated in several places or that one domestication event was followed by several episodes of admixture between dogs and wolves. They concluded that dogs had a diverse origin involving more than one wolf population. When they compared the amount of substitutions possible within wolves and dogs, it was determined that the rate of substitution was identical between the two species. Therefore, according to Vila et al., the time required to obtain such diversity was estimated to be about 135,000 years, much older than indicated by the fossil record.

Archaeologists derived time lines of domestication based solely on bone evidence, at dated sites, where the canine's skeletal structure shows distinct changes less resembling wolf and more closely resembling dog. However, the molecular biologists staunchly maintain that 14,000 BP date is wrong and that the dog has a more ancient historical beginning dated at 135,000 BP (Vila et al. 1997). Their assumption is based on mitochondrial DNA analyses in which control regions are sequenced. Differences are observed and calculations are done to estimate how much time has lapsed from the date of divergence. However, the conflicting theories of canine domestication have given rise to numerous questions. Such as, why is there such a large discrepancy between the dates presented by the archaeologists and molecular geneticists? Which date is correct? Is this confusion solvable?

In reviewing both molecular and archaeological research, few studies were found which incorporated evidence from both arenas of research. The molecular biologists rely heavily on their sequencing data in order to identify the date of divergence from the wolf to the dog. This divergence is labeled as domestication without any further exploration of other probable causes. The archaeologists also do not draw from the vast amount of complicated molecular data by citing the evidence from the fossil record, which exhibits no evidence of such an ancient origin at any location worldwide.

Researchers have previously proposed two contrasting hypotheses for the date of canine domestication. On the basis of the fossil record, most archaeologists argue that canines were not incorporated into the human social structure before ca. 14,000 years ago. Recently, molecular geneticists infer a much earlier date of 100,000 to 135,000 years ago have challenged this view. Both hypotheses cannot be correct but neither can be unequivocally rejected at this time. The intent of the purposed research on the domestic dog is four fold: 1) review and analyze archaeological literature on the fossil evidence of dog domestication, 2) review and analyze current molecular literature on the genome structure of canids that relates to the origin of the dog, 3) identify and discuss various evolutionary changes in dog behavior which is unique to the domestic canine, and 4) attempt to resolve the discrepancies between the archaeological and molecular data in order to provide a tentative date for the domestication of the dog. In addition, I will propose an alternate theory of domestication that takes into account molecular genetics, behavioral studies and the archaeological record. I hypothesize that dogs diverged from wolves over 100,000 BP independently of man, as an adaptation to a changing environment. Furthermore, as these animals evolved, mutations in the mtDNA accumulated naturally without the benefit of artificial selection. I hypothesize that these genetically and morphologically different canids began to live in closer proximity to humans at around 15,000 yrs BP, as witnessed in the fossil record. However, these animals that early man domesticated were not wolves, but rather they were primitive dogs that were smaller in size and less threatening than wolves.

The strategy to be employed in this study will be to evaluate the different theories and data used in these two approaches. I will also offer a different prospective of canine evolution that provides an alternate theory in contrast to the current archaeological and molecular hypotheses. This purposed research will attempt to coalesce the archaeological evidence and the molecular theories and attempt to shed light and perhaps add a new dimension concerning the issue of the chronological origin of the domestication of the dog.

CHAPTER II

Basics of Molecular Genetics

What is DNA?

Virtually all species display a tremendous range of variation among its individuals. For example, among horses, not only is there an enormous range in size, but also color, head shape, coat length and color configuration. By informed observation, Clydesdale, Miniature horse, Arabian or Appaloosa are easily identifiable. The same is true of the domesticated dog, *Canis familiaris*. St. Bernards, Old English Sheepdogs, Irish Setters, Bulldogs, Chihuahua's and Yorkshire terriers are among the more than 400 breeds of dog found world-wide (Figs. 1, 2 and 3). Each dog breed is distinctive in its size, head shape, coat color, coat length and so on. These physical differences are the result of DNA. DNA, an organic compound, codes for the proteins that regulate the development, structure and function of an organism.

The largest amount of DNA is found within the chromosomes in the nucleus of a cell. Smaller amounts of DNA are found in the cellular organelles, called mitochondria and also encode genetic information. In the human genome, it is estimated to contain 3 billion nucleotide base pairs. The entire canine genome also contains about 3 billion base pairs. However, genome size will vary from species to species. Thus, DNA is the essential component of genetic information that is responsible for all the variation seen.

In 1953, James Watson and Francis Crick revealed the chemical and physical structure of DNA. The structure consisted of two polynucleotide chains wound together in a clockwise helix. The chains consist of a four-letter alphabet of bases, which represent adenine (A), guanine (G), thymine (T), and cytosine (C). The bases within each chain are bound together by a pentose sugar and phosphate ion, while the opposing strands are held together by weak hydrogen bonds that are relatively easy to break by heating. Each base is precisely paired with a complementary base, A-T and G-C, on the opposite strand. If, for instance one strand has the sequence of 5' – GATC - 3' the other strand will be 3' – CTAG - 5'.

What is a gene?

Within the nucleus of a cell, are sets of chromosomes inherited from the parental stock. In humans there are 46 chromosomes, 23 inherited from the mother and 23 from the father. The canine genome consists of 78 chromosomes (38 pairs from each parent plus an x and y) within the chromosome in the coiled DNA helix. On the DNA are areas called promoter regions, which are letters that signal the start of the gene. Some simple genes, such as those in *E. coli* are on the average of 1000 bases long, however the dystrophin gene, which is an essential protein of muscle, contains more than 2,300,000 bases. At the end of the gene sequence is another recognizable region that indicates that the end of the gene has been reached. In humans each set of chromosomes it is estimated to contain as few as 30,000 or as many as 100,000 genes in the 3 billion nucleotide base pairs, although the most recent research indicates that the 30,000 estimate may be more accurate. Canines, it has been theorized to have around 100,000 genes. Each gene occupies a unique position with a particular chromosome, therefore genes that are linked to particular chromosomes can be mapped and the distance between genes on a chromosome can be deduced. However given the tremendous size of the canine genome, and that sequencing can only occur in 400-700 base pair sections, the task of producing a high resolution genetic map is quite formidable.

What is mitochondrial DNA?

Within the cytoplasm of a cell are organelles, specialized structures within specific functions. One type of organelle is called mitochondria, which carry DNA molecules that encode genetic information and are the principle sources of energy in the cell. Billions of years ago, ancestors of mitochondria were probably prokaryotic organisms, a simple cell within a single copy of DNA, which probably formed a symbiotic relationship with the more complex eukaryotic cells found in animals and plants. Mitochondrial DNA is a supercoiled, circular chromosome and has the same fundamental role in all eukaryotes. In humans, the mitochondria chromosomes consist of 16,569 base pairs, whereas canines have 16,727 base pairs (Fig. 4). Interestingly plants can have considerably more. For example, corn has a mitochondrial genome size of 600,000 base pairs. Although the size of the mitochondrial genome can vary wildly between species, it remains constant within a species. Mitochondrial chromosomes can also be referred to as non-Mendelian genes, extranuclear genes, organelle genes or extra chromosomal genes.

Mitochondria have multiple copies of the DNA molecule and each cell can have several hundred mitochondria within it. Since mitochondria encoded proteins essential for cellular respiration, any deletions or mutations in the base pairs can cause degenerative conditions in those tissues with high physiological demands (Williams 2002: 610). Ischemic heart disease, and neurological disease such as Parkinson's, can accelerate the rate at which variant forms of mtDNA are generated in tissues (Williams 2002: 610).

Fig. 1. Over 400 varieties of dogs exist today, ranging in size, shape and color. From top left to right, Norwich terriers, wheaten colored Scottish terrier, Otterhounds, English setters, parti-colored Cocker spaniel, Blenham spaniel (photos M. Raisor).

Fig. 2. Modern breeds of dogs exhibit many differences in head shapes. From top left to right, Basset hounds wearing protective ear snoods, rough-coated Collie, Bull terrier and Boxers (photos M. Raisor).

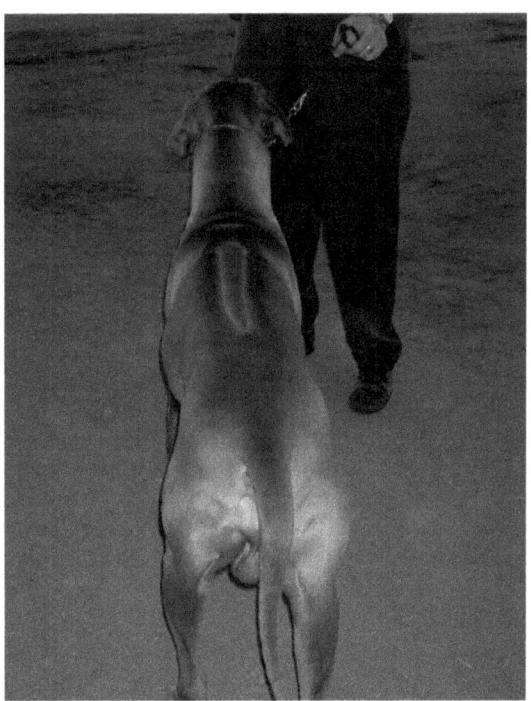

Fig. 3. Mastiff-like breeds were depicted on Egyptian tombs, similar to the mastiff above (top). Rhodesian Ridgeback with its unique hair pattern was bred to hunt lions (bottom) (photos M. Raisor).

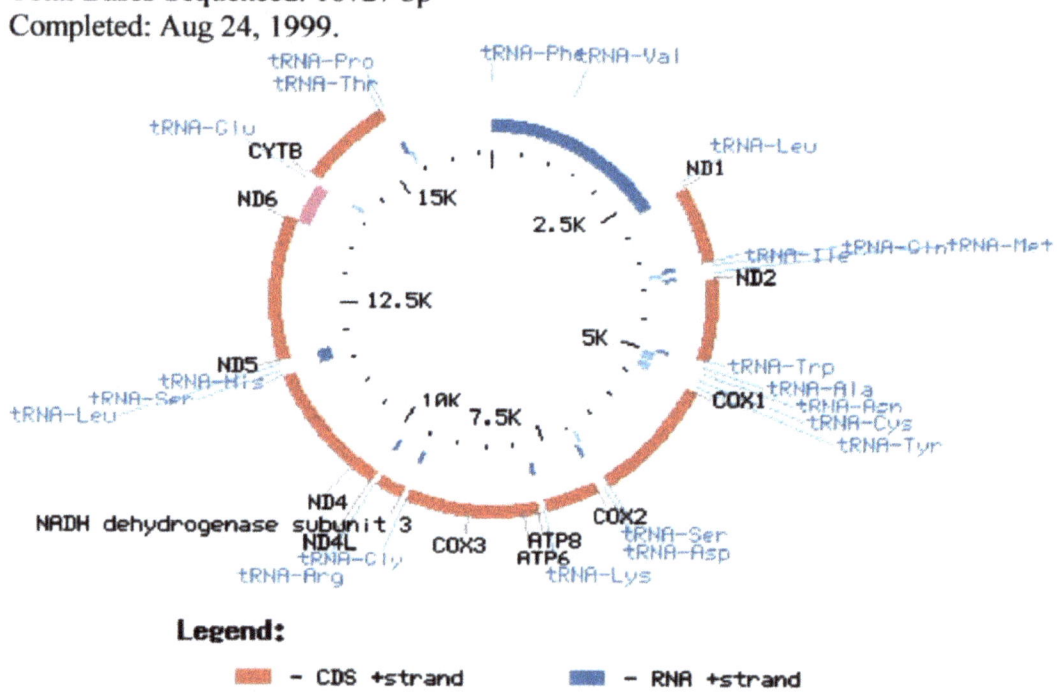

Fig. 4. Canine mitochondrion, complete genome (http://www.ncbi.nlm.ni.gov).

Mitochondrial inheritance

Mitochondria are located in the maternal cytoplasm of the oocyte (egg) and sperm. However, sperm mitochondria disappear in early embryogenesis by selective destruction, inactivation or simple dilution by the vast surplus of oocyte mitochondria (Cummings et al. 1997:213; Schwartz and Vissing 2002:576). Any mitochondria that are abundant in the tail structures are believed to be incapable of gaining access to the interior of the oocyte (Williams 2002: 610). Replication, transcription and translation of the mitochondrial genes occur within the matrix with assistance of enzymes produced by the nuclear genes that have been imported in by the mitochondria (Clayton 2000: 11).

It has long been believed that mitochondria are transmitted from generation to generation only through the cytoplasm of the egg with no contribution from paternal inheritance, although recently that theory has come into question (Schwartz and Vissing 2002: 579). Therefore, the maternal line plays an important role in the transmission of genetic information, unlike the Mendelian model of inheritance which derives its genetic information from the chromosomes in the nucleus that is contributed from both the paternal and maternal ancestry. In mammals, any disorder in the mitochondrial sequence is passed on from the mother to the offspring, with both sexes being affected with only the females transmitting the defect. Regardless of the size of the defect, a single base pair or a large-scale deletion, the mutation can proliferate with time and outnumber wild-type mtDNA (Schwartz and Vissing 2002: 578). Knowledge of the mammalian mitochondrial DNA model of inheritance has become a fundamental biological principle of the molecular theory of evolution.

What is a microsatellite?

Microsatellites, also known as genetic markers have been crucial in mapping the canine genome. Located on the chromosomes are short base pair sequences repeated dozens or hundreds of times. These short repeats, composed of 1-6 bases, are present at hundred of sites throughout the canine genome. Frequently these markers are linked to a gene coding for a disease and can be used to determine where a disease is most likely to be expressed. If the marker is extremely close to a disease, the microsatellites may be inherited along with the defective sequence. Microsatellites have also been used to identify differences in the mitochondrial genome to make evolutionary assumptions about the divergence and domestication of the wolf and dog.

Nuclear and mitochondrial size

The size of the DNA found within the nucleus (nuclear DNA) is variable depending on the complexity of the species. Algae, an extremely simple organism, has a genome size of 660,000 (6.6×10^5) base pairs, whereas yeast, a slightly more complex organism contains 13,000,000 (1.2×10^7) base pairs. Birds have a genome size of 1.2×10^9, however mammals, the most complex have a genome size of over 3 billion base pairs.

With the larger genome size, there is also an increase in the number of genes expressed. Many genomes of different species have been sequenced and it has provided insight as to how much of the DNA codes for specific genes and what percentage codes for other functions such as metabolism, cell structure or cell transport of components. For instance *E. coli, which* has a genome size of 4.6×10^6, has 4,288 genes, with each gene having approximately 950 bp and having a separation of 118 bp between each gene. In humans, and probably other mammals, it has been estimated that the genome codes for 30,000 to 100,000 genes. Because of the large number of genes it is theorized that there could be substantial overlap with possibly three to four genes for every function.

Mitochondrial size in mammal genomes is significantly smaller and more compact than nuclear genomes with size usually falling within the range of 16,5000 base pairs in mammals. A major portion of the mitochondrion is delegated for respiration. The relatively low gene content of mtDNA compared with the nuclear genomes appears to imply a relatively rapid and extensive loss or transfer of genetic information at an early stage in evolution (Gray et al. 1999: 1479). As additional complete mitochondrial genome sequences have appeared, it has also been evident that elimination of genes from mtDNA is not only an ongoing evolutionary process but that certain genes have been lost on more than one occasion (Gray et al. 1999: 1479).

What is PCR?

In 1985 a new technique was developed that accelerated the field of molecular biology (Mullis 1990). Polymerase chain reaction (PCR) has become the cornerstone of genetic analyses because of its ability to rapidly produce large amounts of DNA both selectively and repeatedly. PCR uses single stranded DNA as a template and synthesizes a complementary strand over and over again, until extensive quantities are produced. This technique is first done by taking 'double' stranded DNA and uncoiling the strands by heating at a temperature of 94°C. This is followed by the addition of primers consisting of short nucleotide sequences of 20-30 bp and annealing (combining) the primers to complementary regions on the single-stranded DNA. In the third step, the enzyme DNA polymerase called Taq, begins at the primer and synthesizes a DNA strand complementary to the primer. These three steps (known as cycles) are repeated over and over by heating and cooling until multiple copies of the DNA is produced. The amount of DNA increases geometrically with each cycle at the rate of 2n with n being the number of cycles. For example, one molecule of DNA after one cycle produces 2 molecules of DNA. If a sample is amplified with 20 cycles, 1,048,576 copies will be produced. Each cycle is extremely rapid, lasting only a few minutes. The use of a thermal cycler expedites the efficiency and specificity of the amplified reaction.

PCR has been used extensively for clinical diagnosis and forensic application. The advantage of using PCR is that the DNA does not have to be in large amounts or even purified to be amplified. It has also been successfully used to amplify ancient DNA (Hofreiter et al. 2001). DNA sequences have been reproduced from mummies to determine kinship, mastodons, insects in amber and fossils. Evolutionary relationships are hypothesized by comparing sequences of amplified ancient DNA to modern samples to examine how changes have evolved over time.

Development of the canine genetic map

Mapping of the canine genome was initially developed as an aid in identifying genetic disorders in humans. Dogs were considered to be an excellent experimental model since half of all described canine diseases resemble specific human pathological conditions (Ostrander and Kruglyak 2000: 1271; Patterson 2000:1). This is especially true of cancer. For example, it has been reported that dogs develop cancer twice as frequently as humans, and the presentation, histology and biology of several canine cancers closely parallel those of human cancers (MacEwer 1990: 125; Ostrander and Kruglyak 2000: 1272; Withrow and MacEwer 1989). Using canines as a molecular model for humans has numerous advantages from a research approach. Unlike mouse models, which often require that certain disorders to be induced, such as an exposure to a carcinogen, many disorders in canines are naturally occurring. Diseases that are hypothesized to be appropriate models for human disease includes osteosarcomas, mammary carcinoma, oral melanoma, lung carcinomas, and malignant non-Hodgkin's lymphoma (MacEwer 1990: 125). Second, with the purebred dog population consisting of >300 partially inbred genetic isolates called breeds, the gene flow between breeds is restricted (Ostrander and Kruglyak 2000: 1271). This has resulted in specific breeds having a high susceptibility to distinct diseases, which strongly suggests that these breeds have a greater number of risk alleles (Ostrander and Kruglyak 2000: 1271). Thirdly, breeders of purebred dogs keep meticulous pedigrees of their dogs. In trying to map inheritance of disease in a human it is necessary to construct a genealogical record, which is sometimes quite difficult to do. However in purebred canines, this is routinely done and therefore patterns of inheritance are easier to establish. Fourth, breeders often inbreed in order to select for certain desirable characteristics. This artificial section has a profound impact on how much genetic variation for a particular trait will exist. A decrease in heterogeneity increases the possibility of recessive inherited disease to be expressed. This makes mapping of the canine genome more ideal than selection of a genetically isolated population of humans. Fifth, as a result of "popular sire" effect and many breeds having been propagated from small founding populations, an artificially induced bottleneck effect in many breeds of purebred dogs has been produced. Bottlenecks occur when a population has been drastically reduced in size, such as by a natural disaster or by intentional manipulation. During this reduction, genes that would have normally contributed to the gene pool are lost, and allele frequencies are altered. In humans, there are few cases were a population has undergone inbreeding and long-term isolation and therefore gene frequencies are widely variant. In contrast dogs offer a preferable research model without having to pool information from a large sample size. Finally, dogs are a companion animal whose has monitoring of their health is monitored on a daily basis, similar to humans. Everything from diet, exercise, vaccinations and overall physical condition are detailed not only by their caregivers but more importantly by veterinary professionals using the same laboratory and medical differential approaches that are used on humans. This increases the possibility that genes of interest for human medicine might be most quickly identified by mapping the corresponding illness in dogs.

The completion of the sequencing of the canine genome has provided an excellent resource to expedite the study of inherited diseases (Table 1). To date, the most extensively studied diseases are either homologs of human conditions or diseases that are widespread and threatening within a particular breed (Ostrander and Kruglyak 2000:1272). For example, achromatopsia, a severe congenital deficiency in color perception often associated with reduced visual acuity, and x-linked inherited retinal degeneration, the dog is the only known animal counterpart of the human disorder (Aguirre, Ray and Acland 1999: 1). In 1997 an International Workshop on Canine Genetics, reported that studies of the canine chromosome 9 will be pivotal in understanding the inherited susceptibility of breast cancer and retinal photoreceptor dysfunction and disease. Other diseases such as hemophilia B (Christmas disease), proteolipid protein deficiency, muscular dystrophy, retinitis pigmentosa and liptocytosis are homologous in both humans and canines (Aguirre et al. 1999: 1). The study of canine narcolepsy, and autosomal recessive trait with full penetrance in Doberman pinschers and Labrador retrievers (Fig. 5), has given researchers insight as to how to approach the study of the molecular inheritance of human narcolepsy (Lin et al. 1999; Mellersh et al. 1998; Ostrander and Kruglyak 2000; Ostrander et al. 2000). A severe x-linked immunodeficiency syndrome in dogs called X-SCID, which is associated with recurrent bacterial, fungal, protozoal, and viral infections caused by severe depressed cellular immunity, has been shown to be caused by the same gene that produces a human form of SCID (Jezyk et al. 1989).

Mapping of the canine genome has not only been beneficial in identifying human disease, but has also helped pinpoint a multitude of canine-specific genetic markers and modes of inheritance of disease, some which are breed specific. Gergits and Casna (1998) using a multi-locus DNA probe have been able to prove the presence of genetic markers unique to specific breeds, indicating that there is genetically identifiable differences which influence the diversity between breeds of dogs. Lingaas and colleagues (1998: 36) studying the level of genetics of inter-breed polymorphism, have been able to determine the amount of interbreeding and genetic drift of several wild and domesticated breeds that are endangered. Whereas, Sutton (Sutton et al. 1998: 37) has reported that it is possible to efficiently resolve parentage in dogs by using both DNA fingerprinting and microsatellite analyses.

However, a more important application of the mapping of the canine genome has been the identification of genes related to numerous genetically inherited diseases affecting various dog breeds. The problem of disease heterogeneity, which often confounds human linkage studies, may be avoided in dogs, because breeding practices often ensure that a small number of genes, or even a single gene, will underlie a given disease in a specific breed (Wayne and Ostrander 1999: 253). More than 300 medical genetic disorders have been described in domestic dogs, constituting the largest known number of naturally occurring genetic disorders in any nonhuman species (Gorden et al. 2003: 5; Patterson 2000, 2001). Copper toxicoses, a fatal autosomal recessive disorder that causes progressive hepatic disease from the accumulation of copper in the liver, is very prevalent in Bedlington Terriers. For many years it was thought to be similar to Wilson's disease seen in humans. Mapping of this disorder in humans revealed its location to chromosome 13 q, however this was not proven to be true in canines. Yuzbasiyan et al. (1997) although unable to identify the gene, were able to identify a closely positioned marker which is suitable for diagnostic use.

Several other genes have been targeted that are linked to canine disease. Of particular interest has been identifying the gene that causes progressive retinal atrophy (PRA), a male specific inherited eye disease similar to retinitis pigmentosum in humans (Petersen-Jones et al. 1994; Acland et al. 1994). Additionally, canine thyroid cancers have been linked to somatic mutations in P53 (Deville et al. 1994). There also appears to be a correlation between the human TNF-alpha cDNA and the canine TNF-alpha gene which causes hemophilia B (Evans et al. 1989). Other canine diseases which are showing promises in being pinpointed on the genetic map are BRCA1, possibly related to mammary tumors, Collie eye anomaly, melanoma, epilepsy, hip dysplasia, diabetes, renal cystadenocarcinoma, blindness and deafness (Gordon et al. 2003: 2).

Organization of the canine genetic map

Dogs have a high karyotype number in comparison to humans (2n=78 vs. 2n=23). Of the 78 chromosomes in dogs, two of these chromosomes (X and Y) are involved in the process of sex determination and are known as sex chromosomes. The remaining 76 chromosomes (38 pairs) are known as autosomes. Microscopic examination and arrangement of the chromosome pairs according to size and location of the centromere is known as a karyotype construction. Staining of the chromosomes reveals the presence of light and dark bands. The staining can be accomplished by several different methods, with thirty-two canine specific paints having been developed (Langford et al. 1998: 38). Staining produces distinctive banding patterns unique to each chromosome. The arms of the chromosome are further delineated by designation of the short arm as the p arm, with the longer arm labeled as the q arm. Each arm is divided into smaller numbered regions and each band within the region also represented by a number. For example 12p3.4 is a descriptive address where 12 is the chromosome number, p is the arm, 3 is the region, and 4 is the band number. The chromosomes can range in size from 137 Mb (X chromosome) to 27 Mb (Y chromosome) (Breen 1998: 37).

According to Lewin (2000), mapping of genes can be done with several approaches. Lewin states that one technique, a genetic (or linkage) map is constructed by identifying the distance between mutations in terms of recombination frequencies. A second method involves construction of a linkage map by measuring the amount of recombination between sites in genomic DNA. These sites have sequence variations that generate differences in the susceptibility to cleavage (cutting) by restriction enzymes and map

TABLE 1. Key citations in the study of canid molecular genetics from oldest to most recent.

YEAR	RESEARCH TOPIC	CITATION
1976	Blood Proteins/ Domestic Dog/ Canidae	Simonsen
1977	Genetic differentiation of dingo and domestic dog	Cole et al.
1990	Allozyme differences of Black-backed Jackal	Wayne et al.
1991	Red Wolf and Hybridization	Wayne and Jenks
1991	Blood Polymorphisms in Asian dog breeds	Tanabe
1992	Gray Wolf mitochondrial variability	Wayne et al.
1992	Red Wolf and hybridization	Nowak
1993	Molecular evolution of Canidae	Wayne
1994	Molecular genetics of museum specimens/ Ethiopian wolves/ Red wolf	Roy et al.
1994	Molecular genetics of Ethiopian Wolf	Gottlelli et al.
1995	Molecular genetics of Red Wolf	Wayne and Gittleman
1995	Evolution of Dingo	Corbett
1996	Molecular origins of Japanese dog breeds	Okumura et al.
1996	Molecular taxonomy of Red Wolf and endangered Carnivores	Brownlow
1997	Molecular genetics and origins of domestic dog	Vila et al.
1997	Polymorphisms in the Asiatic domestic dog/ Grey Wolf	Tsuda et al.
1997	Microsatellites between dog breeds	Zajc et al.

YEAR	RESEARCH TOPIC	CITATION
1999	Hybridization between Grey Wolf and dog	Vila et al.
1999	Domestic dog and genetic diversity	Vila et al.
1999	Genome structure of domestic dog	Wayne and Ostrander
1999	Mitochondrial Evolution	Gray et al.
1999	Red Wolf and Hybridization	Reich et al.
1999	Microsatellites and Dingo	Wilton et al.
1999	Origin of primitive dogs: Carolina Dogs and NGSD	Brisban and Glenn
2000	Canine genetics	Ostrander er al.
2000	DNA profile of Canadian Wolf/ Red Wolf/ Coyote	Wilson et al.
2001	Molecular genetics of Scandinavian Wolves	Sundqvist et al.
2001	Genetic variability of African wild dog	Girman et al.
2001	Mammalian evolution	Killian et al.
2002	Molecular genetics and origin of domestic dog	Savolainen et al.
2002	Molecular genetics and origin of New World dogs	Leonard et al.
2002	MHC class genes in dogs and European Wolves	Sheddon and Ellegren
2002	Canine linkage analysis	Gordon et al.
2002	Paternal inheritance of mtDNA	Schwartz and Vissing
2002	Paternal inheritance mtDNA	Williams
2004	Genetic relationship between purebred dog breeds to assign classification	Parker et al.

Fig. 5. Labrador retrievers have been used to study the genetic inheritance of narcolepsy (www.my.netian.com).

construction can be accomplished irrespective of the occurrence of mutants. In a third approach, a restriction map is constructed by cleaving DNA into fragments with restriction enzymes and measuring the distances between the sites of cleavage. This type of map represents distances in terms of the length of DNA, and aids in construction of providing a physical map of the genetic material. However a restriction map does not identify sites of genetic interest but it can detect large changes in the genome that can be recognized because they affect the sizes of even numbers of restriction fragments. A fourth research design and the most informative, is to determine the sequence of the DNA. From the sequence, genes are identified and the distance between them measured. Analysis of the protein coding potential of the DNA sequence will determine whether or not the sequences represent proteins. The basic assumption is that sequences coding for proteins will be least likely to have mutations. Therefore by comparing the sequence of a wild-type DNA with that of a mutant allele, it can be determined the exact site of where a mutation has occurred.

The most important key to constructing a restriction map of a genome is the selection of restriction enzymes which are designed to recognize specific sequences of base pairs and cut the DNA at those targeted sites. The fragments can be visualized and further separated by gel electrophoresis. Bands seen on the gel can be measured in kb (kilobase = 10³ bp) or in Mb (megabase pair = 10⁶ bp). Usually it is necessary to use several different types of enzymes, such as EcoR1, HindIII or BamH1, to accurately get a series of overlapping fragments in order that a continuous map can be constructed. The DNA fragments on the gel are transferred to nitrocellulose paper by a technique known as a Southern blot. The nitrocellular paper is treated with a radioactive probe which binds to any complementary DNA fragment. The gel is exposed to X-ray film where distances of the bands can be measured and a restriction map can be constructed.

Microsatellites as genetic markers

Microsatellites have quickly become the standard for usage as a genetic marker in DNA fingerprinting. They consist of short segments of DNA that are composed of 1-6 bases. They are not to be confused with minisatellites which are repeated sequences units ranging from 11 to 60 bp in size (Gupta et al. 1996: 45). Microsatellite bases can be repeated up to around 60 times but typically 5-30. Microsatellites are more randomly and evenly dispersed within the genome than minisatellites (Webber 1990: 388). The short DNA segments are made up of mono, di, tri or tetranucleotides (Mellersh and Ostrander 1997: 199; Stallings et al. 1991: 807; Tautz and Renz 1984: 4127). At each area where a gene occurs in the chromosome (locus), the pattern of repeats can vary. Because of the variation, the banding pattern seen is unique to each individual making them the preferred marker for genetic mapping. This pattern of polymorphic bands is called DNA fingerprinting.

Microsatellites are important for map building since the distribution of this sequence repeats within the genome is random (Mellersh and Ostrander 1997:199) and act as landmarks for the organization of the DNA. For example, both humans and dogs have a dinucleotide repeat (CA) on the average every 30-60 kilobase (kb) (Stallings et al. 1991:807).

Why microsatellites form in the DNA is unknown. However, two theories do exist. One theory is that microsatellites occur during meiosis because of unequal crossing-over. Another theory proposes that it is caused by strand-slippage that probably occurs during lagging strand synthesis. This theory seems to have the most merit among molecular geneticists.

At present, over 400 canine-specific microsatellite based markers have been identified (Mellersh et al. 1998: 38). The markers have been determined through linkage analysis using reference families composed of 26 three-generation pedigrees from 351 individuals (Mellersh et al. 1998: 38). According to the researchers, these markers display a pattern of tetra-nucleotide (4) repeats, which appear to be more specific to purebred dogs than repeats consisting of two nucleotides. Identification of these markers will be pivotal in highlighting those genes that contribute to our disease.

Evolutionary relationships of canids

Prior to the advances in molecular genetics, evolutionary relationships of canids were determined through comparative studies of fossils and extinct species of canids, much of the fossil mammal taxonomy relied upon features of the dentition (Olsen 1985: 2). The earliest fossil carnivores originated 40-60 million years ago (Olsen 1985: 2; Vila et al. 1999a: 72; Wayne 1993: 218). The earliest forms of canids, the now extinct Miacids, were long bodied quadrapedal carnivores with relatively short legs (Vesey-Fitzgerald 1957: 1-2). The oldest known Miacid skeleton, from the early Eocene of Wyoming, indicated that it was an arboreal animal that weighed about 1.3 kg (Nowak 1999: 634). Shortly after the first mammalian carnivores evolved, they differentiated into many distinct families including the cat, hyena, mongoose, bear, raccoon, otter, skunk, seal, fox, wolf and dog families (Wayne 1993: 219, Wayne and Ostrander 1999: 247-248).

Within the order Carnivora are two basic groups, the cat-like carnivores (superfamily Feloidea) and those carnivores more closely aligned with canids (superfamily Canoidea) (Tables 2, 3 and 4). Within Canoidea there are four families: Canidae, Ursidae, Procyonidae, and Mustelidae. The family Canidae is composed of dogs, wolves, coyotes, jackals, and foxes. Ursidae represents bears, with Procyonidae composed of raccoons, coatis and other raccoon relatives. Weasels, badgers, skunks, and otters designate Mustelidae. Carnivores are characterized by unique physical characteristics such as having four to five toes on each limb, open-and-shut (not side-to-side) jaw articulation, a rooted number of teeth, and highly developed carnassials specialized for crushing/shearing. Male carnivores typically have a baculum. Females exhibit a variable number of mammae on the abdomen, and the pectoral region (Nowak 1999: 632). Most carnivores can swim with some species such as the polar bear and otter, being semiaquatic (Nowak 1999: 632).

Within the family Canidae, 16 genera comprising 36 species are distributed throughout the world except the West Indies, Madagascar, Taiwan, the Philippines, Borneo, and the islands of New Guinea, Australia, New Zealand, Antarctica, and most oceanic islands (Nowak 1999: 634). The smallest species of Canidae is *Fennus zerda*, with the largest being *Canis lupus*. Canids have exceptional senses of smell, sight and hearing that heightens their ability in the pursuit of prey. Most canids have four digits on their rear feet and five on the front, except for the African wild dog which has only four on the front and back. They walk, trot tirelessly, amble, canter or gallop at full speed on their digits or partly on more of the foot (Nowak 1999: 635). Except for *Canis familiaris*, females and males reach sexual maturity after 1-2 years of age, with females generally giving birth once per year.

Four species of canids have common names containing the designation of "dog" which often results in confusion of these taxon with domesticated dogs. However these species, the raccoon dog (*Nyctereutes*), small-eared dog (*Atelocynus*), bush dog (*Speothos*) and African wild dog (*Lycaon*) are separate distinct species and not related to *Canis familiaris*. For instance, the African wild dog (*Lycaon pictus*) also called the African hunting dog, is neither a dog nor a wolf although its scientific name means painted wolf. It is a unique species of Canidae, with a social organization, dominance hierarchy, care of offspring, and hunting behavior closely mimicking wolves. African wild dogs have a general canid body shape, with modifications accumulated over 3 million years of divergence from the rest of the dog family, such as the absence of the fifth toe called a dewclaw (Creel and Creel 2002: 1). Although it was once thought to be related the hyena, karotyping has revealed that it has the same number of chromosomes as the domestic dog. They are 65-75 cm in height and weigh from 17-36 kg. Their coloring is very unusual and is a mottled brown, black, yellow and white color that occurs in almost every conceivable arrangement and proportion (Nowak 1999: 676). Reproductively the African wild dog has a longer gestational period consisting of 79-80 days than is typical of dogs that have a gestational period of 61-64 days (Nowak 1999). They are extremely fast moving animals that have been known to approach speeds up to 66 km/hr for 10-60 minutes. *Lycaon* hunt cooperatively in groups when pursuing large game such as gazelle, impala, wildebeest, and zebra.

Reproductively, only the highest ranking male and female African wild dog breed. Pups are fed by adult members by regurgitation and are given first priority to kills once they are eating solid food. By the time they are 9-11 months old, they are able to kill prey on their own. At 1-2 years of age, both males and females disperse from their natal packs, eventually joining with groups of the opposite sex (Nowak 1999: 676).

Creel and Creel (2002: 4) report that molecular studies have revealed that based on a 736 base pair sequence, African wild dogs are phylogenetically distinct from other wolf-like canids (wolf, coyote, jackal), which justifies their current placement in a monotypic genus. They state that wild dogs showed an 11.3-13.7% sequence divergence from the other species, and the single most parsimonious phylogenetic tree placed the divergence of the wild dog just basal to the radiation of the *Canis* clade. It was further noted that the 1% difference within the species indicates that two geographically isolated subspecies probably occupied Africa.

Lycaon is classified as an endangered species due to being indiscriminately hunted and poisoned. In addition, the decline of the African wild dog has also been attributed to recurrent outbreaks of viral disease. At present there are efforts to draw attention to the conservation of these animals. In Botswana, Kenya, South Africa, Tanzania, Zambia, and Zimbabwe where the African wild dog is protected, population numbers have significantly increased. However persecution of these animals continues to further reduce the population in those areas where humans have expanded into the wild dog habitats, making their future uncertain.

TABLE 2. Phylogenetic listing of Carnivora by order, superfamily, family and common name (Nowak 1999). Carnivora is composed of dogs, bears, raccoons, weasels, mongooses, hyenas, and cats. It consists of 7 families, 92 genera and 240 species.

Superfamily	Family	Common Name
Canoidea	Canidae	Dogs, Wolves, Coyotes, Jackals, and Foxes
	Ursidae	Bears
	Procyonidae	Raccoons and Relatives
	Mustelidae	Weasels, Badgers, Skunks, and Otters

TABLE 3. Phylogenetic listing of Canidae by family and genus (Nowak 1999). (**) Denotes common names that are labeled as dog although they have no relationship to domesticated dog. The use of "dog" as a part of the common name often results in confusion of these taxon with domesticated dogs. Canidae is represented by 16 genera and 36 species.

Family	Genus	Common Name
Canidae	Vulpes	Foxes
	Fennecus	Fennec Fox
	Urocyon	Gray Foxes
	Alopex	Arctic Fox
	Lycalopex	Hoary Fox
	Pseudalopex	South American Foxes
	Dusicyon	Falkland Island Fox
	Cerdocyon	Crab-eating Fox
	Nyctereutes	Raccoon Dog**
	Atelocynus	Small-eared Dog**
	Speothos	Bush Dog**
	Canis	Dogs, Wolves, Coyotes and Jackals
	Chrysocyon	Maned Wolf
	Otocyon	Bat-eared Fox
	Cuon	Dhole
	Lycaon	African Wild Dog (also known as African Hunting Dog)**

TABLE 4. Phylogenetic listing of Canis, consisting of 8 species (Nowak 1999).

Genus and Species	Common Name	Distribution
Canis simensis	Simien Jackal	Mountains of central Ethiopia.
Canis adustus	Side-striped Jackal	Open country from Senegal to Somalia, and south to northern Namibia and eastern South Africa.
Canis mesomelas	Black-backed Jackal	Open country from Sudan to South Africa.
Canis aureus	Golden Jackal	Balkan Peninsula to Thailand, Sri Lanka, Morocco to Egypt and northern Tanzania.
Canis latrans	Coyote	Alaska to Nova Scotia and Panama.
Canis lupus	Gray Wolf	Eurasia except tropical forests of southeastern corner, Egypt, Libya, Alaska, Canada, Greenland, conterminous United States except southeastern quarter and most of California, highlands of Mexico.
Canis rufus	Red Wolf	Central Texas to southern Pennsylvania and Florida.
Canis familiaris	Domestic Dog	Worldwide distribution with feral populations in New Guinea and Australia.

Molecular evolution of canids

The Canidae are the most phylogenetically distinct with the canine karotype exhibiting little similarity to the other 35 extant species in the carnivore family (Wayne and Ostrander 1999: 248). Although there have been attempts to domesticate other species within the Canidae family, only *Canis familiaris* has been fully domesticated (Clutton-Brock 1995: 8). Consequently, understanding the genetic diversity, which distinguishes dogs from other species of carnivores, has been instrumental in constructing an evolutionary model.

However, Wayne and Ostrander (1999: 248) have proposed four different phylogenetic divisions within the Canidae family based upon DNA analysis that differs from the traditional phylogenetic classifications (Figs. 6 and 7). They propose: 1) red fox-like canids, including red, kit, and Arctic foxes with a chromosomal diploid number of 36-64; 2) the South American foxes with a chromosomal diploid number of 74; 3) wolf-like canids, which includes the domestic dog, gray wolf, coyote and jackals with a chromosomal diploid number of 78, and 4) a monotypic genera based upon a more primitive chromosome complement, with a separate, ancient evolutionary history that includes the gray fox (chromosomal number of 66), raccoon dog (chromosomal number of 42+), and bat-eared fox (chromosomal number of 72). Wayne and Ostrander (1999: 248) speculate that this radiation occurred about 12-15 million years ago.

Wayne et al. (1989) and Vila et al. (1999a) have been able to distinguish through DNA hybridization that Carnivora are divided into two superfamilies, Canoidea and Feloidea. Wayne (1993: 219; Wayne et al. 1987; Wayne et al. 1997) was able to determine patterns of Canidae evolution by the use of electrophoresis to study allozyme variants and by comparison of G-banded chromosomes. Wayne asserts that comparative analysis of chromosomes has been the most informative since canids have a broad diversity in chromosomal morphology and number, ranging from the red fox which has a low diploid chromosome number of 36, to the gray wolf and dog which have a high diploid number of 78. However, Wayne states the differences seen in the allele frequencies for a large number of loci has been used to calculate the genetic distance between pairs of species with the genetic distance being used to discern clusters of species. All *Canis* species have identical chromosome number (Vila et al. 1999a: 73; Wayne et al. 1987: 123; Wayne 1993: 219). Additionally, all species in the genus Canis are known to hybridize (Gray 1954). By reconstructing and comparing DNA sequences, Vila et al. (1999a: 72) concluded that the gray wolf (*C. lupus*), coyote (*C. latrans*), and Ethiopian wolf (*C. simensis*) and dog (*C. familiaris*) form a monophyletic group. Based on taxonomic studies, it has been suggested that the dog was probably a descendent of the gray wolf and the golden jackal, with each wild species giving rise to different breeds of dogs (Coppinger and Schneider 1995: 32; Vila et al. 1999a: 73). However, recent genetic analysis of limited mtDNA restriction fragments of various dog breeds and numerous gray wolf populations from different locations around the world has shown that the mtDNA genotypes of dogs and wolves are either identical or differ by the loss or gain of only one or two restriction sites (Ostrander et al. 2000: 117; Pennisi 2002: 1541; Tsuda et al. 1997: 230; Vila et al. 1997: 1687; 1999a: 73; Wayne 1993: 220). There was no indication that dogs were descended from jackals or coyotes. Wayne (1993: 220) also states that the domestic dog is the closest relative of the gray wolf, differing at most by 0.2% of the mtDNA sequence. Vila et al. (1999a: 71) confirms this interpretation by further adding that dog and wolf sequences differed by 0-12 substitutions, while dogs, coyotes, Ethiopian wolves and jackals differed by at least 20 substitutions. The coyote, the closest wild relative of the wolf, differs by 0.2- 1.5% of the mtDNA sequence to the wolf and by 7.5% difference when compared to dogs (Wayne 1993: 220; Wayne and Ostrander 1997: 249). Tsuda and colleagues (1997: 232, 236) found evidence that repetitive sequences appeared in the identical positions near the 3' end of the mtDNA D-loop region among dogs, wolves, foxes, and raccoon dog. These types of repetitive sequences are not unusual in mammals, according to Tsuda, although the types of sequences seen in the repeat units are species specific. In Tsuda's examination of the D-loop region, it was found that only one exception occurred between dogs and wolves. Therefore it was concluded that dogs and wolves were members of the same species.

One important note to remember is that mitochondrial DNA is inherited through the maternal line. Therefore matings between male jackals or coyotes and female dogs would not be detected in the mitochondrial haplotype. It is also especially pertinent to remember that all members of the Canis family can interbreed and produce hybrids. However, given new understanding of molecular genetics, these sporadic matings didn't contribute to the mtDNA sequence and doesn't change the extensive data supporting a wolf ancestry to the dog.

Timing of genetic divergence

Estimating evolutionary divergence by geneticists has been based on changes in the mitochondrial DNA. Since inheritance in the mitochondria is primarily uniparental, there is no recombination of genetic material between the paternal and maternal lines, unlike inheritance which occurs inside the nucleus. Observation of the mitochondria has revealed to researchers that mutations accumulate more rapidly than in nuclear DNA. Additionally it is more sensitive to size reductions in a breeding population. These factors make mtDNA an extremely useful instrument for explaining evolutionary events in matriarchal lineages. In domesticated animals the mtDNA polymorphisms can be used to determine which wild species was the matriarchal ancestor of a domesticated animal (Tsuda et al. 1997: 230).

According to Brown et al. (1979: 1967) and Tsuda et al. (1997: 236) mutations among mammalian mitochondrial DNA accumulates at a rate of 2-4% per million years. If for instance, there was a difference of 0.57% in mitochondrial DNA between an ancient ancestor and modern population, it is possible to determine that divergence occurred over an evolutionary period of 142,500-285,000 years.

Tsuda et al. (1997: 236) further tested the rate of divergence theory by analyzing the mtDNA D-loop region in domestic dogs, wolves, foxes and a raccoon dog. It was discovered that the average divergence values of dogs and wolves when compared to foxes was 19.71%, between foxes and the raccoon dog it was 20.28%, and between the dog and wolf versus the raccoon dog was 21.01%. Tsuda concluded that based upon the rate of divergence of 2-4% per millions years, the divergence of the 3 genera occurred around 5-10 million years. This falls nicely within the predicted range of the fossil record, which has estimated the division of canines between 7-10 million years ago.

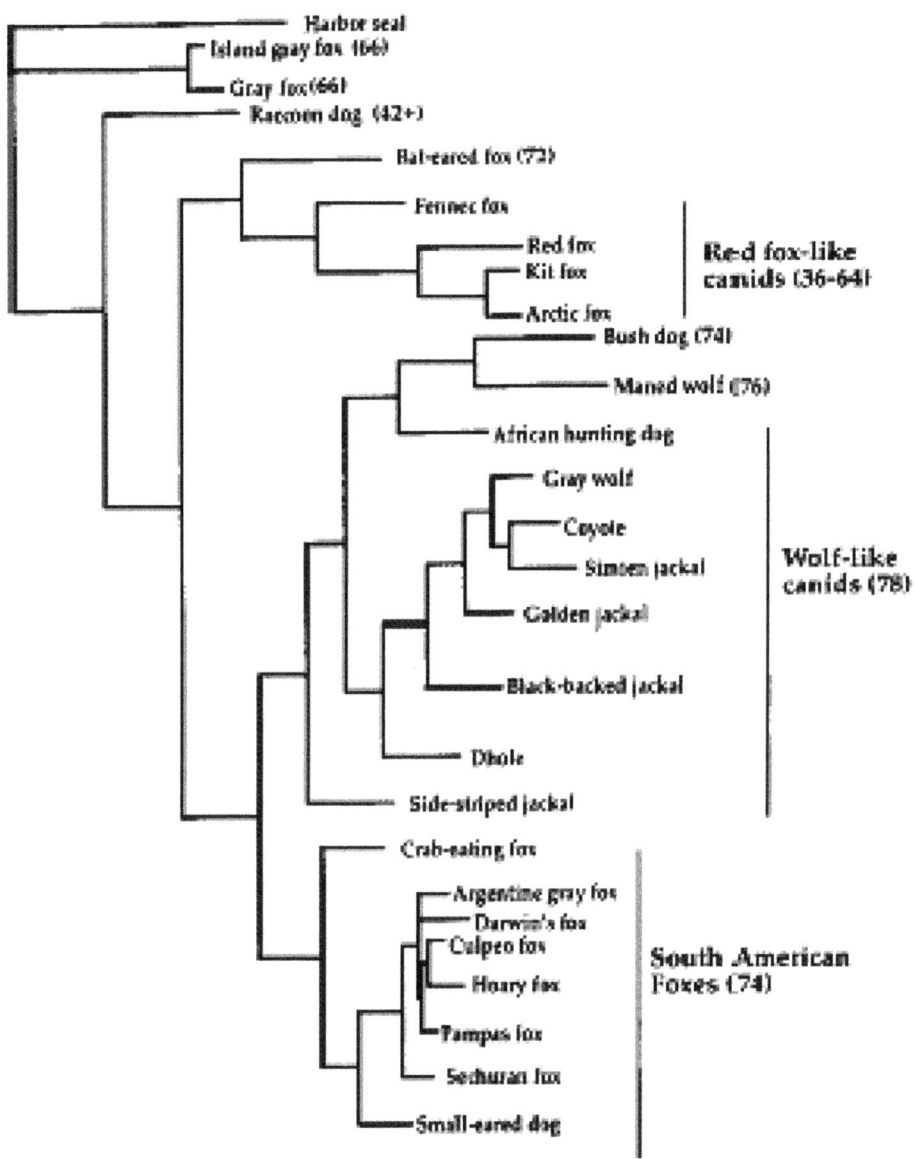

Fig. 6. Four phylogenetic divisions proposed by Wayne and Ostrander (1999) based upon DNA analysis.

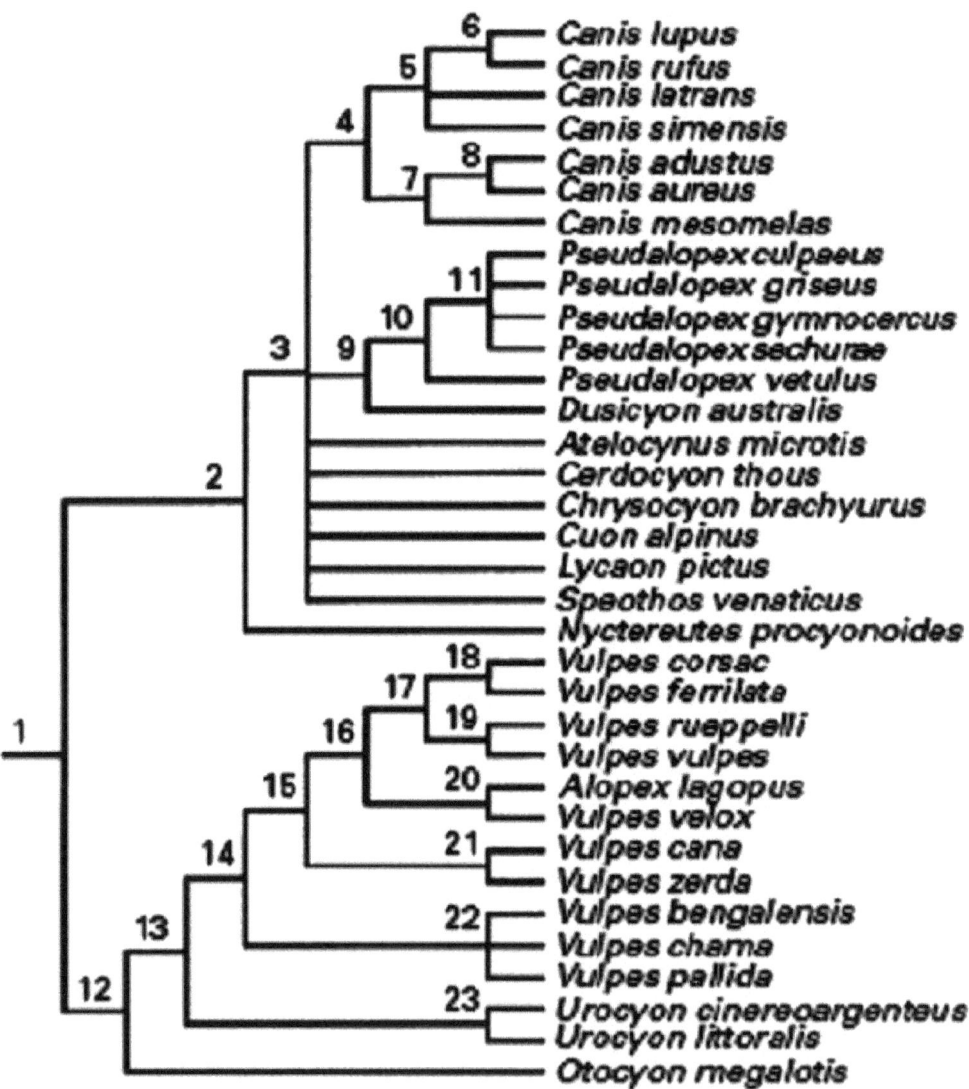

Fig. 7. Composite family tree of canids.

Phylogenetic tree of the dog and wolf

Vila and colleagues (1997) have been the dominant researchers in establishing an origin of the domestic dog from wolves from sequencing of the mtDNA. Their work has been instrumental in stimulating additional research in molecular genetics on dog domestication. Since Vila and fellow researchers first reported his findings in 1997, it has provided the groundwork for all the studies that followed and will be discussed at length here.

Vila's et al. (1997) research was quite thorough with 140 dogs representing 67 breeds and five crossbred dogs, as well as 162 wolves. The wolf population was derived from 27 different populations and included numerous geographic areas from Europe, Asia and North America. Additionally, five coyotes, two golden jackals, two blackback jackals and eight Simien jackals were examined since it is possible for these species to interbreed with dogs. From sequencing of the mitochondrial control region in wolves and dogs, Vila et al. were able to propose a phylogenetic analysis. In Vila et al. (1997) opinion, all analyses supported a grouping of dog haplotypes into four distinct clades. Later studies will expand on Vila et al. early work and propose the possibility of more clades, however this will be discussed later in this paper.

Vila et al. (1997) suggested that four clades were representative of different geographic areas as well as distinct dog breeds. A clade is a purported monophyletic group in which all members share a single common ancestor at some point in the past (Wayne and Ostrander 1999: 249-250). Vila et al.'s description of the clades is as follows (Hodges 2002: 1; Vila et al. 1997: 1687) (Fig. 8):

Clade IV, contained three dog haplotypes, D6, D10, and D24 that were identical or similar to a wolf haplotype found in Romania and western Russia, and resembled closely related wolf sequences from eastern Europe (Greece, Italy, Romania, and western Russia). It is suggestive of recent hybridization between dogs and wolves, of no more than 20,000 years.

Clade III, contained three dog haplotypes, D7, D19, and D21, and is found among a variety of breeds, such as the German shepherd, Siberian Husky, and Mexican hairless. This clade is proposed to be approximately 50,000 years old.

Clade II, included dog haplotype D8, from two Scandinavian breeds, Norwegian elkhound and a Jämthund. This haplotype sequence was closely related to two wolf haplotypes, W4 and W5, found in Italy, France, Romania, and Greece. It is also related to sequences seen in western Russia.

Clade I, included 18 of the 26 haplotypes in dogs. It is considered to be the most ancient and diverse. It suggests that either wolves were domesticated in several places at different times or that there was one domesticated event followed by several episodes of admixture between dogs and wolves. According to Hodges (2002) this clade consists of several different branches. The southern and eastern branch, included types D1, D23, D18, D9, D2, and DH. It includes the Asian breeds and dingo, New Guinea singing dog, Basenji, Eskimo dog and Chinese Crested. This clade is mostly seen in the Scandinavian breeds, as well. A second branch is of European origin and consists of D12, D15, D20, D26, D17, and D16. A third branch is found in breeds all over the world. It contains DNA type, D3, which appears to be similar to the common type from which Group I is derived. Branch four is formed from D14, D22 and D25. Lastly, branch five is seen in mostly European breeds and consists of D4, D5, and D13.

Vila et al. (1997: 1687; 1999a: 73) and Wayne et al. (1999: 249) concluded that the four clades of dog reflect establishment of the dog by an ancestral wolf population possibly in more than one region and at different times. Alternatively, it was theorized that there was possibly only one domestication event but followed by multiple instances of interbreeding between dogs and wolves.

Timing of these events, as outlined by Wayne, Vila and colleagues, has lead to much controversy within the molecular genetics and paleontology fields. The sequence seen in Clade 4 was identical in both dog and wolf sequence and was considered to indicate a very recent interbreeding or origination event of no more than 20,000 years. However, Clade 2 appeared to be only seen in Norwegian breeds and exhibited a vast amount of divergences. They suggested that this clade illustrated an ancient and independent origin from wolves, now extinct. Clade 3 was estimated to be no more than 50,000 years old. However, Clade 1, the most ancient of all four clades was deduced to be about 135,000 years old. They reasoned that since Clade 1 had 18 of the 26 haplotypes found in dogs, and assuming a calibration rate of evolution between wolves and coyotes of one million years, this indicates that the diversity seen in dogs and wolves would take 135,000 years to obtain. The six haplotype difference seen in the control region sequence of 1,030 base pairs was inferred by the researchers to indicate an origin more ancient than the 14,000 years proposed by the archaeological record. However, they do concede that changes seen in the mtDNA may not translate to visible morphological changes seen in the wild dogs that were conceivably identical structurally to the ancient wolves. They argue that the changes seen between 10,000 to 15,000 years ago may have been the result of selection imposed by the nomadic hunter-gatherers and later the establishment of sedentary

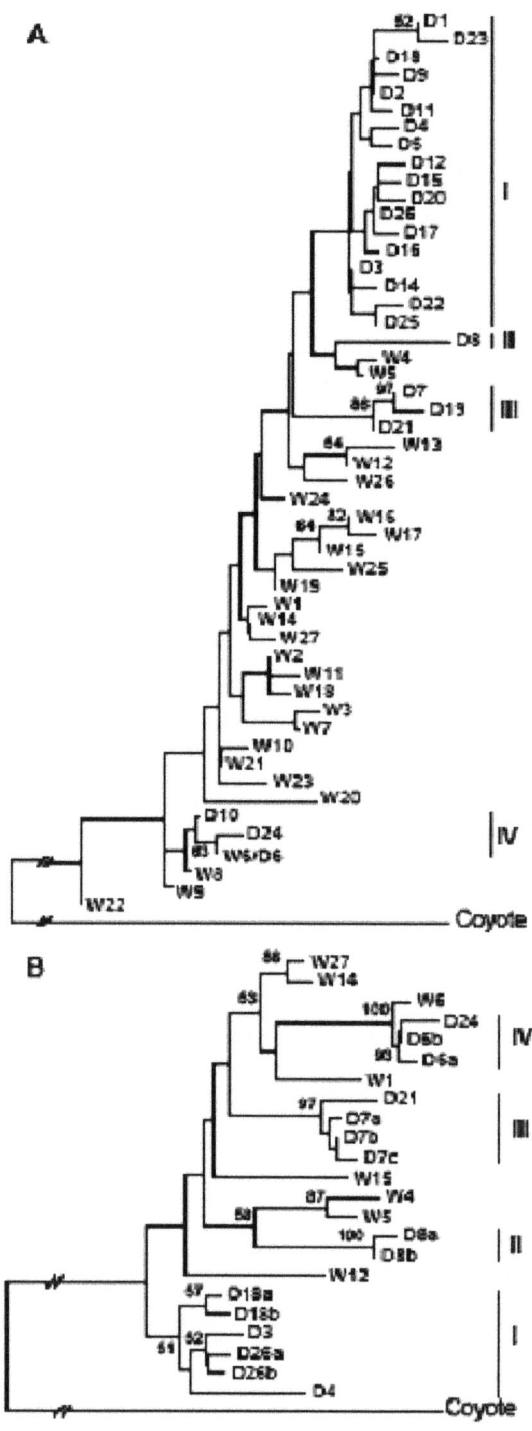

Fig. 8. A) Neighboring-joining tree of wolf and dog haplotypes based on 261 bp of control region sequence. B) Neighboring-joining tree of 8 wolf and 15 dog genotypes based on 1030 bp of control region sequence (Vila et al. 1997).

agricultural societies may have stimulated the phenotypic changes found in the fossil record.

A more recent study however, disagrees with Vila and Wayne's (1997; 1999a) conclusion of a 135,000 BP domestication date. Savolainen et al. (2002) examined 582 base pairs in the mtDNA of 654 domestic dogs from Europe, Asia, Africa, and Arctic America in addition to 38 Eurasian wolves. Although they used same phylogenetic clade groups used by Vila, they also assigned two more groups, which were not included in the earlier study. However, rather than using the Clade I, II, III, IV nomenclature imposed by Vila, they renamed the clades as A,B,C,D respectively, and they added two new additional groups as E and F.

In Savolainen and colleagues' (2002: 1612) study, they concluded that the domestic dog did not originate from four female wolf lines as previously reported, but from at least five female wolf lines. They reported that Clade A contained wolf haplotypes seen in China and Mongolia whereas Clade B had haplotypes seen in eastern Europe. This suggested to them that Clade A had an east Asian origin and Clade B was indicative of a European or southwest Asian origin.

Savolainen et al. (2002: 1611) also reported that out of the 654 domestic dogs analyzed, 71.3% of the dogs had haplotypes belonging to Clade A. Also, 95.9% of the dogs had haplotypes belonging to A, B or C. The other haplotypes belonging to Clade D, E or F were found sporadically and localized only regionally in Turkey, Spain and Scandinavia, Japan and Korea, and Japan and Siberia. Since Clade D, E and F were expressed in miniscule amounts Savolainen and colleagues concentrated on the analysis of Clades A, B and C since it seemed to comprise the largest proportion of the mtDNA genetic variation seen world-wide in the dog.

In Savolainen et al. (2002: 1611-1612) study it was determined that the eastern part of the world contained more distinctly different haplotypes (51.5%) than the 28.1% seen in the west (as defined as a line separating the east and the west from the Himalayas to the Ural mountains). They concluded that the greater number of unique haplotypes seen in Clade A implies that east Asia provided the foundation of the haplotypes seen in the West.

It was also reported that the same pattern was found in Clade B and Clade C. Clade B had 41.2% more distinct haplotypes than seen in the West (6.8%). Savolainen et al. (p. 1612) stated that Clade C exhibited less variation but resembled Clades A and B in that the West had only shared types, whereas the east had two unique haplotypes.

From this data they concluded that both Clade A and B point to an East Asia origin for the domestic dog. To lend support to this conclusion they cited the larger genetic variation seen in East Asia and the pattern of disbursal seen in the different geographic areas of the world.

Savolainen and colleagues (2002) also tried to estimate the amount of time it would take for the divergence between the different clades to occur when compared to the wolf haplotype. By comparing the mutation rates expected in the 582 bp control region of the mtDNA, and assuming that wolves and coyotes diverged one million years ago, they were able to estimate the relative age of several subclusters seen in Clade A. These subclusters were assumed to represent several different wolf haplotypes which had contributed to the gene pool (Fig. 9). According to their calculations, the mean genetic distances of three subclusters were estimated to be 11,000 ± 4,000 years, 16,000 ± 3,000 years, and 26,000 ± 8,000 years, for an average of approximately 15,000 years. Estimated ages for Clade B was asserted to be 13,000 ± 3,000 years whereas Clade C was suggested to be 17,000 ± 3,000 years. However, Savolainen and fellow researchers theorized that if there was only a single origin, the estimated age of Clade A would fall in the range of 41,000 ± 4,000 years.

The dates of 11,000 to 41,000 years reported in Savolainen et al. (2002) study contradict Vila et al. (1997) who believe that dogs became domesticated approximately 135,000 years ago. When compared to the archaeological record, the date estimated for the multiple haplotype origin (~15,000 years) is much closer to the date of the earliest archaeological evidence of domestic dog age of origin seen in the fossil record (~13,000 years). However if a single founding event is used for comparison to Vila et al. study, Savolainen's reported 40,000 years ago origin date is still considerably less than Vila et al. calculated date of origin (135,000 BP). Additionally, Savolainen's location of dog domestication as east Asia also conflicts with Wayne and Ostrander's study (1999) which concluded that dogs likely originated from a large founding stock derived from wolf populations existing in different places world-wide and at different times. Savolainen et al.(2002) asserts that based on the fossil record worldwide, the earliest canid remains are dated at ~ 12,000 BP with other remains exhibiting morphology typical of canines appearing only by 9,000 yr BP. Therefore, Savolainen et al. (2002: 1613) concludes that if you incorporate the origin dates seen in the fossil record throughout the world, as well as the information gleaned from their mtDNA study, all indications imply an east Asian point of origin for domestication at approximately 15,000 yr BP. Savolainen and colleagues also suggests that there were several wolf haplotypes that contributed to Clade A.

In a study done by Leonard et al. (2002), statistical components as well as inferences made by Vila in his studies, were used to determine the origin of New World dogs. Leonard and colleagues wanted to determine if domestic dogs in the Americas were derived from independently from gray wolves in the New World or

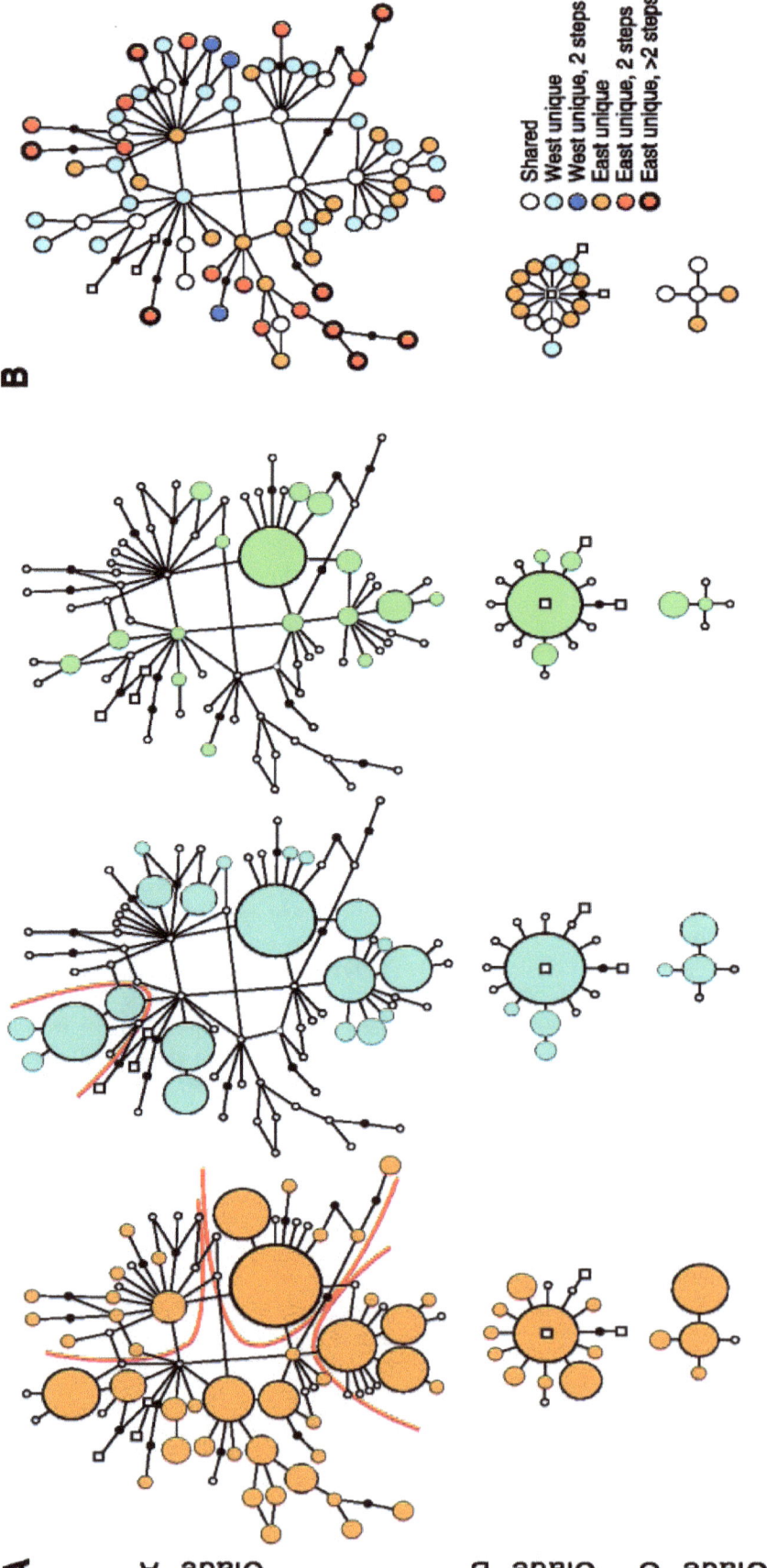

Fig. 9. A) Haplotypes found in East Asia, Europe, and Southwest Asia are indicated in separate networks with orange, blue, and green. Subclusters of clade A, three in the East Asian and one in the European network, are marked by red lines. B) Haplotypes shared between and unique to East and West. (Savolainen et al. 2002).

Fig. 10. Siberian Husky (photo M. Raisor).

were they ancestors of dogs brought to the New World by late Pleistocene humans that crossed the Bering Strait from Asia. Leonard et al. extracted DNA from the bones of 37 dog specimens from several archaeological sites in Peru, Bolivia and Mexico. The specimens were chosen for their extreme antiquity which dated before the arrival of Columbus. Leonard and researchers (2002: 1614) stated that they felt that selection of more recent dog remains might not be unbiased since it would have been possible for dogs brought over with the Europeans to interbreed with the native American dogs. A control region of 425 base pairs was amplified in the mtDNA of 13 archaeological specimens (37 dog specimens were attempted). An additional 11 dog specimens recovered from the permafrost in Alaskan goldmines were also sequenced and were also dated prior to the arrival of Europeans. These sequences were compared to the Vila et al. (1997; 1999a) studies in the area of the control region consisting of a 257 base pair fragment. Special attention was paid to those sequences representing dogs known to have originated in the New World, such as the Chesapeake Bay retriever, Newfoundland, Eskimo dog, Siberian Husky, and Mexican hairless (Figs. 10 and 11). The Australian dingo and the New Guinea Singing Dog were alsoanalyzed since they are believed to be unique breeds that have lived in relative isolation due to geographic barriers. Leonard et al. (2002: 1614) reported that base on the 13 archaeological specimens analyzed from Latin America, 11 haplotype sequences were defined. Using Vila et al. (1997) four clade classification system, Leonard et al. was able to assign ten of those samples to Clade I, and one sequence to Clade IV. As previously reported by Vila et al., Clade I is comprised of 80% of the dog haplotypes and is representative of many of the common dog breeds as well as those ancient breeds such as the greyhound, dingo, basenji, and New Guinea Singing dog. Additionally, Leonard and researchers discovered that three of the ancient sequences were identical to those sequences derived from Eurasian dogs, and on sequence was identical to those seen in modern dogs.

Leonard and colleagues examined the 11 dog remains from the Alaskan sites approximately dated at 1450 and 1675 C.E. Based on the 257 base pair sequence, eight haplotypes were identified. From those eight haplotypes, all contained Clade I, five had unique sequences and three exhibited sequences that were identifiable to modern domesticated dogs.

On the basis of their analysis, Leonard et al. (2002: 1614-1615) was able to infer parallels between the patterns observed in Vila et al. study and those seen in their New World samples. The Bolivian remains were found to contain haplotype D28 which is ancestral to a unique clade seen in the New World haplotypes. Leonard et al. suggests that this unique haplotype would be consistent with a history of isolation. By contrast, the Alaskan samples contained haplotype D36 or D2, which has been observed to be common in Old World dogs. They further note that the sequences derived from the ancient Native American dogs were extremely well differentiated from those sequences obtained from North American wolf samples. They also suggest that the North American gray wolf sequences do not indicate that interbreeding of gray wolves with dogs occurred or was uncommon as previously theorized by other researchers, but rather supports the hypothesis that ancient and modern dogs share a common origin from Old World gray wolves.

In characterizing the genetic evidence, Leonard et al. (2002: 1616) infers that based upon the analyses of the ancient sequences from the New World dog remains when compared to those sequences acquired from ancient and modern dogs worldwide, they support an Old World gray wolf ancestry for dogs. They further assert that the phylogenetic analysis suggest that minimally, about five founding dog lineages invaded North America.

The unique Latin American haplotype seen in the Bolivia, Peru and Mexico samples, Leonard classified as Clade A (not to be confused with Clade A reported in Savolainen's 2002 study). Clade A was not found in any of the 350 modern dog sequences. Leonard and researchers speculate why the unique New World Clade A has seemed to disappear from the modern breeds. They hypothesize that the absence of Clade A is indicative of an extensive replacement of native American dogs by those introduced by Europeans. They tried to prove this theory by examining the DNA of the 19 samples of the Xoloitzcunitle, sometimes better known as the Mexican hairless. This breed is known to be present in Mexico for over 2000 years and would have predated European contact. However the sequencing data revealed that the Xoloitzcunitle contained only sequences seen in dogs of Eurasian origin. Leonard et al. observed that these could be the result of close inbreeding for several hundred

Fig. 11. Hairless breeds of dogs from top left to bottom, Chinese crested, Xoloitzcuintli (Mexican hairless), and Peruvian Inca Orchid (Chinese crested photo, M.Raisor).

generations which reduced the amount of genetic variation that could have been seen. Another possible explanation is that the Mexican hairless had a separate derivation from the New World wolves (Vila et al. 1999a: 74). Vila et al. believed that because of the Xoloitzcuinitlis special religious association and its medicinal value for relieving pain associated with rheumatism (Cordy-Collins 1994: 40), the native tribes went to considerable effort to protect this breed from the Spanish. According to Vila and colleagues (1999a: 74-75) citing Valdez (1995), the natives hid the dogs in mountain villages in the western Mexican states, where their breeding was strictly controlled and was not crossed with other dogs. Vila et al. also assert that the likelihood that the Xoloitzcuintli escaped from these villages and interbred with other dogs would not have occurred. Vila and fellow researchers believe that the fragile physical health of the breed, which made it extremely sensitive to sunburn and cold, would make it unlikely to survive outside the confines of the villages. However Vila and fellow researchers (1999a: 75-76) sequencing data did not support this theory of isolation. It appeared that no unique Xoloitzcuintli haplotypes were found nor were the sequences similar to those found in New World wolves. Vila et al. (1999a: 76) state that only haplotype D6, a haplotype shared between dogs and wolves but only presently found in wolves in Romania and European Russia, was the most common haplotype seen in five of the Xoloitzcuintli. Additionally, when Vila et al. compared the Xoloitzcuintli sequence to the sequence of the Chinese crested dog, another hairless breed of dog that was believe to be related to the Xoloitzcuintli, no shared haplotypes were present. This indicated that the Chinese crested dog and Xoloitzcuintli were not related (Fig. 11). However Vila et al. did identify seven distinct sequences within the control region which Vila et al. suggested that the founding population was quite diverse genetically. Therefore, Vila et al. concluded that the Xoloitzcuintli was derived from a large number of founding females of Old World origin and not derived by an independent origination from North American wolves. However, Leonard et al. (2002: 1616) concluded that the absence of ancient North and South American dog haplotypes from a large diversity of modern breeds, including the Xoloitzcuintli, illustrates the considerable impact that invading Europeans had on native cultures. This also implies, according to Leonard et al., that the mtDNA lineages seen in the New World dogs prove that the ancestral population originated in Eurasia and not the New World.

Tsuda et al. (1997), in a study similar to Leonard's, compared Asiatic breeds of dogs assumed to be indigenous to Japan, to European dog breeds (bred in Japan) and three species of gray wolf (*Canis lupus lupus, Canis lupus pallipes*) including Chinese gray wolf *(Canis lupus chanco)*. Tsuda et al. performed a sequence comparison of the mtDNA D-loop region among 24 dog breeds and gray wolves. When analyzing the sequences, Tsuda and researchers specifically tried to identify nucleotide substitution and length of variations. Their results indicated that there were no significant differences in the sequence divergence values among dogs and wolves. They inferred that the wolf was the matriarchal ancestor to the dog. The gray wolf sequences were found to fall within two clades, A and B. Tsuda et al. stated that the Asiatic wolves (*C. l. chanco*) were limited to Clade A, the Indian wolves *(C. l. pallipes)* were limited to Clade B, whereas the European wolves *(C. l. lupus)* contained both Clades A and B. Tsuda et al. postulated two theories to explain this. One hypothesis is that the European subspecies is ancestral to the Asiatic subspecies. Their second hypothesis implied that the haplotypes found in the Asiatic subspecies were introduced to the European subspecies.

Tsuda and colleagues (1997: 236) also found that the Chinese subspecies of wolves showed extensive subspecies-specific mtDNA polymorphism whereas, the European subspecies did not. Domesticated dogs also exhibited extensive polymorphisms which were not breed specific. In studies done of Japanese breeds, such as the Shiba and Ryukyu, many of the haplotypes were identical. This was found to be true of both Japanese breeds as well as non-Japanese breeds. Tsuda et al. deduced that interbreeding occurred in the ancestral lines of domestic dogs. Based upon the seven different haplotypes seen in the Shibu, Tsuda and researchers concluded that the domestication from wolves to dogs occurred in more than two places. However Tsuda et al. refined this statement by suggesting that it was possible that dogs were domesticated in a single place, but mated with wolves along the migration route of humans. Therefore in Tsuda and colleagues opinion it would be difficult to determine if domestication occurred in a single place or in multiple locales.

Tsuda et al. (1997: 236) concluded that the parallels between the repetitive sequences seen in the wolves and dogs were similar to those patterns seen in other mammalian species. In any case, Tsuda et al. work indicates that there is strong experimental evidence to infer that dogs and wolves are members of the same species, with breeds of domestic dogs maintaining a large degree of mtDNA polymorphisms introduced from their ancestral wolf populations.

Seddon and Ellegren (2002) took a different approach in their study of dog domestication by examining the class II genes of the major histocompatibility complex (MHC). The MHC locus is a small segment of a single chromosome which contains many genes coding for functions concerned with immune responses. The locus has been determined to be highly polymorphic with individual genomes showing allelic variation such as changes that produce differing phenotypes or changes in the DNA that affect the restriction pattern. The histocompatibility antigens are classified into three types based upon their immunological functions. Class I proteins are found on every cell of the mammal and are responsible for the rejection of foreign tissue. Class II proteins are found on the surface of the B and T lymphocytes and macrophages, and are necessary for the communication between cells that execute the immune response. The Class III proteins cause the lysis of cells as a part of the humoral response (Lewin 2000: 705-708).

In Sheddon and Ellegren's research (2002), they attempted to study the MHC genes in European wolves, North American wolves and dogs to determine the variation that occurred during the process of domestication. Their study focused on the Class II DQA, DQB1 and DRB1 alleles. They were able to determine that in the nine DQA alleles derived from the European wolves, all alleles from the European wolves were shared with North American wolves, dogs or both. The coyote which had 5 alleles at DRB1, only shared 1 allele out of the 17 DRB1 alleles with wolves or dogs. At the DQA locus, the coyote had a unique allele not seen in dogs or wolves. Ten alleles were identified at the DQB locus in European wolves.

Sheddon and Ellegren (2002: 498) determined that both North American and European wolves retained a large amount of diversity in the MHC Class II loci. They attribute this to the large founding population size which was distributed throughout multiple geographic locations worldwide and extensive migration of the historical population. They also found this to be true in dogs. According to their research, they were able to observe that dogs carried a full range of MHC Class II allelic lineages through their domestication from gray wolves in the Old World, with the majority of alleles present in modern-day dogs being derived from wolves. The diversity seen between the European and North American wolves was thought to be the result of genetic drift. Geographic separation of the two populations could also have restricted gene flow which could attribute to the loss of some alleles. However Sheddon and Ellegren infer that the MHC pattern seen in dogs represent the genetically diverse origin of dogs as reported in previous mtDNA studies. However both authors assert that the formation of dog breeds will trap alleles in the dog population and will reduce intra-breed variability at both microsatellite and MHC loci. Sheddon and Ellegren had expected to see a progression of shared allelic lineages with differentiation of species following domestication. However, they found following domestication. However, they found this not to be true. What they did conclude was despite the high mobility of wolves, there appears to be a genetic structuring among the wolf populations. They further inferred that the northern European wolves contributed little to the domestication of dogs, which has been suggested from other studies of mtDNA that point to an Asiatic origin of dog domestication (Tsuda et al. 1997).

Vila, Wayne and other researchers have periodically suggested that the diversity seen in the mtDNA of dogs has originated from the interbreeding of dogs to wolves throughout history. Vila (et al. 2003) have proven this theory in a recent study of hybridization of endangered Scandinavian wolf populations. Using autosomal markers of both paternally (y chromosome) and maternally (mtDNA) inherited microsatellites, they were able to confirm that hybridization does occur between wolves and dogs in the wild. From data collected on wolves from Scandinavia, Finland, Russia, Latvia and Estonia, as well as 44 domestic dogs from diverse breeds, they were able to identify a suspected wolf-dog hybrid. However, the researchers agree that hybridization is a rare event. If interbreeding between wolf and dog populations do occur, the researchers infer that this event would be the result of a disruption in the population density of the wolves (Vila and Wayne 1999: 197). They indicated that wolf behavior predetermines that wolves form social pack units. If hybridization did occur, the researchers felt that the most likely direction would be a male dog crossing with a female wolf. However, since the researchers didn't observe any obvious effects of dog genotypes in a small endangered wolf population, they concluded that wolf hybrids would be less likely to reach maturity since dog sires do not help raise offspring like wolf family units do. Therefore the hybrids would be less likely to able to integrate into a wolf pack. However with this in mind, the researchers' identification of a hybrid offspring from a wild female wolf indicates that interbreeding events although rare, can occur with offspring living to adulthood.

Ethiopian wolf

Similar genetic studies have been done on the highly endangered Ethiopian wolf *(Canis simensis)*. Fewer than 500 of these species live in the wild which have been severely impacted by the loss of habitat and a civil war. Gottelli et al. (1994) conducted nuclear and mitochondria DNA analysis to determine how phylogentically distinct Ethiopian wolves are from other canids and to assess the amount of genetic variability exists within the population. Canid species used for comparison consisted of gray wolves *(C. lupus)*, coyotes *(C. latrans)*, golden jackals *(C. aureus)*, black-backed jackals *(C. mesomelas)*, African wild dog *(Lycaon pictus)*, side-striped jackal *(C. adustus)*, gray fox *(Urocyon cinereoargenteus)*, and 32 different domestic dog breeds.

Gottelli and researchers (1994: 305) were able to infer from mtDNA and microsatellite analysis that the Ethiopian wolf is most similar to coyotes and gray wolf having the fewest number of substitutions in the control region and a mean divergence value of about $5 \pm 0.52\%$. When they compared the other African wolf-like canids, the mean divergence values ranged from $6 \pm 0.57\%$ to $11 \pm 0.82\%$, with the African wild dog showing the most number of substitutions in the control region (204 bp substitutions in 2001 bp protein coding sequence). The data also revealed that the golden jackal is a sister taxon to the clade containing the gray wolf, coyote and Ethiopian wolf.

Fig. 12. Coyote (*Canis latrans*)
(http://katherine.as.arizona.edu/~ksu/su/new_photo/gatespass/coyote).

When Gottelli et al. (1994: 306) compared the Ethiopian wolf to the domestic dogs, they found that the mtDNA sequence differed by about 3.5%. However, microsatellite analysis revealed that the Ethiopian wolves had 8 alleles out of 19 alleles that were unique only to them, whereas the domestic dog had 47 out of 57 alleles that were not found in phenotypically normal Ethiopian wolves.

Gottelli et al. (1994: 310) hypothesized that based on the molecular genetic analysis, the Ethiopian wolf could be an evolutionary relic of a past invasion of gray wolf-like ancestors which migrated into North Africa during the Late Pleistocene. Gottelli et al. inferred that because gray wolves occupy alpine and temperate environments, ancestors of the Ethiopian wolves would have been well suited to the cold-temperate Ethiopian highlands. Therefore, the ancestral population would not have advanced into the savanna regions where they would have been in direct competition with the African wild dog *(Lycan pictus)*. This theory is partially supported by the mtDNA evidence which shows no evidence of the African wild dog and Ethiopian wolf having a direct ancestor relationship. Additionally, no domesticated dogs exhibit any evidence of the presence of alleles associated with the Ethiopian wolves. According to Gottelli et al., all evidence indicates that the Ethiopian wolf is a phylogenetically distinct canid related to the gray wolf *(Canis lupus)*, and coyote.

Coyote

Mitochondrial DNA studies of the coyote *(C. latrans)* have also proven insightful. Similar parallels between the research done on other canids have provided comparable information on not only the geographical origin of the coyote, but also their Pleistocene diversification (Fig. 12). In an earlier study done by Wayne et al. (1992), genetic variability in the mtDNA genotypes was compared between the gray wolf and domestic dog using coyote as the foundation for the analysis. In expansion of this study was later done by Vila et al. (1999b) to further define the genetic variability, origin and diversification of gray wolves and coyotes. From these studies they were able to determine that the haplotype diversity of coyotes was much greater than those haplotypes seen in wolves. The average divergence estimates were calculated to be 9.6% between coyotes and wolves, which suggested that the coyote mitochondrial control region sequences diverged at a more ancient time than the sequences in the gray wolf.

In previous studies, the sequence divergence time period for coyotes was predicted to be on the order of 1 million years ago (Lehman et al. 1991). Vila et al. (1999b: 2098) however, hypothesizes that coyote's actually diverged 420,000 years ago based on the view that the divergence rate is 10% per million years with coyotes exhibiting a mean divergence rate of 4.2%. This conflicts with Brown et al. (1979: 1970) who ascertain a mutation rate of mtDNA of 2-4% per million years in mammals which would date coyote divergence at approximately one to two million years ago. If Vila et al. 10% mutation rate is used for predicting divergence, it would infer a difference of 580,000 years then was predicted by Brown's original calculation. Vila et al. also maintains that a mean sequence divergence of 2.9% in gray wolves would imply a formation of wolf haplotypes of about 290,000 years ago. Therefore the lack of consistency between researchers using a common baseline for divergence for ancestral species can dramatically skew divergence predictions.

Vila et al. (1999b: 2098-2100) infers that the more recent separation of coyotes and wolves sequences that is projected in his study may be the result of the effect of population fluctuations during the Pleistocene glacial cycles on the harmonic mean of the effective population size. Vila et al. citing Avise et al. (1984) study which stated that historical fluctuation in population size causes the harmonic mean of the effective population size to be much smaller than the average census population size, and results in a more recent coalescence than predicted from census population size alone. Vila et al. concludes that both coyotes and wolves were more diverse than current populations in the past but coyotes were less diverse than wolves. Vila et al. state that the differences now seen by the substitutions seen in the control region is reflective of dramatic population fluctuations. These changes mirrored environmental upheavals as Ice Ages inflicted reductions in geographic territories inhabited by coyotes and wolves. During interglacial periods, expansion of habitats would follow. The fluctuations seen in the environment would be mirrored in the canid populations. Therefore, during the Pleistocene, both coyotes and wolves would be subject to decreased genetic variability due to the greatly reduced population size.

However Vila et al. (1999b: 2098-2100) point out that the normal distribution of wolves is limited to forest habitats whereas, coyotes roam plains and deserts. They suggest that coyotes would be less sensitive to climatic changes induced by the glacial expansion given that the plains and desert regions of North America would have been less affected by Pleistocene climatic changes. Wolves on the other hand, would be more likely to be affected by glacial expansion due to the fragmentation and reduction of their geographical ranges. Therefore, Vila et al. concludes that the genetic variability of coyotes may have been better preserved than that of wolves although their geographic distribution was less extensive. However the authors observe that the coyotes have been more adaptable than wolves to changes in their habitat territories as well as tolerating periodic human interaction. This has led to an explosion in the coyote population size and expansion of the geographic range, whereas wolves have diminished both in available habitat territory as well as in population size. According to Vila et al., the reduction in the wolf population would decrease the genetic diversity which would explain the diminished haplotype variety seen in the sequence analysis.

Red wolf

Considerable attention has been focused on the evolutionary history of the red wolf *(Canis rufus)* since Ronald Nowak first reported in 1979 that the red wolf first appeared one million years ago (Fig. 13). Nowak reported that both skeletal differences and dental measurements from the fossil record not only indicated that the red wolf was a separate and distinct species, but that it was perhaps the ancestral foundation from which the coyote and gray wolf emerged. This idea of identifying the red wolf as a recognizable species was further championed by Phillips and Henry (1992) who reported their evidence of behavioral and ecological differences which supported Nowak's hypothesis that the red wolf was a distinct species. However, because the red wolf is an intermediate in both size and stature between the coyotes and gray wolves (Nowak 1979, 1992), many molecular biologists are not persuaded that the data supported a distinct species status. As molecular techniques have become more refined, numerous articles have been published attempting to refute Nowak's previous work (Brownlow 1996; Roy et al. 1994a, 1994b, 1996; Reich et al. 1999; Wayne and Jenks 1991; Wayne and Gittleman 1995). Virtually all the molecular genetic studies concluded that the red wolf was a hybrid consisting of shared alleles that were found in both coyotes and gray wolves. These results caused an immediate uproar among conservationists who had devoted considerable time, money and effort to prevent extinction of this species. The molecular genetic results

Fig. 13. Red wolf (*Canis rufus*)
(http://www.nhptv.org/natureworks/graphics/redwolf.jpg)

were especially controversial given that since the red wolf had been protected under the Endangered Species Act (ESA), it had according to the U.S. Government was heralded as "the most significant success stories" in bringing a species back from the bring of extinction (U.S. Fish and Wildlife Service, 1994). Almost immediately there were attempts to delist the red wolf on the basis of a "hybrid policy" which would have compromised any future conservation efforts. In a counter-attack, the conservationists, zooarchaeologists and some molecular researchers simultaneously challenged the results of Wayne and colleagues, both on the basis of genetics (Dowling et al. 1992) and paleontology and morphology (Nowak 1992). As many researchers rallied to the defense of the red wolf, they noted the potential bias in Wayne and Jenk's study (1991) calling it nothing more than "molecular chauvinism" (Avise 1989; Brownlow 1996: 396). A short review of previous research on the red wolf will follow that will highlight the research results that have lead to the controversy surrounding the classification of the red wolf. These studies have been particularly important in that there is so much contention over the interpretation of the molecular genetics, even among the molecular scientists.

In 1991 Wayne and Jenks performed DNA analysis by comparing segments of mitochondrial DNA from red wolves that were collected from the coastal regions of Texas and southwestern Louisiana. These individuals were a part of a captured breeding program. Of the 400 red wolves caught, only 40 were considered pure enough for breeding, while the others were destroyed because of infiltration of coyote genetic material (Jenks and Wayne, 1992: 237-251). The authors using mtDNA from the red wolves and similar control region sequences from both the gray wolf and coyote were able to compare the three species. Wayne and Jenks (1991: 567) concluded that the red wolf sequences contained no alleles that were not also found in the coyote and gray wolf.

However questions arose on whether or not if the hybridization of the red wolves had an ancient origin of if it was the result of intense eradication efforts as settlers moved west and habitat fragmentation occurred. Roy et al. (1994b, 1996) in an attempt to answer these questions obtained DNA from six museum skins that had been collected prior to 1930 before, according to Nowak (1992; 1995), when the red wolves began to interbreed with gray wolves and coyotes. In both studies, Roy et al. concluded that hybridization was extensive prior to 1940 and that no phylogenetically distinct clade of red wolf genotypes were identified, which would have been expected if the wolf had been a distinct species. Roy et al. (1996: 555) asserted that even if hybridization had obscured the genetic structure of the red wolf, it would be expected to find some evidence of phylogenetically distinct red wolf genotypes in the pre-1940 samples. Roy et al. further reported that the microsatellite analysis of the museum skins showed that nearly all alleles in the red wolf are shared with coyotes. Roy et al.(1996: 1420) states that the lack of unique genetic red wolf markers, was not consistent with an ancient origin since other canid species have 17-27% unique alleles when compared to other canids. In the museum specimens only 3 unique alleles were found, and Roy et al. maintained that 6 unique alleles would have to be the minimum expected given sampling consideration.

In 1999 Reich, Wayne and Goldstein attempted to determine the date in which the hybridization occurred since previous data supported the theory that interbreeding was apparent before 100 years ago but was perhaps not as ancient as the Pleistocene predictions. Samples were obtained from 144 coyotes, 141 gray wolves and 56 red wolves. The red wolf sample consisted of the individuals from the Texas captive breeding program and 17 museum specimens. The gray wolf and coyote samples were gathered from numerous geographic areas including Canada, Alaska and the Northwest Territories. The authors focused on eight alleles at four loci and extrapolated a mutation rate. The mutation rate was calculated based upon data gathered from two isolated California Channel Island fox populations known to have diverged approximately 11,500 years ago. Reich et al. postulated that the mutation rate for red wolves would be 3.7×10^{-5} per year which would give an approximate limit on the date of hybridization, conservatively at 12,800 years. However the authors were quick to point out that half of the calculations also fall less than 2500 years. Reich et al. infers that red wolf lineages are young enough not to have accumulated any mutations since hybridization. However, the authors still support the hypothesis of a recent hybridization associated with the appearance of European settlers beginning around 250 years ago. This study is of particular importance since it implies a "softening" of Wayne's earlier work which inferred that the red wolf had always been a hybrid with no distinct evolutionary history.

In 2000, a Canadian study on the red wolf population provided some clarity on the red wolf hybrid debate. Wilson et al. (2000) compared recent molecular studies and evolutionary history of the eastern Canadian wolf *(C. latrans)* to the red wolf to suggest an alternative evolutionary history.

Wilson et al. (2000) obtained DNA samples from captive red wolves, Texas coyotes and from wolf teeth collected in Algonquin Park and elsewhere in Ontario during the 1960's. The wolf teeth represented individuals which had only had contact will coyotes less than 30 years. The researchers followed the methods for analysis of the allele frequencies at 8 loci as previously reported by Roy et al. (1994a, 1994b, 1996). The allele frequencies of the Algonquin Park and red wolf populations were compared to other North American populations of wolves and coyotes. Microsatellite analysis was used to establish the genetic origins of red wolves to determine if it was similar coyote genetic material.

Wilson et al. (2000: 2158) concluded that the genetic similarity between red wolves and eastern Canadian wolves was not heavily influenced by the introgression of coyote genetic material. They further concluded that alleles that were prevalent in Texas and other coyote populations as reported by Roy et al. (1994a, 1994b) were absent or present at very low frequency in red wolves. Their results found that the majority of the captive red wolves overlapped the distribution of the eastern Canadian wolf population. The researchers hypothesize that if the red wolf had more closely related to the coyote genetic material, the distribution would have overlapped or fall within a closer distribution to the Texas coyote population and not that of the geographically distant population of eastern Canadian wolves in Algonquin Park.

Wilson et al. (2000: 2158-2159) additionally determined that the eastern Canadian wolves in Algonquin Park and red wolves clustered together in their allele frequencies and away from the gray wolf. This implied, according to the researchers, that there was little or no gray wolf *(C. lupus)* genetic material in these populations.

Further testing of the mitochondrial DNA control region sequences found no gray wolf control region sequences in any red wolf or historical samples collected in the Algonquin Park. These mtDNA findings supported the results obtained from the microsatellite analysis. Wilson et al. (2000) was also able to identify one unique haplotype (C1) in the eastern Canadian wolves that was not found in coyotes. The researchers were also able to identify a unique haplotype in red wolves (C2) that was not seen in coyotes. They concluded that the presence of the C1 and C2 sequences in the geographically separated red wolves and eastern Canadian wolves but not in the Texas coyote, were consistent with a common origin of these two wolves. However they qualified their conclusions that due to the fact that a few samples contained coyote mtDNA sequences, some level of hybridization had recently occurred.

When Wilson et al. (2000: 2159) calculated the sequence divergent rate between the eastern Canadian wolf and the red wolf haplotypes, they determined that it was 2.1%. Calculation of sequence divergence between the eastern Canadian wolf and the coyote was calculated at 3.2% based on the C1 haplotype. When the same comparison was made between the coyote *(C. latrans)* and red wolf, it was determined to be 2.3%. The researchers also found that the sequence divergence between the gray wolf *(C. lupus)*, red wolf and eastern Canadian wolf was approximately 8.0%. Comparison between the gray wolf and coyote sequences was judged to be 10.0%. Using a mammalian divergence rate of 1-2% per 100,000 years as previously reported by Stewart and Baker (1994), Wilson et al. determined that sequence differences seen between the eastern Canadian wolf and coyote was consistent with a separation of 150,000-300,000 years during the late Pleistocene.

Wilson et al. (2000: 2160, 2164) concluded that the mtDNA data and the microsatellite results indicate that the red wolf and eastern Canadian wolf are not hybrids. The researchers state that in their opinion that the North American canid mtDNA lineage diverged into the red wolf and eastern Canadian wolf and separately the coyote. They further state that the North American wolves and coyotes evolved independently of the gray wolf *(C. lupus)* which evolved in Eurasia. The foregoing inferences suggest that if the North American wolves evolved from the gray wolf *(C. lupus)* the mtDNA of the North American wolves would contain sequences more similar to the gray wolf and not the coyote. However the North American wolves were closer to the coyote haplotypes. Wilson et al. characterized the parallels seen in the North American wolf haplotypes as evidence of a sharing of a common lineage with the coyote until 150,000-300,000 years ago.

Although Wilson and colleagues (2000: 2164-2165) findings contradicted previous studies that the red wolf was a hybrid of the gray wolf and coyote, it is unlikely that debate concerning classification of these species will cease. In fact, they suggest that the red wolf be moved to the *C. l. lycaon (eastern Canadian wolf)* classification. In any case, the work of Wilson et al. indicates that the red wolf *(C. rufus)* and the eastern Canadian wolf *(C. l. lycaon)* have a common origin and they present three additional points to support this conclusion. First, a small wolf has been identified from Pleistocene fossil samples uncovered in North America. Second, the historic territorial ranges of the red wolf and eastern Canadian wolf overlap today, and both would have existed in southern refugia during the Pleistocene. And finally, the lack of introgression of coyote DNA in western gray wolves and Mexican gray wolves suggests that the smaller size of the eastern wolves is not the reason for hybridization but would infer that species that evolved together in the New world would be more likely to have hybridized with each other.

It is important to remember that when using molecular genetics to define evolutionary phylogeny, this field is still in its infancy. When reviewing the molecular research done on the evolutionary history of red wolves, it becomes very apparent that molecular genetics is not yet an exact science. Molecular geneticists working on the same species frequently disagree when interpreting results. Slight differences in sequencing data can be deemed insignificant by one researcher but will be interpreted by others as highly relevant. Yet neither conclusion can be rejected.

Jackals

It has been speculated that domestic dogs originated from jackals and gray wolves, first by Darwin (1871) and later by Lorenz (1954). It was theorized that each wild species possibly gave rise to different breeds of dogs (Vila et al. 1999a: 73). Given that jackals have the same chromosome number as other Canis species (2n=78) and can hybridize, this theory didn't seem unlikely. However, comparative analyses of gene sequences in jackals, dogs, coyotes, and wolves has proven that there is extensive genetic differences in jackals that would exclude them as being ancestral to domestic dogs.

In a study conducted by Wayne (1993), phylogenetic analysis of a 736 base pair region of the mitochondria was used for comparison between gray wolves, dogs, coyotes and four jackal species. Surprisingly, it was discovered that the Simien jackals, based on the genetic analysis, should be redesignated as a wolf rather than a jackal. Wayne infers because of the remote area of the Ethiopian highlands where it is found, the Simien jackal is probably an evolutionary relic of a past African invasion of gray wolf-like ancestors. Comparison of the mtDNA sequences in two of the black-backed jackals resulted in an 8% divergence between the two jackals. Such a large divergence percentage within a single population that is freely interbreeding is not typical. Wayne proposed that two mtDNA sequences evolved at significantly different rates and diverged before the speciation event that gave rise to black-backed jackals.

In an additional study done by Roy et al. (1996) on pre-1940 red wolves, they also compared allele frequency differences between wolf and wolf-like canids. In an examination of 92 alleles in coyotes, 17% were not found in gray wolves. In gray wolves, of the 95 alleles examined, 20% were not found in coyotes. Golden jackals had the greatest proportion of unique alleles, 25% when compared with coyotes, 27% when compared with gray wolves and 50% when compared to pre-1940 red wolves (Roy et al. 1996: 1419).

Considering that the domestic dog is closely related to the gray wolf, different by at the most from 0.2% to 1.8% of the mtDNA sequence (Wayne et al. 1990; Wayne and Jenks 1991: 565; Wayne et al. 1992: 563; Wayne 1993: 220) several inferences can be drawn. When comparisons of the mtDNA sequence of gray wolf to coyote, the closest wild relative, a difference of 4% is derived. Additionally, a comparison of black-backed jackals to wolves and coyotes yields a difference of about 8% in the mtDNA sequence (Wayne and Gittleman 1995: 38). Therefore, according to molecular researchers, the difference between domestic dog and jackal would at least be 8%, the same difference that is seen in wolves and jackals. It can be concluded that jackals are not ancestral to dogs given the greater sequence divergence values than those values calculated for wolves and dogs. On an evolutionary time scale, if divergence of wolves and coyotes is estimated to be one million years, jackal's divergence would have an even older evolutionary time estimate.

Variability of wild-type dog breeds

As the dog genome has been mapped, additional studies have been conducted to determine if it is possible to distinguish specific sequencing patterns that can be used to identify specific dog breeds as well as establishing when a breed was originated. Zajc, Mellersh and Sampson (1997) examined microsatellite sequences between three purebred dog breeds to ascertain evolutionary relationships including breed specific alleles. Fifty unrelated individuals were chosen from the German Shepherd, Greyhound and Labrador retriever dog breeds. Microsatellite analysis was done based on allele frequencies at 19 loci. The authors wanted to learn if because of intense artificial selection and major inbreeding, would it be possible to identify allele variations in spite of the relatively high genetic homogenetic composition within specific pure breeds. Zajc et al. (1994: 545-547) suspected that based on previous dog paternity testing research which employed microsatellite technology, the same techniques could be used to identify dog breeds and evolutionary history.

The researchers found that all three breeds of dogs differed significantly in their allele frequency distributions for most of the microsatellite markers that were polymorphic. stated that although they observed some breed-specific alleles, the significant differences were not in the presence or absence of certain alleles or their size range at individual loci but in the relative frequency and distribution of these alleles across loci. The researchers found that this was very similar to investigations done on human populations and to studies of North American canids (Wall et al. 1993; Roy et al. 1994; Zajc et al.1997: 183).

With respect to the phylogenetic relationships among the three dog breeds, Zajc and colleagues (1997: 184) found based on microsatellite genetic distances, Greyhounds and German Shepherds were significantly further apart genetically which suggested that the two lineages had separated at an early stage of canine domestication. They conclude that this finding is consistent with art artifacts dated from around 5000 BC which depicts two breeds of dogs that closely resembled the present-day German Shepherd and Greyhound. The genetic distance estimated for Labrador retrievers however, indicated that they were a much younger breed. The distance between the Labrador when compared to the Greyhounds and shepherd was almost equidistant. Zajc and colleagues inferred that the Labrador was selected from one or more breeds from both the Greyhound and German shepherd lineages. Additionally, they found that the Labrador population showed less intrabreed variation than the other two breeds. Since Labradors are believed to have originated in Newfoundland, the reduced variation would be consistent with a high inbreeding coefficient due to a small breeding population in a limited geographic area.

Fig. 14. (Top) Australian dingo, *Canis lupus dingo* (www.caravanning-oz.com).
(Bottom) Australian cattle dogs are believed to be derived from the Australian dingo (photo M. Raisor).

Zajc et al. (1997: 184) summarized that the microsatellite genetic markers revealed significant information about domestication. When compared to humans, dogs have a very low amount of population variation. However when compared to other domesticated animals, such as the horse or bovine, the dogs show parallel distributions which would indicate intentional inbreeding selection.

Genetic variability of primitive dog breeds

Australian dingo

Dingoes are a type of Asian dog that are possibly derived from the Indian or Arabian wolf by domestication by not more than 10,000 years before present (Corbett 1995: 12). Although dingoes have been associated as being indigenous to Australia, there is fossil evidence that the earliest Dingoes evolved in Asia (Fig. 14). The distribution and antiquity of dingo fossils throughout Asia and Australia fit in with the Asian seafarer theory (Corbett 1995: 14, 17; Dayton 2003: 556). Corbett suggests that during the Pleistocene, migration of humans from mainland Asia through the islands of Southeast Asia and into the Pacific, introduced dingoes into Australia perhaps on several occasions over many centuries. More than likely, according to Corbett, the dingoes accompanied the Asian seafarers as a source of fresh food during sea voyages. He bases this hypothesis on historical and modern evidence that dingoes have been and are commonly eaten throughout Asia.

The importance of the dingo (*Canis lupus dingo*) in the evolutionary pathway of canids has been largely overlooked. For the last 200 years in Australia, the dingo has been persecuted and hunted ruthlessly, first by European settlers and later by ranchers who viewed them as "pests" and "sheep killers" (Mullally 1994: 23-24). Even today in many areas of Australia, they are classified as vermin and are only protected in National Parks where preservation of native fauna is a priority. Although some research has been done on morphological differences between the domestic dog and dingo (Newsome et al. 1980; Newsome and Corbett 1982; 1985), scant research has been accomplished on trying to identify diagnostic DNA markers that can be used to assess the genetic background of dingoes (Wilton et al. 1999). Current evolutionary information on the dingo has largely been derived through the fossil record by archaeologists, zoologists and paleontologists. The dingo has been mostly ignored by molecular geneticists who view the animals as a subspecies of wolf-like canid and indistinguishable from domestic dogs.

One of the earliest molecular studies of the dingo was conducted in 1977 (Cole et al. 1977: 230-231). Blood was collected from domestic dogs and dingoes, and 20 enzyme systems were used to detect electrophoretic differences at 16 loci. Cole et al. found very little biochemical differentiation between the dingoes and the domestic dog. They concluded that the homogeneity of the dingo and dog blood enzymes reflected homogeneity of the gene pools. Cole et al. stated that the failure to discover an enzyme system that differentiates between domestic dogs and dingoes meant that it would be extremely difficult to determine gene flow or unique haplotypes.

Wilton, Steward and Zafiris (1999) is the latest molecular study which has tried to identify specific microsatellite variations in order to detect differences between domestic dogs and dingoes. DNA was extracted from blood samples from 16 dingoes and 16 crossbred dogs. Fourteen microsatellites were examined for possible variation based upon earlier studies of microsatellite structure used in other canids (Mellersh et al. 1994; Ostrander et al. 1993).

Although the results of Wilton et al.'s (1999: 110) study were less dramatic than molecular research done on wolves and coyotes, it was promising. At one locus, a difference of one base pair was detected in dingoes. They were also able to identify one locus, a dinucleotide repeat, in which the dingoes have an odd numbered allele size while dog alleles are of even size. The researchers also noticed that there was more homogeneity in the dingoes than dogs which may be the result of a small founding population. However, the researchers concluded that this locus would have to be repeated on a much larger sample size to make sure that this site was consistent as a diagnostic marker. In a more recent study Wilton (2001:51, 55) found six additional microsatellite loci that were not shared between dogs and dingoes. Wilton suspects that additional microsatellites may be found if "pure" dingoes that have not been hybridized are found for testing. Wilton (2003) proposes that more molecular research be conducted on tanned dingo skins from museum collections, as well as bones and teeth collected by anthropologists working on Pacific Island dingo remains. Wilton further proposes that molecular data be collected on the Australian cattle dog, a breed that was deliberately crossed with dingoes.

New Guinea Singing Dog

One of the most endangered wild canids, the New Guinea Singing Dog (NGSD) was first discovered in 1957 (Fig. 15). Named for their unique vocalizations, their howls are similar to wolf howls with overtones of whale song and other barks sounding like birdcalls (Koler-Matznick 2003a; 2003c). Originally declared a unique species, it was designated *Canis hallstromi*. However, in 1969, the breed was grouped with the Australian dingo as a feral subspecies of the domestic dog and reclassified as *Canis lupus dingo* (Koler-Matznick 2003a; 2003c). Because of the reclassification, zoos and some conservation groups lost interest in the breed, and extinction is an imminent threat. As a result of the current discover of some unique breed characteristics, there has been some debate that the NGSD should be returned to the *Canis hallstromi* classification which would provide it some protection under the Endangered Species Act.

Almost all the NGSD's living in North America are derived from a single breeding pair captured in 1957 in New Guinea and later given to the Taronga Zoo in Australia. At present approximately 200 NGSD's are believed to be living in captivity. Of the 200 dogs, half are known to be in breeding programs in North America, with a small percentage of the dogs in breeding programs in Europe. The remaining dogs are believed to be owned by exotic animal breeders (Koler-Matznick, personal communication, 2003b).

The NGSD is a small canine, 18-20 inches at the shoulder and weighing 20-25 pounds. They are a sable color when born and change to a tawny color in adulthood. They characteristically have white socks and a bushy tail tipped with white. Their skull is wide with flared zygomatic arches. They have the appearance of being a smaller version of the Australian dingo.

As a result of the rarity of the NGSD's and given the limited access to pedigreed captive stock, very little molecular research has been done on this unique breed. One of the earliest studies that included the NGSD was Simonsen's (1976) electrophoretic research on the blood proteins in domestic dogs and other Canidae. Simonsen (1976: 15) concluded from his study that there were no differences in the blood enzymes of *Canis lupus* (gray wolf), *Canis familiaris* (domestic dog), or *Canis dingo* (Australian dingo). However examination of the NGSD revealed some distinct differences. In the NGSD, enzyme 6-phosphogluconate dehydrogenase matched *Canis latrans* (coyote). Simonsen also discovered that glucose-6-phosphate dehydrogenase in the NGSD matched *Canis latrans* (coyote) and *Vulpes vulpes* (red fox).

Recent examination of the mtDNA in NGSD's revealed three maternal lines, with none shared with *Canis lupus* or *Canis latrans* (Koler-Matznick 2003c; Vila et al.1997). One NGSD haplotype was seen in many common breeds as well as ancient breeds such as the dingo, basenji and greyhound in Clade I (Vila et al. 1997: 1688).

Fig. 15. Examples of primitive dogs. (Top) Carolina dog (photo L. Brisban). (Bottom) New Guinea singing dog (Canis hallstromi or Canis lupus dingo) (http://rarebreed.com/breeds/ngsd_club.html).

Further molecular examination of this unique breed is of critical importance in the debate of the origin of the domestic dog. Due to the general assumption that the NGSD were a feral domestic canine, little attention has been paid to this breed.

Although NGSD's display discernable morphological differences from domestic canines, as well as behavioral, physiological and vocalization variants, minimal research has been done to discover the evolutionary significance of NGSD's. Current studies that have included the NGSD in mtDNA analysis have used small sample sizes (n=2) and depended on exotic animal breeders to supply specimens for study (Koler-Matznick, personal communication 2003b; Vila et al. 1997: 1687). In order to gain more reliable data on this breed, future studies would have to include a larger sample size of pedigreed captive NGSD's that have not been hybridized with domestic dogs. Having evolved for many thousands of years in an environment free of other members of the

Canis (e.g. wolves and coyotes), the NGSD can be used to study the most primitive characteristics of the dog-wolf complex (Brisbin and Risch 1997:1124). NGSD's provide an opportunity to study a dog breed that some zoologists have identified as not only a living relic of Stone Age tribes, but also a critical link in the evolutionary pathway of canids (Koler-Matznick 2003c).

Carolina dogs

For over twenty years Lehr Brisbin, Jr. and colleagues at the Savannah River Ecology Lab (SREL) in Aiken, South Carolina have studied a shy, feral nature dog which Brisbin designated as the Carolina dog (Fig. 15). Located on 300 square miles of protective land, SERL researchers often spotted what locals had called a "yallar" dog. However, Brisbin happened to notice that the overall physical appearance of these feral dogs was very similar to the Australian dingo. Yellow in color, with white feet, erect ears, curved sickle-tail and short coat, at first glance it seems to be a typical dog of mixed heritage. However, certain behavioral attributes of the Carolina dog are more similar to wild-type canids. Differences in estrus cycles, a propensity of digging "snout pits", underground den construction, tail signaling, and hunting behavior have distinguished the Carolina dog from domesticated canines.

At present, no molecular data has been published on this breed, although Brisbin has conducted some preliminary studies on the mtDNA. In an interview Brisbin and co-researcher Travis Glenn, reported that when the mtDNA of Carolina dogs was compared to dingoes, New Guinea Singing dogs and domestic dogs, the Carolina dogs mtDNA sequences tended to group together with dingoes (Weidensaul 1999: 52-54). Brisbin and Glenn believe that these initial results may indicate that the Carolina dogs are a more primitive breed, like the dingoes and NGSD's and are a part of the worldwide distribution of pariah canids. Further molecular research on Carolina dogs is planned by Brisbin and colleagues, which will hopefully add to the evolutionary record. Brisbin hopes to determine if these dogs represent close descendents of dogs that first crossed the Bering Strait Land Bridge.

CHAPTER III

Behavior of Wolves

Researchers, in their discussion of molecular data results, have made one large assumption when making conclusions on the origin of the domestic dog. Molecular geneticists presume that early humans tamed wolves, while selectively breeding them for desired characteristics. That is, they hypothesized that these tamed wolves became precursors to the domestic dog. There are two broad generalizations which are the foundation for domestication theory: 1) wolves when captured as infants can be easily trained and assimilated within a human social unit, and 2) early humans possessed a level of sophisticated modern cognition that allowed him to rationalize the benefits of animal husbandry and strategically selected for specific qualities in wolves that would better adapt them for human exploitation. Even contemporary anthropological models assume the relative ease of taming a wild canid without investigating documented wolf behavior studies. These assumptions however, may not be warranted.

Decades of studying wolf behavior, both in wild populations and captive human-reared wolves, has given much insight into this highly evolved social animal. Indeed it has been speculated that wolves possess a social complexity comparable to gorilla, chimpanzee and man (Fox 1972). To evaluate the plausibility of wolves being tamable, wolf behavior patterns of sociability, aggressiveness, hunting behavior, trainability, context-specific signal communication and cognitive complexity is reviewed below.

Reproductive development

Although domestic dogs can be reproductively mature and have a first estrus at 6-18 months, wolves are much slower to mature. Domesticated dogs have a estrus cycle of two times a year occuring approximately six months or more apart. Wild wolves on the other hand have a yearly estrus with the first cycle occurring not until their second, third, or fourth winters (Mech et al. 1998). In dogs, there is no seasonal sequence to these cycles and they may occur at anytime during the year with the estrus period in dogs lasting approximately three weeks whereas in wolves it lasts about a month. Wolves come into estrus during the late winter with pups born early in spring coinciding with herbivore birth patterns (Mech 1970). Wolves have an identical gestation period to dogs, lasting from 61 to 64 days during which time the pregnant female may begin to restrict her activity to an area in close proximity to the den (Fuller 1989: 185). The dens can consist of a variety of structures depending on what is environmentally available. Mech (1970) and Mech et al. (1998) have documented dens in rock caves, rock crevices, sandy bluffs or dug under the roots of fallen trees. These dens can be dug as early as fall of the previous year with adults and yearlings of both sexes participating in den construction (Ryon 1977: 88; Thiel et al. 1997: 481).

Neonatal development

Like dogs, wolf pups are born blind and deaf with limited motor ability. Between 12-14 days the eyes begin to open in both dog and wolf pups (Fig. 16). However, they are still helpless with poor visual perception. During the first 3-4 weeks of life the lactating mother remains with the pups, with the female depending on the male mate to provide food and defense for the lactating females (Ballard et al. 1991).

At five to ten weeks, wolf pups although they have complete dentition, are still unable to chew pieces of meat requiring regurgitated food (Packard et al. 1992; Mech et al. 1999; Packard 2003: 48) and periodic nursing. When the den is approached by humans, the mother and pups retreat to the den (Packard 2003: 48). If the pups lag, the mother or other adults will pick them up in their mouth and carry them into the den (Packard 2003: 48).

By four to ten months the wolf pups are sufficiently large and coordinated enough to accompany adults on hunts where they begin to sharpen their basic hunting skills (Packard 2003: 52). Much of the hunting behavior has been "practiced" during play where they pounce, stalk, chase and wrestle with siblings. During hunting excursions, the pups accompany the parents and older juvenile siblings. Feeding at the kill sites is first initiated by the parents who consume enough to feed themselves and the pups, with older juveniles sharing the food last (Mech 1988).

On the average, wolf juveniles disperse from the pack (Ballard et al. 1997). However, if food resources become scarce, the older siblings may disperse at a younger age as competition for food escalates (Mech et al. 1998).

Behavioral development

Numerous studies have been conducted on comparisons between wolf and canine social development and behavior (Bekoff 1977; Frank and Frank 1982a, 1984; Scott 1954; Zimen 1972, 1987). It is important to understand wolf behavior since many researchers infer that early humans were able to interact with these animals and form a cooperative relationship. Two studies were done by the Franks(1982a; 1984) and Zimen (1987), comparing the social development between hand-raised timber wolf pups (*C. lupus lycaon*) and Alaskan malamutes (*C. familiaris*). In an earlier study done by Zimen (1972) wolf pups litter raised by their wolf mother exhibited flight behavior by 21 days old and never

Fig. 16. (Top left) Wolf pups are born blind and deaf with limited motor ability. (Top right) Between 12-14 days the eyes begin to open. (Bottom left) By 6 weeks, the wolf pups have comparable motor ability to a small, mature dog. (Bottom right) By 6-9 months, the wolf juveniles can successfully hunt and kill small prey. (www.californiawolfcenter.org; www.rosswarner.com/5659.jpg; www.kerwoodwolf.com/youngpuphowl2.jpg; www.ag.Arizona.edu/~rjsmith/wolf.jpg)

became socialized with humans. Therefore the Franks (1982a) obtained 11-day-old wolf pups which they felt would better bond to their human caregivers. The researchers spent approximately 12 hours per day with the wolves during which time they were bottle-fed and alternately spent nights with the authors or wolf mother.

The Franks (1982a: 510, 513) reported several physiological differences in the wolf pups when compared to the Malamutes. It was first observed that the wolves had superior locomotor abilities than the dogs. At 19 days the wolves were able to scale 45 cm walls whereas the Malamutes at 32 days were unable to climb a 15 cm barrier. The Franksfurther observed that by 6 weeks of age the locomotor ability of the wolves were comparable to small, mature dogs and were fast enough that they could avoid capture by their human caregivers (Fig. 16). Also, the wolf pups were extremely sensitive to dietary changes unlike the Malamutes which had no difficulty in switching from mother's milk, to formula, to solid food. Whereas the Malamutes readily made the transition to solid food in three days with no gastrointestinal disturbance, the wolves were far less adaptable. When separated from their mother, the wolves lost weight and resisted any minor variation in their diet. The Franks reported that it took a period of weeks before the wolf pups successfully made the dietary transition. A third difference noted was that the wolf pups displayed less sexual dimorphism than the Malamutes, nor did they exhibit any sex-related differences in social behavior, that is males were not more assertive. The researchers were able to identify the males or females at a glance quite easily in the Malamute litter but could not identify either sex in the wolves.

In social development, the Franks (1982a: 510) reported that the wolf pups continued to have a tenuous relationship with the human. Even at two weeks of age the wolves would seek out adult canines to hide behind. As the wolves grew, they still exhibited a distinct preference for canine social partners, rather than their human caregivers. This apparent preference had also been seen in an earlier study done by Frank and Frank (1982b: 96) where rewards for task-solving was reinforced by allowing play with other adult dogs.

Another interesting point discovered in the Franks' study was the level of aggression and fighting in the wolf and Malamute litters (Frank and Frank 1982a: 512-513, 516-517). Surprisingly, the Malamutes exhibited more intense aggression with their siblings and occasionally would attack adult members. However the wolf pups engaged in more peaceful play and never challenged adults. The Franks inferred that the wolf's highly ritualized behavioral structure, with its elaborate use of facial expressions and body language acts as a buffer against intra-family conflicts. Even when the Malamute pups were exposed to adult wolves they were unable to recognize the wolves' display of dominance and submission behaviors. Wolves separated from their littermates at a very young age, would nevertheless exhibit ritualized behavior of aggression and dominance ordering. The Franks (1982a: 523) hypothesized that natural selection would operate against intragroup aggression especially in a population that has to hunt cooperatively in order to ensure its genetic survival. Therefore development of a social system which would diffuse indiscriminant aggression is especially important to prevent injury or death.

In another pivotal study done by Zimen (1987), wolves and dogs were compared on approach and flight behavior. This research used both wolves and poodles, and also included wolf-hybrid pups (F1 and F2). In a previous attempt to hand-raise 21 day old wolf pups, Zimen had concluded that wolf pups at that age had already developed flight behavior and never became socialized to humans. In this particular study, Zimen hand-raised the litter on the 14th day after their eyes had opened. In this litter, Zimen stated that he was able to completely tame and socialize the wolf pups to humans. Even when these pups escaped their enclosure, they would eventually return. This positive assimilation to humans was completely different in the litter hand-raised from the 21st day of birth. Zimen (1987: 280) observed that although the pups that had been raised at day 21 had friendly tendencies such as tail wagging when a person entered the enclosure, they still were fearful of humans and could not be approached closer than a few meters.

Zimen (1987: 281-282) also studied another litter which was raised in a natural setting and left alone with their mother and a pack of 13. Zimen reported that the pups were only observed outside the den on the 29th day and when approached they would disappear in the den. By the time the pups were six weeks old their only reaction was flight behavior and would never come out of the den when the author approached.

In wolf hybrids (F1) that Zimen had hand-raised it was observed that the hybrids reacted very similar to the wolves. Zimen reported that before the 21st day, all the hybrid pups exhibited flight reactions when approached. Zimen also noted that even though the hybrids eventually became socialized to the point where they were not fearful of the researcher, they never became socialized toward strangers. In the litter which was raised by the mother, the hybrid pups were extremely fearful and behaved very much like wolves. Zimen observed that these pups never became socialized but were more tolerant of a human presence than wolves.

In the F2 hybrid litter, a cross between a wolf and poodle referred to as a "Puwos", Zimen noted that all four pups displayed varying degrees of flight behavior ranging from very fearful to highly socially motivated. In those pups that had exhibited flight behavior, they never became socialized to humans. However those that had low flight tendencies became very friendly and excited when humans approached. It is also interesting to note than even those pups that were raised by friendly, socialized mother, remained non-social and shy. Zimen also noticed that in those litters where some of the pups displayed extreme flight tendencies, they would eventually influence the reactions of the less timid pups, so that by the time the pups were six weeks old, all the pups would retreat when approached.

Zimen's (1987) studies on the domestic dog revealed similar results but the reactions were less severe and they quickly adapted to humans within a few days. As the poodles matured, their reactions to humans became more sociable and sought human contact.

Zimen (1987: 290) concluded that there is a strong genetic fixation of fear and flight, in both wolves and hybrids. Therefore he concluded that a strong social bond between man and wolf could only be achieved by socializing wolf pups at an extremely young age before they have developed firm fear/flight tendencies. Zimen further concludes that socialization is the most successful in those animals obtain at six days old and had no interaction with other wolves. Zimen (1987: 291) hypothesizes that in order for Paleolithic humans to accomplish this, it would have been necessary for women to provide human milk in order to feed the pups.

Many of Zimens' observations were also confirmed in an earlier study conducted by Fentress (1967) who studied the behavioral development in a hand-reared male timber wolf. Although Fentress' study lacks much of the developmental detail that was included in Zimen's research, it provides an interesting look at the adaptability of a wild canid raised as a "pet". In Fentress' work, a wolf pup was obtained at the age of four weeks and raised in a human family environment similar to the way a dog would be raised.

During the first few weeks, the pup had difficulty in adjusting to a new diet and had to be force-fed, but eventually adapted to a meat diet. The pup was sociable with familiar humans but was cautious with strangers. By the age of 13 weeks the pup began to kill chickens and exhibited aggression when there was an attempt to remove the dead animal. By 14 weeks he would regularly kill rodents and became visibly excited around horses and would attempt to nip at their tails. His interaction with dogs remained friendly and he would try to initiate play. At six months the pup killed a cat that the wolf had been raised with however he was still friendly with humans.

After the pup had reached one year of age he became more aggressive in his hunting behavior and attacked cats, chickens, and geese (Fentress 1967: 346). Previously learned tasks were less frequently performed successfully as the wolf became more independent and restless. During this period the wolf would often practice mock attacks and pounces although Fentress noted that the pup still remained friendly with humans.

By his second year, Zimen observed that the wolf's attitude toward small children changed and the wolf began to watch them with the same intensity as cats. Therefore his access to unsupervised children was restructured.

At the end of the three-year study, Fentress (1967: 348) concluded that the wolf had remained sociable towards humans and the dogs. However, if given free run in a fenced field, Fentress reported that he would spend considerable time avoiding direct contact with humans. When exposed to unfamiliar things, the wolf remained easily frightened and difficult to calm. These observations are very similar to Zimen's (1987: 290) study when he observed that frequently even in "tame" wolves, they would show avoidance behavior towards humans although they would wag their tail in a "friendly" manner. Avoidance and flight when exposed to new objects, strangers or situations was also observed in Zimen's study which was also noted in Fentress' research.

Woolpy and Ginsburg (1967) conducted an 8-year study studying wolf socialization towards humans. This research was particularly significant since socialization of the wolves was attempted at various ages and used wolves with varying degrees of exposure to human handling.

In wolf pups born in captivity, Woolpy and Ginsburg (1967: 358-361) observed that during the first six to seven weeks the pups approached anyone readily or at least not move away from them. By the seventh week the pups exhibited a fear response and they also became more difficult to get the animals to respond when they interacted with humans. The researchers also observed that by the time the wolves had reached twelfth weeks of age the fear response had become so heightened that any new or strange stimuli whether it was exposure to a new object or a new person evoked a very negative reaction such as tail tucking, urination, trembling or salivation. The socialized pups were then deprived of human contact for over six months and then reintroduced to humans. Woolpy and Ginsberg found that although the wolf pups had been very friendly towards humans that when isolated from human contact they did not retain their socialization. The researchers concluded that in young wolves the socialization behavior has to be continuously reinforced in order to prevent the fear response to become fixed behavioral reaction. Although in Zimen's (1987: 276) study he first noted a fear response at three weeks, which was also supported in a study by Fox (1970: 56) who reported an avoidance reaction at 24 days, the seventh week avoidance behavior could be the result of being hand-raised at a young age. In a study conducted by Snow (1967: 354) it was noted that captive raised pups often lagged in development than those raised by their mothers. Woolpy and Ginsberg (1967: 361) also ascertained that those pups that had continual social contact with humans through adulthood would stay social and friendly.

When Woolpy and Ginsburg (1967: 359-360) attempted to socialize an adult wolf that had had no human interaction, the fear response was greatly heightened. The wolf would become highly agitated in the new surroundings and when a human would approach the enclosure the animal would attempt to escape. After a month the wolf would not exhibit the extreme escape reaction but would stay as far away from the experimenter as was possible in the enclosure. Any increase of body movements by the researcher would frequently cause the wolf to regress to the escape behavior. Eventually the wolf would approach the experimenter and sniff the clothing. As the animal became less fearful it would attempt to chew at the experimenter's clothing. This stage is followed by the wolf rubbing himself against the human while allowing the experimenter to pet it.

Woolpy and Ginsburg (1967: 360) found that as the adult wolf became more confident with the experimenter the animal also becomes bolder and would bite and tug any protective clothing worn (Fig. 17). They stated that if an attempt is made to prevent biting at the clothes, the wolf would bite harder and more vigorously. They further asserted that attempts to dominate the animal physically at this stage could lead to a full-blown attack or cause a setback to an earlier stage of development. They also reported that if an experimenter retreated too quickly after an attack the wolf was more inclined to be even more aggressive in future human encounters.

The last stage of social development in the adult wolf was marked by the wolf approaching the experimenter in a friendly way soliciting being petted or rubbed with no aggression evident. To get to this particular stage of socialization was very lengthy, taking at least six to seven months of frequent interaction. Woolpy and Ginsburg (1967: 361) also reported that socialization attempts were not successful if more than one animal was present even if the other animal was fully socialized. They reported that the more fearful animal would use the other animal as a barrier and in some cases would launch aggressive attacks while shielding itself behind the other animal.

Woolpy and Ginsburg (1967: 361) concluded that to successfully socialize an animal towards humans was more dependent upon the age of the animal. Although socialization could be achieved at any age, the older animals showed much higher levels of fear response and aggression which resulted in lengthy conditioning taking at least half of a year to achieve. In the wolf pups, socialization was easier to accomplish since it paralleled pack relationships which are formed very early in life. However in all age groups, for successful socialization in order to be maintained, the researchers concluded that lasting social relationships had to be formed over a long period of time so that the animal learned to cope with the fear response. Woolpy and Ginsburg also stated that as the development of fear response increased as the animal got older, it paralleled the increasing difficulty of acquiring socialized behavior.

Facial expressions

All canids have very extensive ritualized patterns of facial expression and postures that are crucial in hierarchy formation and maintaining stability within a pack. The complexity of social organization in each species of Canidae is generally reflected in the diversity of these physical cues assumed during aggressive encounters (Kleiman 1967: 365).

In the wolf, coyote, dingo and New Guinea Singing Dog, a dominant animal, or an animal about to attack, will open its mouth and bare its teeth by wrinkling the muzzle vertically (Kleiman 1967: 369). In the face of an animal demonstrating submission, the lips cover the teeth and the corners of the mouth are pulled tightly back giving the visual appearance of a submissive "grin" (Kleiman 1967: 369). Fox (1970: 56) noted that the submissive grin was seen in 24 day old wolf pups and was directed to either a conspecific or was used to initiate "play". The subordinate may also exhibit licking movements or many lick the mouth of the superior animal. Schenkel (1967: 324) reported that this act of submission has a begging quality that is seen in the infantile begging-for-food ceremony seen in puppies eliciting regurgitated food from an adult female.

Eye contact is also an important behavioral response that can signal either aggression or submission. Avoidance of eye contact by a subordinate as soon as eye to eye contact is made with a dominant conspecific is especially developed in the wolf (Fox 1970: 57). According to Fox, in a wolf pack the subordinates constantly look towards the alpha animal,

Fig. 17. Socialized wolves will become more bold and assertive as they become more confident with their experimenters, sometimes leading to a full blown attack (www.kerwoodwolf.com/bigbad.jpg).

who frequently ignores them. However when the dominant animal makes eye to eye contact with a subordinate, the subordinate clearly looks away. Fox (1972: 60) also states that while the subordinate avoids eye contact, it will approach the dominant animal side ways. Fox also reports that when he directly stared at the wolves used in his study, he got two reactions. Either the animal acted passive submissive or a direct attach was provoked. Similar reactions have been observed and recorded in the domestic dog. Although teeth baring, lateral recumbency and direct eye contact can often be translated differently in dog behavior. Frank and Frank (1982a: 519) infer that in the process of domestication, selection pressures against aggression have relaxed, and in most breeds of dog the wolf's highly predictable dominance rituals has disintegrated into an assortment of independent behavioral fragments. Fox (1970: 71) postulates that the ritualized behavioral ceremonies seen in the wolf often involves mutual submission and defensive aggression associated with food begging and food-giving necessary for group cohesion. However facial expressions and posturing in the dog represent different motivations. Fox (1972: 59) observing aggression interaction in wolves noted that wolves and coyotes exhibit an inhibition of the bite. Fox (1972: 59) reported that when an alpha wolf exerts dominance over a subordinate, it would seize the jaws of the subordinate, however the jaws of the alpha wolf do not close. However in domestic dogs, there is no inhibition of bite and some dogs will bite without provocation.

Similarly the submissive lateral recumbency seen in the wolf is less likely an act of submission in the dog. As Fox (1972: 59) points out, a dog on his back is more probably soliciting attention or a belly-rub and not responding to a threat of domination. Schenkel (1967: 326) suggests that submissive puppy-like behavior seen in wolves regulates the social hierarchy and privilege system. Although dogs exhibit some of these same traits, the submissive responses have lost much of their adaptive function, behavioral integrity and social significance in the dog (Frank and Frank 1982a: 519). Much of these behavioral components have resulted from selective breeding which has altered the wild-type behavioral development and has heightened the dog's ability to be compatible with humans (Frank and Frank 1982a: 519).

Clearly if early man attempted to tame wolves it would have been necessary for them to recognize the wolves' behavioral responses in order to assimilate a wild animal into the human social structure. Early man would have had to be cognizant of his own reflexive reactions that would provoke an attack. For example, smiling or any display of the teeth could be interpreted by a wolf as a challenge for dominance and lead to an attack. The same is true for eye-to-eye contact between a wolf and human. Although a submissive animal would flee when gazed at, an aggressive wolf would view this as a threat and could possible launch a violent attack.

Instinctual vs. cognitive processing

Studies done on cognitive and instinctual learning behaviors in wolves when compared to dogs have proven that there is are dramatic differences in how canids process information. In an early study, Frank and Frank (1982b) tested both dogs and wolves on their ability to perform problem-solving tasks that would require insight to successfully complete a task. The Franks (1980; 1982a; 1982b; 1983; 1984) proposed that natural selection in the wolf had favored a "duplex" system of information processing composed of both instinctual and cognitive components. The cognitive system was defined by the Franks (1982b: 95; 1984: 225) as the ability to use foresight into a means to an end relationship. This system would require, according to the Franks, a capacity for mental representation to achieve a goal. The Franks view the use of cooperation and strategy in group hunting, or the ability to charge strategies in order to successfully complete a goal, as examples of cognitive structuring. In this study (Frank and Frank 1982b) both 6-week-old dog and wolf pups were placed in a series of wooden barriers that they had to navigate around to achieve either a food reward or social reward such as interaction with another dog that the pups were fond of and always eager to greet. The wolf pups consistently performed more successfully that the dogs in navigating all three barriers. This ability of the wolves to maneuver through new obstacles and detours suggests, according to the Franks, a higher-order mental process of complex cognitive functioning. The Franks (1982b: 95) state that dogs have a greatly reduced cognitive function because domestication has selected for animals that require more environmental feedback from humans which buffered against the consequences of behavioral mistakes.

Hare and colleagues (2002) proposed that during the process of domestication dogs had been selected for certain social cognitive abilities that enabled them to communicate with humans in unique ways, not seen in wolves. The basis of this study was to see if dogs and wolves contained the same social cognitive skills seen in primates. Previous studies had shown that nonhuman primates would follow the gaze of conspecfics and humans to outside objects for detection food, predators and social interactions among group mates (Tomasello et al. 1998).

Hare et al. (2002: 1634-1635) tested three different hypotheses on the use of social cues. The first hypothesis examined was that canids in general are highly flexible in exploiting social information since they live cooperatively in hunting social groups which can be generalized to humans. A second hypothesis ascertained that domestic dogs have learned their skills from their repeated contact with humans. Therefore if this hypothesis could not be falsified, young dogs or puppies with relatively very little human contact should perform poorly in using human cues. In the third hypothesis, Hare et al. inferred that there has been selection pressure on dogs during domestication for specific skills of social cognition. To test these three hypotheses, Hare and colleagues used adult dogs and adult wolves raised by humans, and puppies of various ages and amounts of exposure to humans.

In one experiment, Hare et al. (2002: 1635) tested adult dogs and wolves on following social cues to indicate the location of food. The experimenter either gazed/pointed/tapped a container to indicate a food source, or gazed and pointed, or just simply pointed towards a container. A control was also used where no cue was given to indicate where the food was located, with the experimenter looking straight ahead. The results indicated that the dogs consistently were able to use all social cues displayed by the experimenter to find the food, whereas the wolves never performed better than chance on any cue. The only test where both wolves and dogs were equally successful was the control. Since no cue was used in the control, both wolves and dogs did not score above chance.

In another experiment Hare et al. (2002: 1635) let both dogs and wolves see food being placed in a canister but there was a delay before the canister was placed in a location. This experiment was done to test levels of memory retention. It was recorded that dogs and wolves performed above chance, with the wolves displaying

Fig. 18. Various behavioral tests have shown that wolves are unable to skillfully interpret human social cues, facial expressions and lack the ability to have face/eye contact with humans (www.karpaty.edu.pl/teams/ustrzyki/wolf.jpg).

slightly better retention rates than the dogs. In the control where the wolves and dogs did not see the food placed in a container, both groups scored at chance levels. Hare et al. concluded that this ruled out any possibility of the animals locating the food by smell.

In the third experiment, Hare and colleagues (2002: 1635) tested 32 dog puppies at various ages. The puppies had been further sub-divided into those raised with humans and a second group of puppies that had had only minimal contact with humans having lived their lives in a kennel environment. Hare et al. reported that there was no difference between the rearing groups in their use of gazing cues or gazing/pointing cues. They also observed that the effect of age on performance was not a factor in the pups using cues successfully.

Hare and colleagues (2002: 1635-1636) concluded based on the results of the various behavioral tests that domestic dogs are more skilled than wolves at using human social cues (Fig. 17). Even young puppies use human social cues very skillfully, regardless of age or length of exposure to humans. The researchers also determined that domestic dogs and wolves perform equally as well on memory tests which they concluded rules out any possibility that dogs out-perform wolves in all human-guided tasks. Hare et al. surmise that the results of the various tests exclude the hypothesis that dogs have acquired their ability to recognize social cues from wolves. They further conclude that the human exposure hypothesis was also proven not to be valid, since puppies raised with very little human contact performed equally as well as those pups human-reared. Therefore they inferred that the domestication hypothesis has the strongest support, with dogs most likely acquiring social skills as the result of domestication.

In a recent study, Miklosi and colleagues (2003) proposed that the readiness of dogs to look at the human face has lead to complex forms of dog-human communication that cannot be achieved in wolves even after extended socialization. In order to test this hypothesis, the researchers used socialized wolves and compared their behavioral responses to domestic dogs.

In the first test, two containers were placed 1.5 meters apart. One of the containers held hidden food. A human experimenter indicated which container held the food by distal pointing (finger 50 cm from object), proximal pointing (5-10 cm away from object, and touching the object physically. The results of the tests revealed that the wolves perfumed poorly on the distal pointing test but performed over chance in the other gestural cues. The researchers found that when wolves are raised similarly to dogs, they can identify some human gestures that can indicate e the placement of food. However Miklosi and colleagues (2003: 763-764) found that the overall performance of wolves is generally worse that that of dogs when similarly tested. The researchers reasoned that the poorer performance of the wolves on the distal pointing test was the result of the wolves avoiding the gaze of humans. This avoidance inhibited the wolves to recognize the movement of the humans' upper body with the association with food.

The second study consisted of two problem-solving tests. In the first test, the wolves and dogs were taught how to retrieve food by opening a bin. In the second part of the test, the food was placed in a cage with the food being attached to a rope. The animals would have to pull the rope in order to gain access to the food. After the animals had mastered both tasks, the researchers altered the tests so that they were insolvable. The bin was closed mechanically or the hidden in of the rope was attached to the cage so that it could not be pulled.

In the initial phase of the test when the food was accessible, both the wolves and dogs obtained the food equally as fast. The researchers (Miklosi et al. 2003: 764) inferred that both dogs and socialized wolves were equally motivated to solve the task and had all the abilities and physical means to achieve their goal. However, the researchers reported that in the blocked test trials, the dogs spent considerably more time gazing at the human than did the socialized wolves. Miklosi et al. found that out of seven wolves, only two looked in the direction of the human while the exact opposite was true for dogs. The dogs also attempted to retrieve the food for a shorter period of time (1-minute median) than the wolves before gazing at the humans. Wolves, for the most part, tended to ignore the humans and tried to get the meat themselves. However the dogs would interrupt their efforts to get the food and would gaze at the human trying to enlist their help. Based upon the results of the blocked test, Miklosi and colleagues suggested that when the task of obtaining the food was insolvable, the dogs initialized communicative face/eye contact with the human earlier and maintained it for longer periods of time compared to the socialized wolves.

Miklosi et al. (2003: 764-765) concluded that the failure of the socialized wolves to perform equally as well as the dogs resulted from their decreased willingness to look at the human (Fig. 18). They attribute this to a genetic predisposition in dogs since the researchers had a difficult time inducing this behavior even in socialized wolves. Miklosi et al. hypothesizes that "human-like" communicative behaviors were one of the first steps in selection in the domestication of the dog. They further suggest that the communicative interaction of face/eye contact in humans is fundamental for social exchange and would be a corresponding behavior that would be selected for in dogs. They conclude that this subtle change in behavior of dogs provide a starting point for the interaction of dog and human communication systems.

CHAPTER IV

The Archaeological Record

The purpose of this chapter is three-fold. The first is to describe the process of domestication. Throughout human history, man has attempted and succeeded in domesticating a variety of species. Dogs in comparison to all other domesticated animals have been the most exploited and altered through human intervention. In the last three thousand years, hundreds of varieties of dogs have been produced through selective breeding. From tiny toy breeds to massive working dogs, the range and diverseness is enormous. Domestication differs from evolution in that domestication involves human control over reproduction, whereas evolution is considered to be a process that takes place naturally and without man's direct interference. Domestication can alter a species both biologically and culturally and it can simultaneously work in conjunction with the evolutionary process. A discussion of why domestication occurred and how it contributes to the differentiation of a new species will be addressed in both dogs and other domesticated animals.

The second objective is to identify the morphological changes seen in dogs versus its wild canid ancestor, the wolf. A clear understanding of canid domestication lies within the very morphological changes that provide the basis for identification of early domesticated dogs (Morey 1992:182). Dogs, as well as other species, undergo numerous skeletal changes when domesticated. Most often these changes are viewed in the skull, which includes facial shortening, crowding of teeth, tooth size reduction, missing teeth and changes in the shape of the cranium. Additionally, there can be changes in physical size and limb length. These skeletal changes are often described as paedomorphosis, or the retention of neonate characteristics in adult animals. Morphological changes in the skeletal can be approached by visual examination or metrically, with traditionally both approaches being used by archaeologists. The pattern of morphological change from wolf to domesticated dog is of importance to archaeologists trying to resolve the identification of canid remains at archaeological sites.

The third objective is to provide a review of those archaeological sites that have contained canid remains of great antiquity dating to the Pleistocene or early Holocene. With molecular data indicating that dogs may have been domesticated 135,000 years ago, it would seem likely that dog remains would have been discovered that would have approached that time period. However, that has not been the case. At present, there is nothing that even closely reaches the antiquity of the molecular research conclusions. Nor have any transitional forms or "pseudo-dogs" been discovered. However, the archaeological evidence of domesticated dogs is of critical importance in proposing the origin of the dog and its worldwide spread. The lack of canine remains dating close to the molecular results does not imply that the molecular data is wrong. Rather, it simply is more evidence that the domestication issue is a complicated puzzle.

The complicated process of domestication

Although domestication involves altering wild-type morphology, it is not to be confused with evolution. The process of evolution occurs very slowly, over many millenniums. The driving force behind evolution is natural selection, in which certain genetic traits better suited to environmental constraints thrive and become integrated throughout future generations. The results of natural selection are organisms that are better adapted to sustain themselves and successfully reproduce. Forces that can influence natural selection are responses to a changed environmental condition such as food and water availability, predator pressure, disease, migration, genetic drift, reproductive fitness, and random mating. Some individuals that are better adapted to their particular environment, pass these qualities on to their offspring. McKern and McKern (1974: 27) best summarized Darwin's (1860) theory of natural selection which was centered upon three observations and two deductions:

Observation One: All organisms reproduce more than required to replace their own numbers.

Observation Two: Despite this tendency to multiply, the number of members of a given species remains relatively constant.

Observation Three: All living organisms vary. They resemble but do not exactly duplicate their parents.

Deduction One: There occurs a universal struggle for existence, both among and within species.

Deduction Two: Individuals with some advantage have the best chance for surviving and for reproducing their own kind.

The key to evolution is that genetic variation must be present within a population before the population can genetically change and evolve. Although humans can indirectly influence the evolutionary process by causing a shift in environmental conditions, the manipulation is unintentional. An example of humans unintentionally affecting the natural evolutionary process was documented in the peppered moth, *Biston betularia*. In England prior to 1848, all peppered moths were grayish-white with speckled mottling on the wings and body. The color provided perfect camouflage for the nocturnal moths as they rested on the trunks of lichen covered trees. As industrial pollution of the region increased, a new phenotypic mutation was observed in the moths called carbonaria. The moths exhibiting the carbonaria phenotype were mostly dark in color with little or no grey mottling. At the same time it was further observed that the lichens covering the trees were being killed due to the black industrial soot that was blanketing the vegetation. By the 1900's, the carbonaria phenotype had reached a frequency of more than 90 percent of those populations that were in high industrial areas. However in rural areas unaffected by pollution, the carbonaria phenotype was not present and the moths retained the grey mottled coloring (Kettlewell 1973; Russell 1992: 738). As the result of man influencing environmental conditions, the carbonaria form survived as it was better adapted in industrial areas and transmitted their genes to the next generation of moths. This mutation gave the altered moths an advantage and therefore tended to favorably increase the odds in terms of the struggle for survival. It is also an unusual case of "micro-evolution", in that the observed changes took place rather rapidly, in less than fifty years.

Domestication differs from evolution in that humans, not nature, create different strains of a plant or animal through the careful selection of desirable traits. These traits are further continued by the reproduction of those animals or plants. This interference by humans brings about rapid evolutionary change. The process is instrumented by nonrandom matings which can be influenced by either positive assortative mating or negative assortative mating. Positive assortative mating occurs when individuals with similar phenotypes are bred. An example of this is when animals of a particular color or size are selected for. In negative assortative mating, animals that are phenotypically different are chosen for breeding, such as a small animal bred to a larger one or vice versa (Russell 1992: 745). Darwin (1859: 34) was one of the first to recognize the potential outcome of nonrandom matings. However Darwin used the terminology of conscious or methodological selection to describe those breedings in which animals were selected that possessed particular traits (such as size, color or morphology) that were deemed to be of value. Darwin also identified another type of artificial selection which he coined as unconscious or unintentional selection. Darwin proposes that frequently a new trait would appear that was not the result of deliberate selection. If this new trait is recognized as being desirable, it could later be intentionally selected for. In many cases for a trait to become "fixed" it is necessary to inbreed in order to increase homozygosity and reduce genetic variation within a population. According to Tchernbov and Horwitz (1991: 57-58), human manipulation through artificial selection creates an ecological "vacuum" where diversity becomes very low, with negligible interspecific and high intraspecific competition and absence of predation pressure. Although man becomes the predator in the form of culling, it does not have the same effect as a prey/predator relationship. Culling, states Tchernov and Horwitz, reduces male selection, and therefore increases inbreeding and genetic drift and accelerates morphogenetic changes.

However, there is a differing hypothesis of early domestication that dismisses the opinion of the intentionality of humans, but rather views domestication as a symbiotic relationship (Zeuner 1963; O'Connor 1997; Russell 2002). Zeuner views early domestication as deriving from tolerated scavenging, human parasitism on animal herds, or control of crop robbers such as rabbits, cattle or geese. Zuener hypothesizes that this early interaction between humans and animals later gave rise to deliberate domestication of additional animals.

However, Bökönyi (1969: 219) views the earliest attempts of domestication, not so much as the artificial selection of traits, as simply a way to secure animal protein. In his view, the domesticated animal acts as a living food reserve. Bökönyi believes that wild animals were captured and kept in corrals and later killed at appropriate times. This activity, infers Bökönyi, leads to man's breeding of animals under artificial conditions.

Many authors agree that the earliest goal of domestication was to alter the wild-type behavior and produce an animal that had a docile demeanor making it more controllable and easily handled (Scott 1968: 252; Bökönyi 1969: 219; Belyaev 1978: 301; Tchernov and Horowitz 1991: 56; Trut 1999: 160,166; Russell 2002: 286; Leach 2003: 349). However, given the vast number of animal species in the world, what has prevented the majority from being fully domesticated?

Diamond (2002: 702) asserts that there are six criteria that hinder an animal from being successfully domesticated: 1) unusual diet that can not be easily supplied by humans (hence no domestic anteaters), 2) slow growth rate and long birth spacing like is seen in elephants, 3) vicious dispositions (for example, lions, bears and zebras), 4) reluctance to breed in captivity (pandas and cheetahs), 5) lack of follow-the-leader dominance hierarchies (bighorn sheep and antelope), and 6) a tendency to panic in enclosures or when faced with predators (gazelles and deer). According to Diamond, even if five out of six tests are met, many species still can not be domesticated.

Scott (1968: 252) believes that the animals which lived in herds, packs, flocks or groups already had a tendency towards social behavior and were easier to domesticate. Scott states that the high degree of sociality found in wild species such as birds, horses, cattle, goats, sheep, pigs, wolves and even rabbits, makes it easier for attachments to be made to human beings, especially if exposure to humans is done at critical periods of socialization development. An interesting point that Scott (1968: 266) makes is when he makes comparisons between wolf and dog behavior. Scott asserts that in adult behavior patterns of both dog and wolf, almost every behavior pattern that is observed in wolves can also be seen in dogs. Scott states that the process of domestication has had the effect of exaggerating or diminishing the frequency of occurrence of behavior patterns which results in an enormous increase in variation. For instance, the aggressive behavior seen in wolves has been modified in various breeds of dogs in which aggression has been focused towards hunting, herding or protective behaviors.

However according to Trut (1999:166) and Belyaev et al. (1981:272), many polygenes determining behavior may be regulatory, engaged in stabilizing an organism's early development. Trut states that although numerous genes interact to stabilize development, the primary genes which control this function are critical in the functioning of the neural and endocrine systems. In a study done on foxes, Trut and Belyaev et al., found that when an animal is exposed to stress, the adrenal glands releases hormones such as corticosteroids that stimulate the body to extract energy from the reserves of fats and proteins. The researchers also noted that serotonin, thought to be an inhibitor in an animal's aggressive behavior, increased dramatically in domesticated tame foxes. Therefore, artificial selection for docility may have a physiological basis in the endocrine system. Crockford (2000) agrees that hormone systems may have been instrumental in domestication and further suggests that humans may not have played an active role in the early stages of canine domestication. Crockford believes that the adrenal system, specifically the thyroid, mediates not only fetal development, post-natal growth, hair growth, reproduction, skin and hair pigmentation, but also behavioral responses to stimuli. Crockford suggests that thyroxine (T3, T4) production is not only species specific as well as breed specific in dogs, but also individual specific. During critical periods, Crockford states that the amounts of thyroxine produced are essential to target genes in various cells. She believes that slight differences in the pattern of production of thyroid hormone contribute to individual phenotypic variation. As a result of the changes, no matter how slight, Crock infers that thyroxine levels produce profound influences on other systems that cause individual phenotypic variation that allows the first stage of domestication to occur. These small subsets of genetically varied individuals would allow humans to select and create behaviorally distinct animals that are stress tolerant and more suitable to a human dominated environment.

All animals that have undergone domestication exhibit similar changes in morphology, whether it's a dog or bovine. It has been noted that domesticated animals have a tendency toward body size diminution with corresponding proportional changes. It has been speculated that size reduction in the earliest domesticated animals was the result of climatic changes following the Pleistocene/Holocene boundary temperature increase (Davis and Valla 1978: 610). However, domesticates have an even more pronounced size reduction than those seen in their wild counterparts which can not be attributed to just climatic changes. Tchernov and Horowitz (1991: 69) state that body size diminution is the by-product of selection pressure for faster maturity and larger litter size. They argue that this resulted in smaller sized, younger parents with smaller sized offspring, which led to an overall size reduction in the population. However, Clutton-Brock (1995: 16) proposes that size diminution was partly the result of progressive stunting caused by malnutrition from the time of conception. The resulting reduction would be advantageous according to Clutton-Brock, since smaller animals could have survived on less food. However, a multitude of factors could have contributed to the trend of reduced body size without the influence of human intervention such as reduced predator pressure (David 1981), a shift in diet (Tchernov and Valla 1997: 91), brain size requirements at comparable body sizes (Morey 1992:197), increased disease frequency (Brothwell 1975: 399), increased inbreeding (Tchernov and Horowitz 1991: 58) or changed environmental conditions created around and within human habitations (Tchernov and Horowitz 1991: 57).

Another characteristic of domestication and probably one of the most outstanding features, is the retention of juvenile traits by adults known as paedomorphosis. The juvenile traits can include behavioral displays such as whining or acts of submission-like urination, but can also include morphological changes as well. Many of the skeletal changes will be discussed in greater detail later on in this chapter and will be only briefly mentioned here. A common morphological change can be seen in the cranial length and snout shape. In domesticated mammals, a pronounced shortening of the mandibular and maxillary length with a slight reduction of carnassial size are "classical characteristics of early domestication" (Dayan 1994: 637). Although the entire snout is reduced, most of the reduction occurs in the anterior portion of the snout. Consequently, as the result of facial reduction, the teeth can become crowded. Some animals may even exhibit missing teeth or tooth anomalies (Morey 1992: 198). In domesticated dogs, the canine teeth and carnassials are much smaller than those found in wolves. This is even true in those breeds of dogs of similar size to wolves. Tooth size reduction may be a paedomorphic response or could be related to dietary changes. Dayan et al. (1992b: 219) suggests that tooth size best reflects the feeding ecology. In canids, Dayan et al. points out that the teeth are not specialized for killing but to deliver slashing bites. However in domesticated dogs the tooth size would be less significant if the animal was less dependent on killing its own prey and was being supplementally fed by humans.

As previously mentioned, domesticated animals exhibit more rapid growth rate and accelerated maturation than is typically seen in wild herds. This includes early sexual maturity as well as reproductive capacity. Tchernov and Horowitz (1991: 65) state that there are three main differences between wild and domestic animals: 1) age of sexual maturity; 2) trend toward larger litter size; 3) reduction of longevity. It has been found in studies of

Fig. 19. After multiple generations, tame foxes began exhibiting changes in coat texture and color such as piebald spotting (photo Belyaev/Trut).

bighorn sheep, that when fed a diet high in quality, sexual maturity is attained at a much younger age (Risenhoover and Bailey 1988). However, Tchernov and Horowitz (1991: 63) believe that accelerated maturity is not unique only to domesticated animals, but is one of the many variations already existing in wild animals. Quoting Darwin (1874: 2), he best summed up the phenomenon of variability: "If organic beings had not possessed an inherent tendency to vary, man could have done nothing. He unintentionally exposes his animals and plants to various conditions of life, and variability supervenes, which he cannot prevent or check." Therefore, if Darwin's hypothesis is correct, the reproductive changes seen in domesticates is caused by the new selective pressure favoring this natural variation. Man indirectly contributes to morphogenetic change by capturing wild animals that are heterogeneous and by culling or inbreeding which changes the population dynamic into a more homogenous phenotype.

Of course other notable characteristics or traits can be attributed to domestication. Many were not selected for but occurred indirectly as a result of destabilization. For instance in Belyaev's fox study, he noticed that in the tame foxes their seasonal cycle of coat shedding was altered (Belyaev 1978: 305). Not only did the foxes start shedding earlier than was normal, but they also shed for months longer than their more wild counterparts. This trait is clearly seen in most breeds of dogs that shed throughout the year, much to the dismay of their owners. Belyaev also observed that many morphological features, not viewed in wild populations, appeared repeatedly. In dogs, Belyaev noted curled tails, drooping ears, undershot or overshot bites were not seen in wild canids but quite characteristic of some breeds of dogs. In a continuation of Belyaev's study, Trut (1999: 162) also noticed a change in coat texture in that wavy or curly hair would sometimes be exhibited in domesticates, as well as changes in coat length (longer or shorter). Another interesting finding from Belyaev's fox study (1978: 268-269) was the appearance of piebald spotting in the coat of the tame foxes. Initially this variation was seen as a discrete "star" on the head. However, as future litters were produced from those individuals with a high degree of tameness, the piebald variation became expressed in numerous patterns. Color combinations of white collaring (collar pied), belted pied, blaze extending down the face, or spotting on the feet, chest, belly or tail (Fig. 19). However, some animals with the pied markings also exhibited a physical abnormality of deafness. Additionally, other reproductive abnormalities such as monorchism (only one testis is apparent), cryptorchism (failure of descent of a testis) or pathological damage of the vestibular apparatus was also viewed in the piebald animals.

Of all the domesticated animals, dogs have been the most successful in this adaptation. Not only have they been so integrated into human society that they are almost considered to be "furry children", they have also become so diversified that different breeds are highly specialized to perform a multitude of different functions. From lure coursing, obedience, agility, herding, retrieving or search and rescue, dogs fill certain unique niches that no other domesticated species has begun to occupy. However, early man's initial efforts at domesticating the early canid forebearers were attempts to fulfill more basic human needs. The search to understand why man singled out canids as the species to be incorporated into primitive societies may be elusive. As with most wild animals, the early dogs were most likely viewed as a potential food source. However our early human ancestors would have certainly observed what keen and efficient hunters canids were and would have recognized the benefit of having captive animals as a way to reliably obtain protein year-round. According to Brisbin (1976: 24) with the respect to the hunting of game, primitive man, thanks to his primate ancestry, had one distinct handicap in that he essentially lacked the acute sense of smell for tracking quarry. In combination with man's weaponry and the dog's nose, the two became a very efficient hunting team.

In research conducted by Manwell and Baker (1984: 243), they proposed several alternative reasons why canids were selected for domestication. They question whether dogs were of much benefit in hunting. The researchers relate information gathered from previous studies that dispel previous beliefs that dogs were integral in aiding man in the procurement of game. The researchers note that the Yanomano of Venezuela who "love dogs, all dogs" and frequently take them on hunting trips, however consider these animals "useless" for hunting. Additionally they point out that !Kung bushmen in southern Africa only occasionally use dogs for hunting and not an integral part of !Kung hunting.

If dogs were not essential for hunting, Manwell and Baker hypothesize that dogs were used as sentinels or guard dogs. Their barking would alert humans of the presence of animals such as bear and would also warn of approaching humans.

Manwell and Baker (1984: 244-245) also assert that dogs could have been used as a potential food source. Dog-meat is a delicacy that is consumed in many societies today. Archaeological data indicates this was true in prehistory. Native Americans were known to use dog as a dietary protein source, as well as Asian cultures. Many sites contain canine bones that exhibit evidence of butchering such as cutmarks and bone breakage.

Another interesting point that the authors make, is the advantages of having the dog as a "bed-warmer" (Manwell and Baker 1984: 248). In cold regions, the act of huddling together helps retain body heat. For instance they refer to the Australian saying of "it's a two dog night" (up to six dogs) to describe how many dogs you would have to huddle with in order to stay warm. The aboriginal women would also carry dingoes on their backs to keep warm. The researchers also relate that historically it has been documented that poor English farmers would keep livestock in their houses as a means of keeping warm, often huddling with the pigs.

Manwell and Baker (1984: 249) further hypothesize that dogs acted as "garbage disposers", helping to maintain camp hygiene. Not only would they scavenge and eat garbage but they would also consume human feces.

Although the researchers agree that there is no archaeological evidence to suggest that dogs were kept for sanitation.

There is also historical evidence that indicates that dogs were used as transportation. Manwell and Baker note that both Native Americans and northern Amerindian groups used dogs to pull travois and carry packs. There is much validity to this argument and can be further supported by the later development of certain dog breeds in Europe that were specifically bred as draft animals to pull carts.

One of the most convincing arguments presented by the authors is that dogs were kept as emotional objects. Pet owning is a very common activity which probably has some basis in fulfilling a human psychological need for caregiving. In research conducted by Archer (1997), he concluded that the tendency for humans to form strong emotional attachments to pets is an evolutionary characteristic of human feelings programmed to be used towards other humans, principally human offspring. Although early man didn't necessarily domesticate dogs or other species in order to have pets, it does seem very likely that once dogs became integrated into the human social unit, it was easy for attachments to form. Considering that there is world-wide distribution of pet ownership, it would seem likely that there is something physiological or psychologically innate in humans that a human-animal bond occurs. An answer might lie in the human attachment to their own offspring. Human children remain helpless for a longer period of time than any other mammal. It would certainly seem that there is some evolutionary force that programs humans to be nurturing towards their young for such a long period. The fact that domesticated animals retain neonate or juvenile features into adulthood may trigger caregiving responses in humans and release parental feelings. An additional stimulus would be that dogs project an array of emotions and moods that mimic human feelings. Excitement, happiness, attentiveness, loyalty and affection are characteristic of human relationships and could be easily be paralleled in human-animal attachments.

How, when and why domestication occurred in dogs may never be satisfactorily answered and can only be speculated. However it is clear, whatever the initial reason that canids were singled out for domestication, they later fulfilled a variety of human needs. Although most domesticated animals are only used to gratify a dietary demand in humans, dogs have been especially effective in being something more than a culinary side-dish. Whether or not dogs were essential hunting companions or filled some other unique position in human culture, they undoubtedly served man in a variety of purposes.

Morphometric differences in the skeletal remains of dog and wolf

Archaeologists have devoted considerable effort to identify morphological differences in closely related

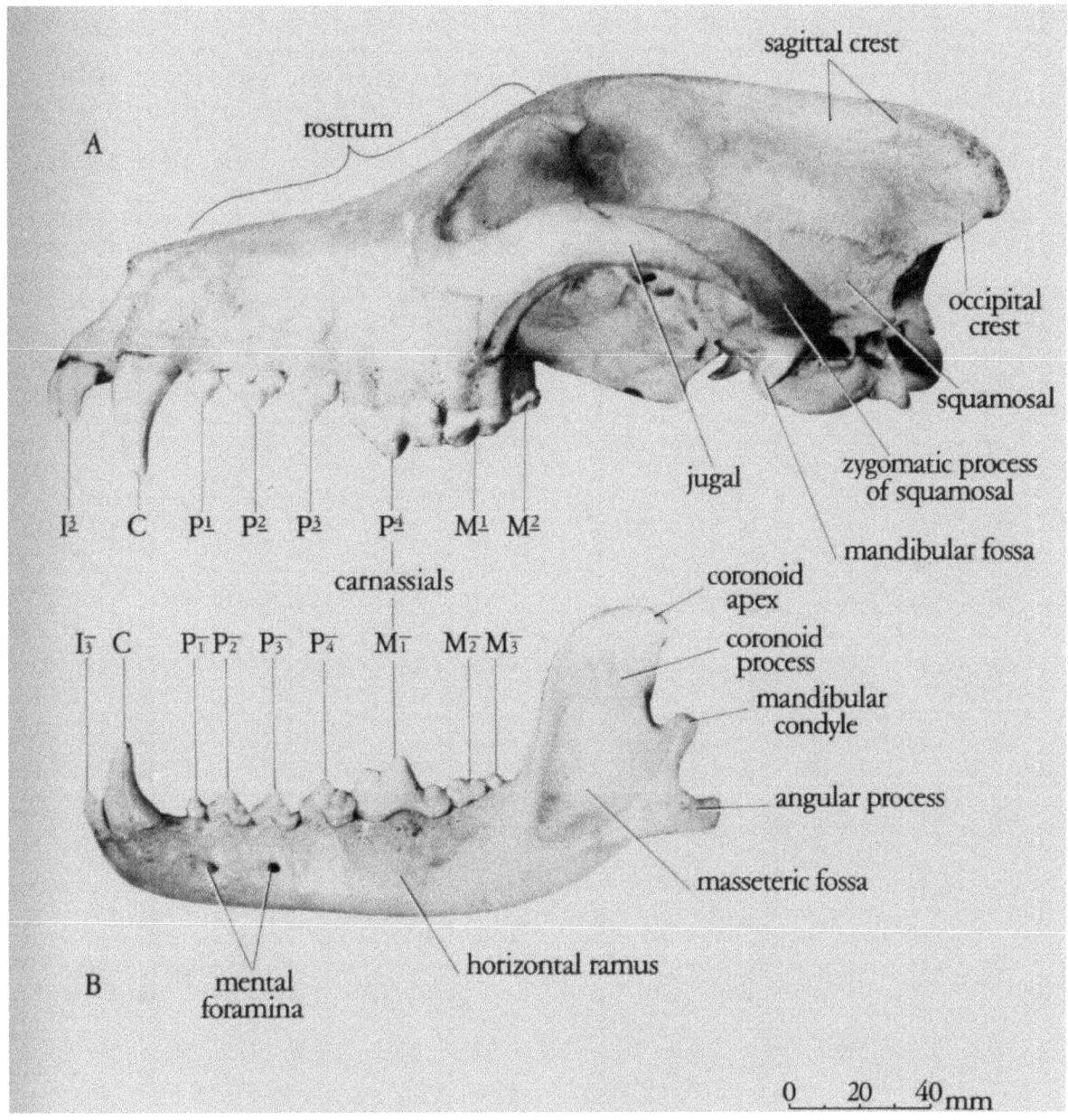

Fig. 20. Elements comprising the canid skull and mandible of a modern wolf, *Canis lupis*.
A) Left lateral; B) left mandible (Olsen 1985:7).

species. In general, both metric and non-metric observations are used to distinguish fossil species. Frequently, contemporary specimens are used as well to characterize developmental differences between subspecies to unravel the evolutionary history and reconstruct information about a population. Consequently, osteologists today rely on multivariate analysis and discriminate functions to distinguish species, sexes or populations.

Substantial attention has been focused on criteria that can decisively distinguish wolf from dog and dog/wolf hybrids. Cranial and dental features are the most reliable; unfortunately, because of the complexity and fragility of the skull, such features are frequently poorly preserved.

Lawrence and Bossert (1967, 1969, 1975; Meadows 2000: 35-48) published extensive statistical data on cranial and dental measurements, as well as discriminant function and linear discrimination analyses, that the authors assert can be used to reliably separate the crania of wolves, coyotes, dogs, and hybrids. Olsen (1985) also provided a similar list of osteological measurements of the skull that he states are diagnostic of *Canis*.

According to Olsen (1985: 93), it is possible to obtain 75 measurements from a complete skull and mandible that reflect the distinctive shape and features of a skull (Fig. 20; Table 5). From these 75 measurements, Olsen ascertains that there are 13 essential measurements that are considered diagnostically critical in separating wild from domestic species of Canis through multivariate computer analysis. Olsen's essential measurements consists of: 1) skull length; 2) cranial length; 3) nasal/premaxillary length; 4) premaxillary/orbital length; 5) tooth row length; 6) molar length; 7) premolar length; 8) zygomatic width; 9) molar width; 10) width of P4; 11) length of P4; 12) width of M1; 13) length of M1. Using a discriminate function in conjunction with the multivariate comparison, Olsen was able to classify different species of Canis into specified groups, as well as assign unknown specimens into a particular group. However, Olsen spent considerable effort to point out that fragmentary bones or teeth can never be classified with complete certainty. Olsen emphasizes that a range of morphological differences can occur within a species thereby making assignment of an individual, perhaps upon a single fragmentary piece of mandible, precarious at best.

Benecke (1987: 33), lists a number of other morphological differences for discriminating between dog and wolf fossil including: 1) facial shortening, 2) differences in the coronoid process, 3) carnassial length, 4) shifting of the palatine border, 5) changes in the zygomatic angle, 6) shape of the sagittal crest, 7) muzzle width, 8) tympanic bulla size, and 9) orbital angle. Benecke observes that a dog's facial region tends to be shorter in relation to the cranium (Fig. 21). This reduction in the muzzle also causes changes in the dentition. Citing Bökönyi (1975:173), Benecke recognizes that facial reduction can cause a shortening of the premolar row by as much as 20% and a slight shortening of 5-10% in the molar region. The shortening causes additional dentition alterations and is witnessed by crowding of the premolars since the distance from the carnassial (P4 and M1) to the canine is too short to accommodate the teeth. This morphological feature was also observed by Olsen (1985:34) and reported that tooth crowding was particularly noticeable in the area of the anterior premolars, rather than lying in a straight line, will be observed to be obliquely positioned. It has also been observed that the shortening of the jaw can result in a congenital absence of P1, a rare abnormality in wild canids but very common in domesticated dogs (Beebe 1980:163-164). A mathematical index of tooth crowding of the premolars can be calculated as the sum total of the lengths of the three anterior premolars correlated with the distance from the posterior border of the alveolus of the canine to the anterior border of the alveolus of the carnassial, mathematically stated as (Degerbøl 1961:39-41):

$$\frac{(\text{Length } p1 + p2 + p3) \times 100}{\text{Length anterior edge } p1 \text{ to anterior edge } p2},$$

and,

$$\frac{(\text{Length } p1 + p2 + p3) \times 100}{\text{Length anterior edge } p1 \text{ to anterior edge } m1}$$

For example, in adult wolves an overlapping index may range from 72 to 87, however wolves reared in captivity and have strongly overlapping teeth may have an index as high as 120 (Degerbøl 1961: 40).

Benecke also identifies distinctive changes in the mandible that are indicative of a dog. Benecke citing Olsen and Olsen (1977: 534) states that one morphological feature diagnostic of domestic dog is a "turned-back" apex of the coronoid process of the ascending ramus (Fig. 22). Neither Benecke or the

TABLE 5. Thirteen measurements of the skull and dentition considered to be the most diagnostic (Olsen 1985: 93-96).

NAME	DESCRIPTION	LANDMARK
Skull Length	Total length of braincase and face	Akrokranion to Prosthion
Cranial Length	Length of braincase only	Akrokranion to Frontal Midpoint
Nasal/Premaxillary Length	Length of face only	Nasion to Prosthion
Zygomatic Width	Maximum facial width	Zygion to Zygion
Premaxillary/Orbital Length	Extension of face beyond eye orbit	Prosthion to Ectorbitale
Molar Width		Measured across outer borders of the alveoli
Molar Length		Mesial M1 to distal end of M2
Premolar Length		Mesial P1 to distal end of P4
Width of M1		Greatest crown breath
Length of M1		Mesial end to distal end
Width of P4		Greatest crown breath
Length of P4		Mesial end to distal end
Tooth Row Length		Mesial end of P1 to distal end of M2

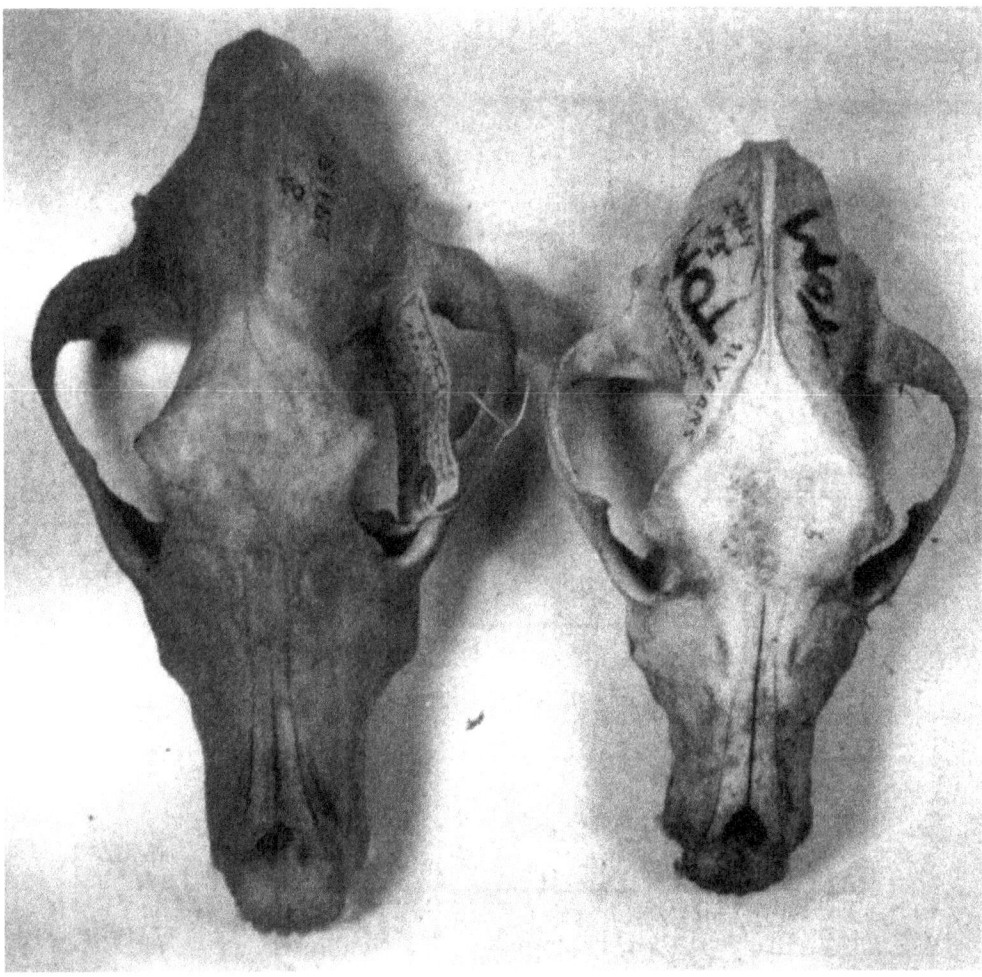

Fig. 21. The skulls of a 43 kg wolf (left) and a 43 kg dog (right) (photo R. Coppinger).

Olsens, can state why only domestic dogs have this feature, as well as the Chinese wolf (*Canis lupus chanco*), however it is absent from other canids such as the North American wolf, coyote or jackal. Although Olsen and Olsen argue that the "hooked" coronoid process occurs consistently in domestic dogs and the Chinese wolf, Crockford (2000a: 302) citing Gollan (1980) disagrees with this assumption. In research conducted by Gollan, a modern purebred Alaskan Malamute and an ancient dog from Iran were identified as having straight coronoid processes. Therefore, Crockford concludes that although the shape of the coronoid process is an important non-metric trait, it can exhibit some variation in shape.

The length of the upper carnassial also exhibits morphological differences. Clark (1996: 214) states that in wolves, the length of the upper carnassial exceeds the sum of the lengths of the two molars. In dogs, Clark states that the summed molar lengths exceed, or are equal to, the length of the carnassial. Dayan et al. (1992a: 317) describes the carnassial length differences in canids as an adaptation to the particular vertebral size and structure most frequently encountered among the prey. Dayan and co-authors (1992a: 325) suggest that canids are not highly specialized carnivores, scavenging and eating vegetable matter as well as live prey. They also infer (1992a: 317) that canids are less specialized in their killing behavior, killing their prey with a series of slashing bites or violent shakes and not by a highly oriented bite. Therefore they conclude that the relatively elongated rostrum indicates a weaker bite region compared with the shearing power of the carnassials. Harrison (1973:189-190) in a study of tooth size also concluded that although the carnassial and first molar appear to be strikingly larger in wolves, when compared to dogs, a narrow zone of overlap exists between the two groups and doesn't provide a distinct morphologic difference as previously believed.

Benecke (1987: 33) also reports that there is a shifting in the border of the palate in dogs. Typically it will be observed that the border of the palate will be located behind the upper second molar in dogs. However in wolves, the palatine border will be positioned in front of the upper second molar.

The zygomatic exhibits differences that can be used to differentiate dog from wolf. Benecke (1987: 33) states that domestic dogs have a zygomatic process that forms a

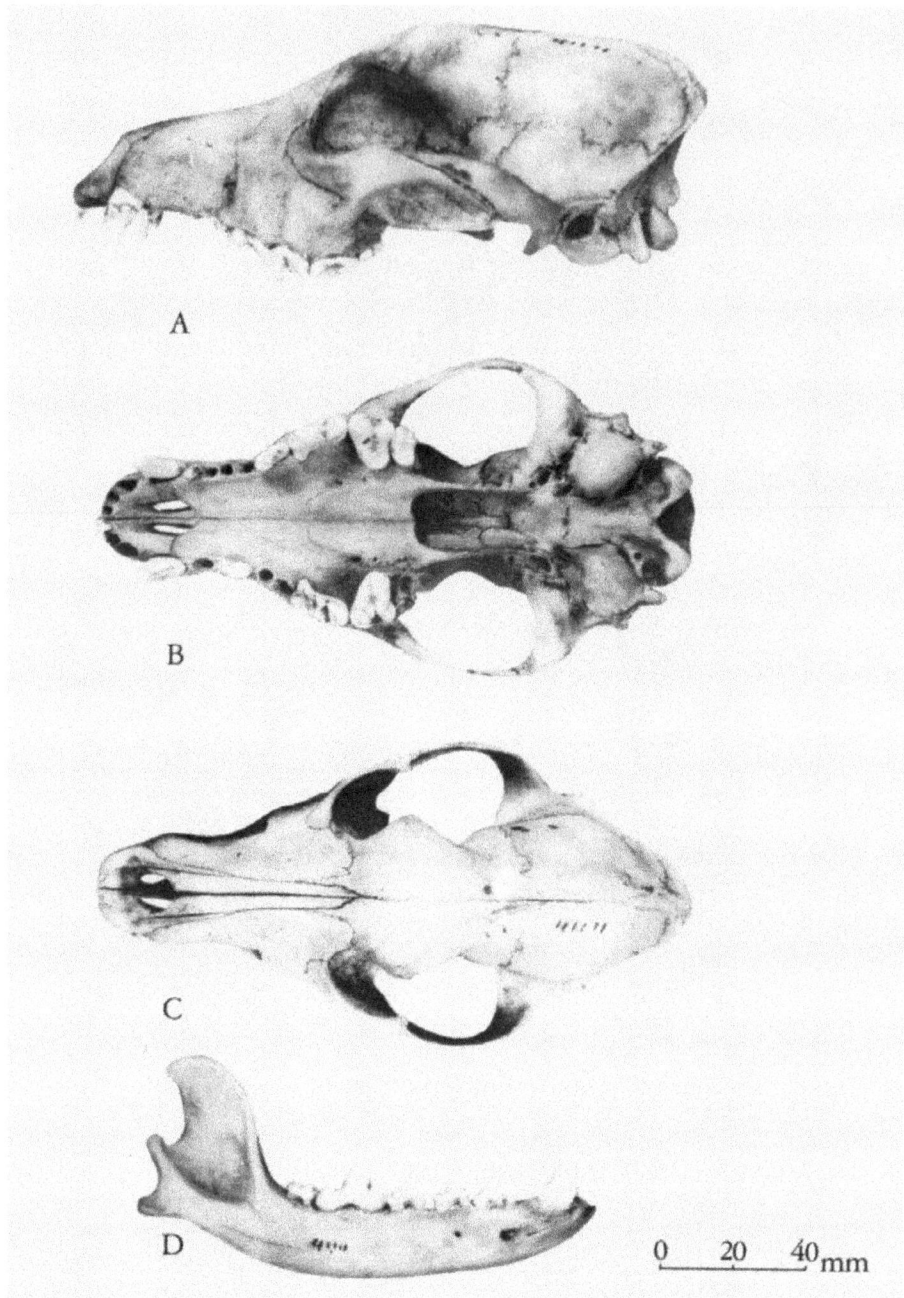

Fig. 22. Skull and mandible of a domestic dog, *Canis familiaris*. A) left lateral aspect of skull; B) palatal aspect of skull; C) dorsal aspect of skull; D) lateral aspect of right mandible (Olsen 1985: 83). right-angle, obtuse angle or straight line in relation to the maxilla. However Benecke reports that in wolves, the zygomatic process forms an acute angle to the maxilla.

Both Olsen (1985: 44) and Benecke (1987: 33) have reported morphological variation of the sagittal crest between dogs and wolves (Fig. 23). Olsen states that the sagittal crest is usually quite prominent in all subspecies of wolves. In dogs, Benecke observes that the sagittal crest is more rounded and projects less posteriorly.

The width of the muzzle can also be informative in identifying a dog from a wolf. Clark (1996: 214) citing Harcourt (1974:153-154) states that although the facial region becomes shortened during domestication, the width of the muzzle will not become narrower and will appear to be broad in comparison to the length. Harcourt's muzzle width index can be calculated as:

$$\frac{\text{Breadth at canine alveoli} \times 100}{\text{Length from nasion to prosthion}}$$

Yates (2000: 269-270) has been able to ascertain distinctive differences in the mastoid region that clearly delineates wolves from dogs and wolf/dog hybrids with

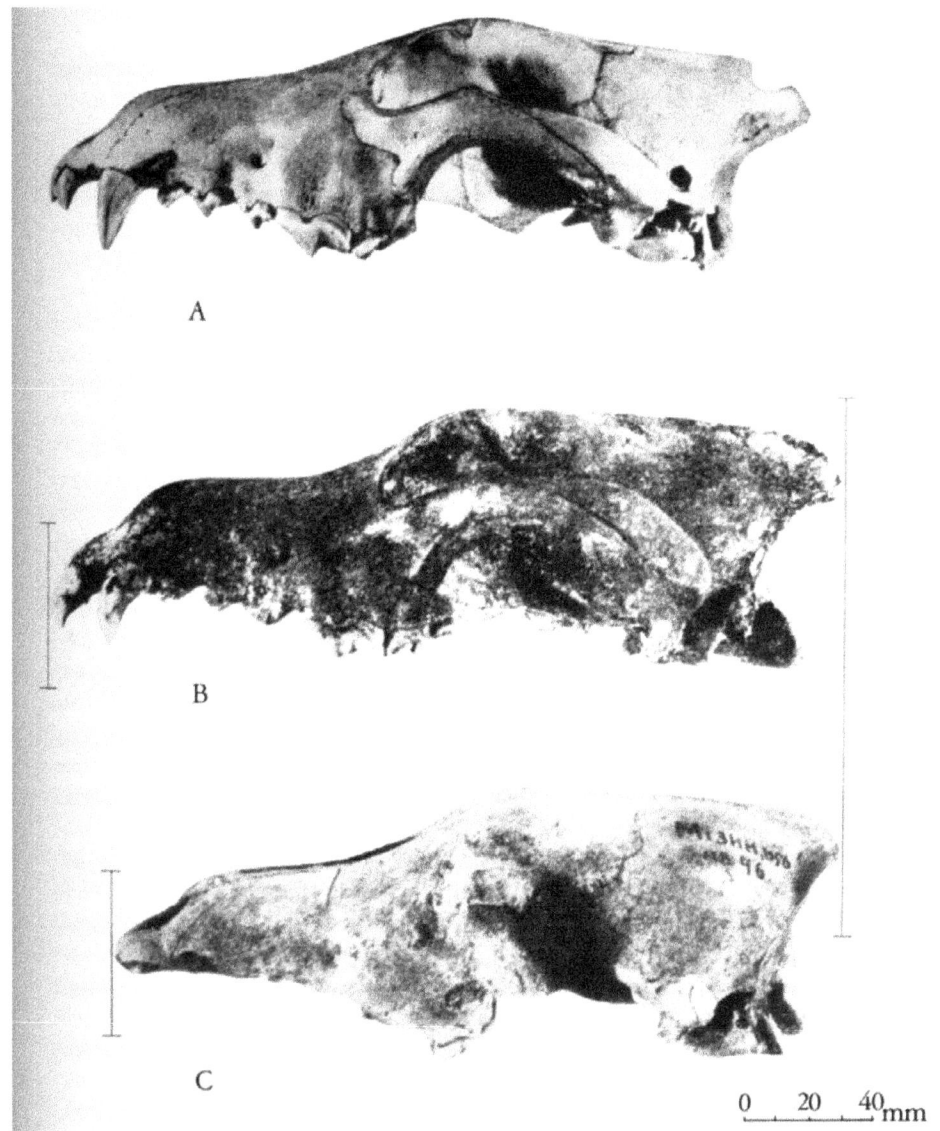

Fig. 23. Comparison of skulls of present-day wolf, late Paleolithic wolf, and late Paleolithic short-faced wolf.
A) Left lateral aspect of present-day wolf, B) left lateral aspect of skull of a late Paleolithic wolf,
C) left lateral aspect of skull of a late Paleolithic short-faced wolf (Olsen 1985: 21).

an accuracy rate of 88%. In this study, Yates found that a channel separated the two insertion areas for the m. sternomastoideus and m. cleidomastoideus in the mastoid region. In adult wolves, Yates observed that there was a greater lateral extension of the cleomastoideus process; while in the domestic dog Yates states that this channel is shallow, narrow and the lateral projection of the cleidomastoideus process is less pronounced. She further observed in wolf/dog hybrids, this process was intermediate in separation and projection. Yates inferred that this morphological difference was due to different gaits exhibited by wild and domestic canids. Yates further hypothesizes that dominance behaviors could also modify this region since submissive, low-ranking female wolves appear to exhibit less separation and projection.

Benecke (1987: 33), Lawrence and Bossert (1967: 230) indicate that the size and shape of the tympanic bulla can also be a distinguishing character for separation of dogs from wolves. Benecke states that the bullae in dogs are small or medium-sized and strongly compressed or slightly crumpled in appearance with marked ribs. However the tympanic bullae in wolves are large, convex and almost spherically shaped.

Additionally morphological changes are seen in the orbital angle. To estimate the orbital angle, a line is drawn through the upper and lower edges of the eye socket and a line is drawn from the ectorbitale to ectorbitale (Benecke 1987: 33). The angle derived from these skeletal regions can be indicative of a wolf if the angle is directed outward and upward, or a dog if the angle is more obtuse.

In 1967, Lawrence and Bossert reported morphologic differences in the brain case which were diagnostic in identifying wolves, dogs or coyotes. The researchers stated that they observed that coyotes had the dorso-posterior part of the brain case well inflated with the maximum width of the brain case in the region of the parieto-temporal suture, the frontal shield not tilted up and the postorbital constrictions close to the postorbital processes. However the authors observed that in wolves and dogs, the maximum width of the brain case was usually at the root of the zygomatics, with an upward tilted frontal shield and an elongated postorbital region, so that the constriction of the anterior part of the brain case and the area behind the postorbital processes are well separated. Lawrence (1967: 50), in an additional study, reported that variation in the size of the brain case, length of breadth of the rostrum and tilting and inflation of the interorbital region is less severe in wolves, coyotes or wild canids. Lawrence further reported that in domestic dog skulls with comparable brain case sizes, there was tremendous variation in the sizes of the rostrum and orbital regions. However, Harrison (1973:190) argued that no reliable cranial distinction could be definitively identified using the brain case. Harrison theorized that finding absolute distinctive differences between the skulls of wild canids and domestic dogs would never be established given the amount of variation seen in canid species world-wide. Additionally, Clark (1995:14) argues that the fragility of the canid skull and poor archaeological retrieval, the planes necessary for the production of cranial measurements prevent making a metric identification.

The length of the muzzle is also a valuable indicator in identification of the domestic dog. Walker and Frison (1982:128), Lawrence (1967: 50), Lawrence and Bossert (1967: 225), Sablin and Khlopachev (2002: 796), Clark (1995:11), Higham, Kijngam, Manly (1980:155), Lawrence and Reed (1983: 486), and Olsen (1985) have all used muzzle length to imply a relationship between domestication and characteristically doglike features. Lawrence and Bossert (1967: 225) reported that coyote and dogs could be identified from wolves by the proportions of the muzzle length and skull length. Although Clark (1995:11) states that to produce a three-dimensional aspect of the head, it is necessary to relate morphology and dimensional indices by making direct comparisons with measurements taken from modern breeds. Higham, Kijngam and Manly (1980:155) found that the depth and thickness of the jaw in the modern dog and prehistoric canid seem to be greater relative to muzzle length than in the wild comparative samples and the dingo.

However they found that the Chinese wolf occupied an intermediate position, being statistically indistinguishable to both the Indian wolf, jackal and modern dog. A prehistoric Thai breed analyzed by Higham et al., was described as wolflike in the shape of the jugular process and mandible but clearly differing from the wolf in having a short snout, broad palate and small auditory bullae, all characteristic features of domestication. Sablin and Khlopachev (2002: 796) assert that a wide palate accompanied with a short snout as an effective criterion for the identification of domestication. They further argue that shortening of the snout in dogs relative to wolves is the clearest single trait distinguishing the two. However, an important point to remember is that snout lengths are only reliable in adult animals as a distinctive morphologic feature. Immature neonatal canids of all species typically exhibit a shortened snout and may be indistinguishable from a domestic dog until the animal has reached maturity.

Another diagnostic feature of dogs is the presence of a "stop". This area is located at the base of the muzzle where it attaches to the frontal bone. In dogs, this area exhibits a bend. Lawrence and Bossert (1967: 225) noted that this area may be modified by the inflation of the frontal sinuses resulting in a steep angle of the forehead. They state that a recognizable bend in the mid-region of the skull so that the rostrum (snout/muzzle) and brain case meet at more of an angle than is usual in wild canids. Lawrence (1967:58) also described this region as highly variable in the degree of tilt in domestic dogs, but a good diagnostic feature of one of the results of domestication.

Using body size to distinguish dogs from wolves or coyotes is more problematic, except when there is an obvious gross difference. According to Clark (1995:13), because shoulder heights are calculated from regression equations derived from the relationship of the overall length of the long bones to the stature of the animal, the ability to produce them relies entirely on the recovery of complete humeri, radii, ulnae, femora, or tibiae. In archaeological samples, this would necessitate recovery of almost completely intact skeletal remains, which becomes difficult. In a study conducted by Clark, she was able to demonstrate that shoulder heights can be estimated from measurements taken from the fourth metacarpal and metatarsals. Using regression equations derived for each of the 8 metapodial elements, Clark (1995: 22-23) was able to determine that metapodia are reliable indicators of shoulder height in modern breeds of dogs and can be used in archaeological skeletons. Harcourt (1974:164-166), assessing shoulder height of dogs from the overall lengths of long bones, found that dogs of the Iron Age were fairly uniform in the height range of 40-60 cm, with a small minority of shorter dogs present. In North America, aboriginal dogs were often described as "wolf-like" due to their large size and apparent superficial external resemblance to wolves (Young and Goldman 1944). This is further complicated by ethnographic reports that Native Americans had dogs of various sizes. Handley (2000: 205, 213) reported preliminary results of prehistoric dog remains in the New England area of the United States, which also seemed to confirm that Native peoples had at least two, perhaps three distinct dog types that differed in size. The largest of the Indian dogs was described as a broad-muzzled Eskimo dog which had a superficial external resemblance to wolves (Walker and Frison 1982:126). Two other types of Indian dogs were described as either "large" or "small" common dogs (Walker and Frison 1982:126). A fourth type was thought to be a wolf/dog hybrid that was only partially domesticated in that it scavenged around campus but was unapproachable (Walker and Frison 1982:126). These height categories designated for the Native American aboriginal dogs are also very similar to results found by Clark (1995:13) in Iron Age skeletal Canis. Clark reported that the estimated shoulder height of domestic dogs was categorized into three height classes: ≤35 cm; 36-50cm; and > 50cm.

Although body size reduction has been used as a criterion of proof of domestication, it remains a controversial generalization. In 1847 Bergman described relationships between morphological variation and the physical environment (Dayan 1994: 633). Bergman proposed that warm-blooded vertebrates tend to be larger in cold environments than those from warmer regions. Bergman related this body size change as a physiological adaptation to producing and maintaining body heat, an obvious benefit in colder environments. Since the formulation of this initial hypothesis, many researchers have offered alternative or complementary explanations such as plant productivity, humidity, competition, latitude, selection pressures, and nutrition (Dayan et al. 1991:189-191). There also seems to be a correlation between the mass of the masticatory apparatus and the size of the animal (Dayan et al. 1991:195). Dayan and colleagues (1991:191) and Davis (1981) concede however, that making generalizations about the decrease or increase of body size based on environmental temperature changes is tenuous, at best. Dayan and researchers assert that different species may respond differently to similar climatic conditions. This hypothesis was proven when they compared body size changes in numerous different species during the same climatic period, which resulted in inconsistent and conflicting size clines. Therefore morphological size change is not necessarily an indication of domestication, but is one of several different possibilities which can affect body size deviations in a population.

At present, the best taxonomic identifier of wild canid remains or domestic dog is based on osteometric analysis of the skull. Cranial measurements combined with discriminate analysis, analysis of dental characteristics, and modifications in the skull which can be visually identified have been the most diagnostic in separating the two species (wolf and dog) in prehistoric samples.

The fossil record of *Canis familiaris*

As previously reviewed, not only is the fossil record limited by the lack of preserved canid material but it is further complicated by the difficulty of identifying a newly domesticated species from its wild progenitor. Few sites have yielded fossil remains of complete dogs. Most fossil localities yield primarily fragments of only a few bones. Although archaeological evidence of dogs have been found world-wide, no skeletal remains have been dated that is comparable to the antiquity of dates suggested by molecular research for the domestication of the dog.

A comprehensive review of archaeological sites found throughout the world will be discussed (Table 6). The purpose of this review does not attempt to formulate a complete list of sites that dog remains have been reported, but rather to highlight those sites that are considered to be the most ancient in different geographic areas throughout the world.

North America

Until the 1960's, skeletal remains of canids found at archaeological sites were given little attention except to be listed in the vast collection of faunal material recovered. However in the late 1960's, zooarchaeologist Barbara Lawrence published a series of four articles on dog domestication that greatly influenced the archaeological community to view canid remains as having diagnostic and historical value (Lawrence 1967, 1968; Lawrence and Bossert 1967, 1969). Lawrence's analysis of dog remains recovered at Jaguar Cave, Idaho was reported to be one of the oldest domestic dog specimens found in North America, with carbon-14 dating determining that the fossil remains were approximately ± 10,370 BP. Although the fossil remains at Jaguar Cave were scant and fragmented, Lawrence was able to secure valuable measurements that were later used for comparative analysis to the wolf. Lawrence concluded that the maxillary and mandibular fragments were far too small to be a wolf but too massive, deeper dorsoventrally and thicker lateromedially, to be a coyote. In addition, the dentition displayed tooth crowding typically seen in domestic dogs. The Jaguar Cave specimen was considered of great importance, not only because it was thought to be one of the oldest dog remains found in North America, but also because of its location. Olsen (1985: 31) pointed out that it was unexpected to find these early dogs in a locality so far south as the Jaguar Cave rock-shelter without finding similar remains in sites closer to the Bering Strait. Olsen also infered that given that the Jaguar Cave dog lacks the typical wolf-like characteristics, it should be expected to find an earlier dog that would be a transitional form bridging the gap between the wolf and Jaguar Cave dog. Olsen asserts that given the harsh environment of this northern region and the poor preservation of skeletal remains, it may not be possible to obtain more ancient remains in proximity to the Bering Strait. However, the dating of the Jaguar Cave remains came into question in 1987 when radiocarbon accelerator dates obtained on two of the dog bones revealed that they may not be as ancient as previously reported.

TABLE 6. Earliest reported canid archaeological material worldwide by region. (*) denotes questionable dating.

SITE	DATE (BP)	SKELETAL ELEMENTS	CITATION
North America			
Jaguar Cave, Idaho	(10,370*); new dating at 3,200 and 940	Maxilla and mandibular fragments	Lawrence and Bossert (1967; 1969), Lawrence (1967; 1968)
Yukon Territory/ Old Crow	11,450-12,660*	Mandible	Beebe (1980)
Koster, Illinois	8,130-8,430	3 complete adult dog skeleton in anatomical position	Morey and Waint (1992)
Agate Basin, Wyoming	10,500	Maxillary fragment	Walker and Frison (1982)
Hogup Cave, Idaho	7,500-8,000	Cranial and mandibular fragments	Haag (1970)
Rodgers Shelter, Missouri	7,540	Long bones, mandible associated with human remains	McMillan (1970)
Fairbanks, Alaska	10,000	Possible wolf or robust dog	Olsen (1985)
Weiser, Idaho	6,600	2 complete dogs, in an intentional burial	Yohe and Pauesic (2000)
White Dog Cave, Arizona	100 AD	2 mummies	Warren (2000)
South America			
Ecuador	5,000	Skeletal fragments in a ceremonial context	Schwartz (1997)
Greenland			
Qaja	3,000-4,000	Numerous dog skeletal elements	Møhl (1986)
England			
Star Carr	9,500-10,000	Skull, fibia, femur of two dogs	Degerbøl (1961)
Germany			
Bonn-Oberkassel	14,000	Single mandible	Nobis (1979; 1981)
Kneigrotte Cave	12,000-13,500	Cranial, maxillary, ulnae, and scapula fragments of possible wolf	Musil (2000)
Teufelsbrucke	12,000-13,000	Metapodial and phalanx fragments	Musil (2000)
Oelknitz	10,900-12,500	Humerus, tibia, metapodial fragments	Musil (2000)
Senekenberg	10,000	Skull, long bones	Degerbøl (1961)
France			
St. Thibaud de Couz	10,000	Skull, mandible, vertebrae, humerus, femur	Chaix (2000)
Ireland			
13 different sites	4,000- 8,000	Present	McCormick
Sweden/ Denmark			
Sites Unknown	8,800	Fragments	Degerbøl (1961)
Hungary			
Vlasac	8,000	1900 bone fragments of a wolf/ dog maybe "transitional"	Bökönyi (1975)
Iraq			
Jarmo	8,500-9,000	Cranial and mandibular	Lawrence and Reed (1983)

SITE	DATE (BP)	SKELETAL ELEMENTS	CITATION
		fragments	
Russia			
Eliseevichi I	12,600-17,340*	2 large crania	Sablin and Khlopachev (2002)
Armenia			
12 Archaeological sites	6,000	Present	Managerial and Antonion (2000)
Israel			
Mallaha	11,300-11,500	Adult fragment and complete puppy skeleton	Davis and Valla (1978)
Atlit Yam	8,000	Mandible, teeth, Rostrum	Dayan and Galili (2000)
Kfar-Galim	6,00-7,000	Complete cranium	Dayan and Galili (2000)
Egypt			
Site Unknown	6,000	Pictures on tablet	Vesey-Fitzgerald (1957)
Kazakhstan			
Botai	5,600	13 canines	Olsen (2000)
Thailand			
Ban Chiang	5,500	Present	Higham et al. (1980)
Australia			
Nullarbor	3,000	Dingo	Wilton et al. (1999)
Japan			
Natsushima Shell Mound	9,300	Possible wolf	Shigehara and Hongo (2000)
Siberia			
Razbonichiya Cave	14,800*	Present	Ovodov (1998)
Siberia			
Lake Baikal	7,000*	Possible wolf	Bazaliiskiy and Savelyev (2000); Olsen (1985)
Ushki	10,000*		Olsen (1985)
China			
Pan po'	7,000	Present	Olsen and Olsen (1985)
Henan	9,000	Mandible	Olsen and Olsen (1985)

Dates on the maxilla were reported at 3200 ± 80 BP and the mandible was given a date of 940 ± 80 BP (Clutton-Brock 1995:13). Although dating of this material may remain problematic, the find is still of great importance in revealing the domestication history of the dog in North America.

Another find of a domestic dog in the Yukon Territory has also been reported as being of equal importance as the Jaguar Cave specimen. A mandible identified as *Canis familiaris* was found among thousands of Pleistocene bones on the Old Crow River (Beebe 1980:161). The specimen recovered consisted of a complete right mandible with preserved teeth that showed no evidence of wear. All faunal remains uncovered at Old Crow ranged in dates from early to terminal Pleistocene (12,660 ± 280 BP to 11,450 ± 200 years). However, Beebe stresses that the status of this canid and its stratigraphic position are "probable", not certain given that the specimen exhibited an abraded surface that is indicative of fluvial transport. Beebe also hypothesizes that the highly evolved morphology of this small animal suggests that it represents a rather late stage in the process of domestication.

The Old Crow mandible displayed several morphological features that are associated with domesticated dogs. The ascending ramus exhibited a pronounced turned-back apex of the coronoid process, a trait recognized as dog. The teeth are reduced in size with decreased molar height. The tooth row also showed a slight bending. The Old Crow specimen also revealed a congenital absence of the first premolar, a trait frequently seen in dogs but rare in wild canids. Due to the shortened snout region, the second premolar was diagonally rotated, another common characteristic of dogs. Beebe concluded that the Old Crow mandible was too small to be regarded as a wolf and smaller than modern sled dogs currently residing in the Old Crow villages. Beebe further stated that because the mandible didn't display any wolf-like proportions, it was believed to be a small dog. Olsen (1985:85-86) states that the Old Crow dog reveals too many characteristics of late stage domestication to be of Pleistocene origin. He suggests two possible interpretations of the Old Crow specimen: 1) the mandible could have been redeposit with the Pleistocene remains as the result of the alternating freezing and thawing conditions typical of the area, or 2) the animal could be the progeny of an older Asian ancestral dog population, that were considerably smaller than the progeny of tamed local wolves. In any case, the dating and the depositional history of the specimens from Jaguar Cave and Old Crow remains problematic.

One site has had solid radiocarbon dates ranging from 8130 ± 90 BP to 8480 ± 110 BP. The Koster site located on the Illinois River Valley has yield an Early Archaic assemblage of human graves, stone and bone tools, as well as faunal remains. The oldest deposit, Horizon 11, contained three complete adult canids in the anatomical position. Preservation of the skeletal remains was good enough to ascertain that two of the canids were males, with the third identified as female.

The Koster canids exhibited two characteristics of domestic dog: wide palates and cranial vaults (Morey and Wiant 1992: 225-227). Cranial length measurements revealed that the Koster remains fall between the means of reference dogs and coyotes. The dentition was crowded with the mandibular ventral borders slightly convex. The coronoid apex of the ascending ramus is turned-back, a typical feature of the morphological patterning seen in domestic dogs. Discriminant analysis identified the Koster sample as falling within the domestic dog reference sample.

Morey and Wiant (1992: 227) conclude that the Koster dogs represent the oldest archaeological discovery of domesticated canids in the world. Another significant conclusion that Morey and Wiant deduce is that the Koster dogs were more than just a utilitarian species. Their intentional burial, they infer, hints at an affectionate relationship with humans.

Another important archaeological find of possible domesticated canids was found at the Agate Basin site in northeastern Wyoming. Walker and Frison (1982:125) reported that the specimens consisted of a partial maxilla and several post-cranial elements recovered from a Folsom occupation site dated approximately 10,500 to 10,800 BP based on material recovered at the site. Walker and Frison compared the Wyoming skeletal material to known prehistoric dogs from North America and Wyoming wolves (1982:133). The researchers hypothesized that if the Wyoming canid skulls were dogs, they would be genetically linked to North American Indian dogs and not to European dog breeds.

Walker and Frison (1982: 160-164) applied cranial criteria established by Iljin (1941) used for separating wolves from dogs to the Agate Basin remains as well as to canid skeletal remains recovered from 17 other Wyoming sites: Vore, Glenrock, Medicine Lodge Creek, Wardell, Piney Creek, Big Goose Creek, Lee, Dead Indian Creek, Bell Cave, Horner, Hawken, Garrett Allen, Laddie Creek, Laramie River, Box Elder Creek, Platte River, and Wolf Jaw Cave. The researchers first examined the orbital angle and concluded that the Wyoming material from all of the 18 sites overlapped wolf/dog hybrids with a slight partiality towards wolf. Examination of the zygomatic maxilla was not reported since preservation was poor. The tympanic bullae exhibited an intermediate shape similar to that seen in hybrids. The size of the tympanic was reported by Walker and Frison to fall between the size seen in pariah dogs and wolves. Another diagnostic character used for identification was the position of the palatine border in relation to the second molar. The Wyoming samples were more characteristic of wolf than dog. Two other criteria (basal skull length and cranial volume) were not used because of the fragmented nature of the skeletal remains.

Walker and Frison (1982:168) concluded that the Agate Basin specimens were larger than most recorded prehistoric dogs (including the Jaguar Cave specimen) but within range of the measurements taken on the Wyoming canids from the Horner, Dead Indian Creek, Big Goose Creek, Vore, Box Elder Creek, and Itasca sites. The researchers reported that the Wyoming skeletal material did not appear to resemble either dog or wolf populations. Walker and Frison (1982:144) state that while the Wyoming canids are related to wolves, they still form a distinct population. Given the degree of overlap between both the dog and wolf species, the Agate Basin skeletal elements represent a domesticated wolf/dog hybrid cross. Both researchers indicate that later ethnographic reports support the theory of intentional breeding of hybrids (Walker and Frison 1982:146) to obtain larger and stronger dogs.

Hogup Cave, Idaho has also yielded bones which were identified as a small domestic dog (Haag 1970). The site was dated 8100-7500 BP. Ten specimens were identified as possible *Canis familiaris* remains. A cranium and one half of a left mandible represented one individual. Most of the teeth were still present in the mandible and were measured for comparative analysis. Haag discovered that the lower carnassial (M1) of the Hogup Cave dog when measured was only 21.99 mm tall. Haag concluded that this was too small for a wolf, even females don't exhibit that extreme amount of sexual dimorphism. Haag inferred that the early dogs of North America were derived from a smaller Asiatic wolf.

A site which also yielded Archaic skeletal dog remains is Rodgers Shelter in Missouri. Radiocarbon dating of carbonized wood on the same level as the dog burial produced a date of 7540 ± 170 BP. McMillan (1970:1246-1247) reported that the dog skeleton exhibited evidence of intentional internment, a shallow basin-shaped pit with capstones covering the remains. Although intentional burial of dogs is not unusual, McMillan states that the Rodgers Shelter burial is particularly unusual given that this practice is not usually seen until 1500 to 2000 years later.

The Rodgers Shelter dog skeleton was represented by ulnae, radii, humerus, femur, skull fragments and mandible. The bones were badly crushed but McMillan was able to reconstruct stature estimates by comparative analysis from other museum specimens. McMillan estimated the dog to be a rather small dog approximately 40 to 50 cm at the shoulder. The muzzle was reported to be massive, a feature that McMillan felt was extremely atypical given the body height of the canine. Upon examination of the teeth, McMillan reported that the height of the right carnassial averaged 4 to 5 mm more than the same measurement taken on modern dog breeds of similar size. The width of the carnassial also extended the modern dogs by 1 to 2 mm.

Although the Rodgers Shelter dogs are not dated as ancient as some other dog remains, it is nevertheless an important archaeological find for several reasons. The reduced size of the animal infers intentional breeding by Native Americans for selective traits. The shortened muzzle and robust mandible, as well as the absence of any wolf-like feature would also seem to support the theory that the morphological changes were due to selective breeding. Lastly, the intentional internment of the animal also raises the possibility that the Rodgers Shelter dog was more of a companion animal and not specifically bred as a food item.

Possible early dog remains have also been recovered near Fairbanks, Alaska. Dredging operations, starting in 1932 and lasting for over twenty years, produced a large number of wolf skulls. Based upon the discovery of late Pleistocene age artifacts found in association with the skulls, the remains were dated at 10,000 BP. Olsen (1985:20-22) later examined the canid skulls and did comparisons between Pleistocene wolves and Holocene specimens, as well as Eskimo dogs from Greenland and Siberia.

He discovered that although the skulls were quite robust and larger than Eskimo dogs, many of the skulls exhibited a shortened facial region. Two of the twenty-eight skulls also revealed a congenital absence of the anterior premolars. Olsen also noted that in several animals that had complete dentition, the teeth were crowded with the position of the premolar turned at an oblique angle. Olsen further observed that many of the skulls had occipital and supraoccipital crests that were visibly reduced than typical of wolves and further reported the one animal had dentition characteristic of the tooth size seen in Eskimo dogs.

Olsen hypothesizes that the short-faced Alaskan skeletal remains probably represent a precursor or forerunner to the later, domesticated Eskimo dog. However, he notes that the way the site was excavated raises many questions as to the antiquity of the material. Since the site was dredged, it is possible that the Paleolithic artifacts and wolf skulls were actually mixed together and therefore are not of the same time period. Another possibility that Olsen raises is that the variations seen in the Alaskan material may be representative of the normal amount of variation that would be seen in a population and therefore not unusual or atypical.

In Weiser, Idaho the Braden site, dated at 6,600 BP ± 90 BP was found to contain dog remains in context with human burials. Yohe and Pauesic (2000:93) suggest that these dog remains are among the oldest known in North America and perhaps the earliest know intentional dog burials directly associated with human burials in the Americas.

The Braden site consisted of a mass grave of twelve human burials and two dogs. Dog 1 was fairly complete *in situ*, while Dog 2 was fragmentary. Both animals were determined to be adults and male. Dog 1 appears to be more robust but both animals are approximately 50 cm at the shoulder. Both dogs had the congenital absence of the lower first premolar, a common trait of domestic dogs. Neither dog exhibited cut-marks indicative of butchering. However given the position of the dogs, the authors believe that the dogs were likely sacrificed at the death of their owner (Yohe and Pauesic 1998:101).

There are numerous archaeological sites throughout North America that have yielded dog remains, however none have been found that have reached the antiquity as those sites previously mentioned. Throughout the Southwest, dogs have been found in conjunction with Pueblo sites. Canyon de Chelly and White Dog Cave in Arizona, Cliff Palace at Mesa Verde, Colorado Pecos Pueblo and Zuni Pueblo, New Mexico are just a few of the vast number of sites that domesticated Pueblo Indian dogs have been found. The dogs are of various sizes with morphological differences in the skulls. A unique aspect of the Southwest is how the environment can frequently preserve organic remains so that their physical appearance becomes visibly apparent. This is found to be true at White Dog Cave where the mummified remains of two dogs that still retained their coats so that coat length and color were easily seen. Other dog remains have also been reported throughout North America but as in the case of the Pueblo Indian dogs, they are associated with human occupation settlements dating anywhere from 8000 BP to 1000 BP ago (Warren 2000).

Meso America and South America

No domestic dog remains older than 5000 BP have been reported from Meso America (Schwartz 1997: 65). Schwartz hypothesizes that the domestication of dogs coincided with the dwindling wild resources and were used as an animal protein supplement. In South America, one of the oldest possible domestic dog burial sites was recovered in Ecuador (Schwartz 1997:122). Dated at approximately 5100 BP, these canid remains were recovered in a ceremonial site. At Fell's Cave (6000-10,700 BP), Los Todos (4800-7200BP), and La Moderna (6500 BP) possible dog remains have been discovered. However, several researchers recently have identified these remains as those belonging to an extinct species of canid called *Dusicyon avus* or a canis species but not *Canis familiaris* (Schwartz 1997: 18). Elsewhere in South America, there are no domestic dog remains known to be dated older than 3500 BP.

If it is accepted that the gray wolf is the ancestral to the dog, the lack of ancient dog remains in both Mesoamerica and South America is not surprising since the gray wolf, although almost world-wide in distribution, has never been found south of the equator (Scott 1968: 250). The lack of wolves in the South America as well as the deficiency of archaeological sites that contain dog remains of great antiquity would imply that dogs were introduced from North America and slowly spread southward. Although the Spanish had reported that this region of the world had local native varieties of dogs, for the most part these animals disappeared under pressure from European dog breeds introduced by explorers or immigrants (Scott 1968: 264).

Greenland

The oldest known site of domesticated dog remains in west Greenland was found in a abandoned Eskimo village known as Qajâ, located on a low foreland stretching northward into the Jakobshavn Icefjord. Excavated by Møhl in 1982, the site was rich in organic remains that were in remarkably good state of preservation. Møhl (1986: 81) states that based on implements found and C-14 dating, the Qajâ site spanned a period from 3975 BP to 2925 BP. Over 44,000 groups of bones were recovered during the exaction consisting of mammal and avian species. After an initial presorting, 18 bones were identified by Møhl to be dog. The discovery of the dog bones was of particular importance since, according to Møhl, the presence of dogs has never been documented in either the Sarqaq (dated 3800 to 2300 BP) or Dorset (dated 2550 BP to 1100 AD) cultures.

The dog bones consisted of one individual that was approximately six months of age and two adults. The younger animal was represented by four vertebrae, two clavicles, scapula and eight ribs. The older animals were represented by two humeri. Møhl compared measurements of the greatest width and greatest length of the two humeri to wolf and sled dog samples. Møhl (1986: 88) concluded that the two humeri were much too small to be considered wolf but fell within the predicted range expected in sled dogs. According to carbon-14 dating, it was determined that the dog remains were approximately 4,000 years old.

Møhl (1986: 88) believes that the dogs arrived in Greenland contemporaneously with the Sarqaq people. Møhl states that he assumes from the organic remains found at the settlement, the Sarqaq people used the dogs as helpers while traveling and/or hunting.

According to Morey and Aris-Sørensen (2002: 44), although Greenland was populated by humans some 4500 years ago, the keeping of large numbers of dogs was a phenomenon of the last thousand years. The authors maintain that based on the archaeological record, the presence of dogs was sparse and sometimes totally absent for substantial periods. This is apparently true of the Qajâ site given the vast amount of mammalian and bird remains but only a handful of dog remains recovered. The researchers maintain that sled teams were virtually unknown until the introduction of rifles and a trapping economy. Prior to that, Morey and Aris-Sørensen (2002: 44-45) assert that dogs were most frequently used as pack animals given that ethnographic summaries from North American Arctic peoples make reference to the role of dogs in transportation and other tasks.

Morey and Aris-Sørensen (2002: 45) hypothesize that the reason dogs are not commonly seen in the Arctic archaeological record is because they come with a liability, a very high maintenance demand. Based upon present day Siberian Eskimo communities, the authors estimate that one adult dog requires 1000 pounds of meat and fat per year for basic dietary requirements. Both Morey and Aris-Sørensen assert that it would be difficult for Arctic peoples to support large numbers of dogs since an abundance of food is not always available in the Arctic. During lean years, the dogs would be in direct competition for the communities' food supply. Morey and Aris-Sørensen (2002: 53) state that it is to be expected dogs would only occasionally be encountered in the archaeological record given the maintenance demands. They conclude that it is doubtful if future discoveries reveal that the early people of the eastern Arctic ever maintained dogs consistently or in substantial numbers.

Great Britain

The oldest known skeletal material of domestic dog in England was discovered in the 1950's. The site known as Star Carr, located in the Vale of Pickering in Yorkshire, contained the fragmentary remains of a skull, tibia and femur. Based upon C-14 method of dating, it was determined that the skeletal remains were dated at 9488 ±

350 BP. Degerbøl (1961) examined the fragments and did a comparative analysis using the bones of Danish Maglemosian dogs. Based upon his analysis, Degerbøl concluded that the Star Carr animal was a dog and not an immature wolf, as was previously suspected.

Analysis of the skull of the Star Carr animal revealed it to be a young dog of approximately six months old. This age was determined from the open cranial and facial sutures and the dental eruption visible from alveoli. The bulla is very small, as well as the frontal bones. Measurements of the bull and frontal revealed it to be much smaller than Norwegian and Maalov wolves. The premolars of the animal are visibly crowded with an overlapping index of 130 that is considerably large even for dogs. The overlapping index for wolves, according to Degerbøl is 85.2 to 100.2, which is much smaller than the Star Carr animal.

The tibia and femur exhibit fused epiphysis, which led Degerbøl to conclude that these bones represented an older adult dog. Given the small size of the skull and the large, robust nature of the long bones, Degerbøl concluded that the skeletal remains at Star Carr represented at least two dogs.

In 1985, excavations near Star Carr at Seamer Carr revealed an interesting find of a cervical vertebra that matched the Star Carr skull. When radiocarbon accelerator dating was done, an even older date of 9940 ± 110 BP was produced, making the Star Carr dog one of the oldest finds of a domesticated dog in the world (Clutton-Brock and Noe-Nygaard 1990).

However, Olsen (1985:71) is less convinced that the Star Carr skeletal remains are those of a dog. Olsen cautions that the canid skull is from an immature individual and is therefore not a reliable indicator of a specific taxonomic category. Olsen also points out that the Star Carr canid consists of extremely fragmentary remains, which makes taxonomic identification very speculative, at best.

Another Mesolithic dog was also discovered at Thatcham in southern England near the town of Newbury in Yorkshire. Details are scant given that only an upper part of a femur was recovered. The shaft width of the femur was 14 mm which was very similar to the size of the Star Carr dog which was determined to be 14.9 mm (Harcourt 1974:154-155).

The number of Mesolithic dogs discovered in Great Britain totals only four animals. Harcourt (1974:151) concludes that there is very little variability in these animals, which probably indicates a single population. Harcourt estimates that the shoulder height of these dogs fell within the range of about 60-cm.

Throughout the Neolithic and Bronze Age, dog remains in Great Britain are meager. Harcourt (1974:159) believes that during these time periods, the dogs were most likely village scavengers consisting of a single and probably uncontrolled breeding population. It is not until the Iron Age (2800 BP- 43 AD) that an abundance of dog skeletal remains is found. However it is during the later Romano-British period (500 BC – 43 AD) that vast numbers of dog remains, with tremendous skeletal variability, is discovered. It was during this time period that small "lap" or "house" dogs are seen, that are as diminutive as 9 inches at the shoulder (Harcourt 1974:166). Additionally, large robust dogs are also found that reach a shoulder height of 28 inches (Harcourt 1974:166). According to Clark (2000:176-177), excavations at the Roman town of Silchester, England have shown numerous dogs that exhibited characteristics of achondroplasia with the long bones, especially the humerus and tibia, extremely stout and twisted, typical of breeding from a gene for dwarfism. Clark implies that the discovery of the achondroplastic dogs indicates that the Romans in Britain produced these dogs from controlled breedings with a basic understanding of animal husbandry practices.

Germany

One of the earliest domestic dog remains in Germany was reported by Nobis (1979, 1981). The site, a late Paleolithic grave at Bonn-Oberkassel, was dated at 14,000 BP. Although the exact location of the site was not given, it is probably located near the cities of Bonn and Oberkassel. The remains consist of a single mandible that was recovered in a human burial comprised of an adult male approximately 50 years old and an adult female approximately 20-25 years in age. The time period of this find is known as the Magdalenian cultural period, which spanned from 18,000-11,000 BP in western Europe. The Magdalenian period is characterized by dramatic changes in hunting strategy, with little evidence for the use of vegetal foods and a dominance in hunting of large herd animals (Enloe 2001:200). Lithics recovered from this period indicate that there was a switch from the heavy stone axes known in the Paleolithic, to small stone microliths attached to arrows. Clutton-Brock (1995: 10) hypothesizes that the success of the long-distance projectiles could have possibly propagated a working relationship with dogs that could track down and bring wounded animals to bay.

Several additional sites in Germany have been reported by Musil (2000) to contain ancient domestic dog remains. Musil examined faunal remains of three cave sites located in central Germany near Thuringer Wald: Kniegrotte (50 40° N, 11 33° E), Oelknitz (50 50° N, 11 40° E) and Teufelsbruecke (50 35° N, 11 25° E). All three of the sites fell within the Magdalenian culture period that existed in Europe.

The Kniegrotte Cave Magdalenian layer was dated at 12,230 ± 90 to 13,585 ± 165 BP. The layers were divided into four horizons, but according to Musil (2000: 22), the precise time periods of each horizon is difficult to determine due to the excavation methods used in 1974. In the uppermost layer, Canis fragments of a single individual were discovered consisting of cranial, maxilla, ulna, calcaneus, and scapula. The maxilla fragment, which also contained teeth, was measured and compared to dog and wolf maxilla. According to Musil the animal was a small adult. Musil determined that the total tooth row length was 80.1 mm, which falls within the range of domestic dog. The maxilla also exhibited tooth crowding with P2 – P2 overlapping.

The Kniegrotte Cave remains present an interesting problem. Musil (2000: 22) questions whether or not the suspected canine remains could be representative of "small" wolves known from other localities. Musil measured and compared wolf remains that had been dated from $29,300 \pm (750\text{-}690)$ BP to $24,560 \pm (660\text{-}610)$ BP. Based upon results from the measurements of these collections, Musil was able to divide the finds into two groups of "large" and "small" animals. It was determined that when the Kniegrotte Cave material was compared to the wolf measurements, the Kniegrotte find fell within the small end of the range of variation for the "small" wolves. Musil also observed that the "small" specimens exhibited tooth crowding and facial shortening more common in dogs. Musil concluded that the "small" wolves were not "typical" wolves but the first canid finds exhibiting the earliest skeletal changes commonly seen with domestication.

The second locality that Musil (2000: 26) examined was Teufelsbrücke Cave. Four dates were determine from this site: $12,300 \pm 85$, $12,315 \pm 100$, $13,025 \pm 85$, $12,480 \pm 90$ BP. The canid material was represented by a proximal fragment of a metapodial and a first phalanx. Measurements of the phalanx determined that it is smaller than the "typical" wolves used for comparison in the Kniegrotte Cave material.

The third site, Oelknitz, a long-term settlement contained numerous faunal remains including large amounts of horse skeletal material indicating that horses were being hunted. This site was dated to five different periods; the oldest dated at $12,545 \pm 80$ BP with the youngest horizon dated at $10,990 \pm 85$ BP. The canid remains were composed of phalanges, metapodia, humerus and tibia. Musil noticed perceptible differences in the phalanges and metapodia that were smaller and more slender than those in a "typical" wolf. Measurements taken of the humerus and tibia also indicated that the animal was smaller than ancient wolves. Again, Musil hypothesized that this smaller canid was an intermediate canid that bridges the gap between wolves and a true domestic dog, possibly indicating some of the first attempts at domestication. Unfortunately Musil did not consider the possibility that this intermediate canid occurred naturally, simply by a dog/wolf breeding.

Another canid skeletal remain found in Germany is known as the Senekenberg dog. Excavated in 1914, the dating of the material has been based on pollen analysis and stratigraphy. It was determined that the dog was contemporaneous with the Star Carr dog with an estimated date of 9,000 BP. Degerbøl (1961: 43-45) reexamined this material, although his examination was not done on the original skeleton but a plaster cast since the original material was destroyed during WWII. Degerbøl noticed that the Senekenberg dog was small and similar in size to Australian dingoes. Degerbøl proposed that the Senekenberg dog might be renamed as a "European Mesolithic dingo", given its close resemblance to the Australian breed.

Examination of the Senekenberg skull revealed it to be robust in appearance. Degerbøl noted that the sagittal crest was high and well delineated. The zygomatic arch is also high and strong. Degerbøl believes that the sturdiness of the sagittal crest and zygomatic arch indicates strong masticatory muscles. The ratio of the braincase to facial length was determined by Degerbøl to be far to small for a wolf but in the same range as the dingo. Additionally, the facial region in the Senekenberg skull was broader than typically seen in wolves. The premolars were positioned close together but were not overlapped. The second molar was not developed and if it had been present, the dentition might have become crowded. When Degerbøl compared the teeth of the Senekenberg dog to the Star Carr dog, he found them to be smaller.

Unfortunately no limb bones exist from the Senekenberg dog. Degerbøl was able to obtain measurements based upon reports done in the 1930's and was able to estimate that the Senekenberg dog was approximately the same size as the Star Carr animal. Although the Senekenberg dog differs in skull features, Degerbøl ascertains that given that both animals are over 9,000 years old, they still represent an early form of a domestic dog.

France

The earliest evidence of domesticated dog in France was found in a rockshelter of Saint-Thibaud-de-Couz on the western slope of Chartreuse in the French Alps. The rockshelter designated as Jean-Pierre I, contained numerous faunal remains as well as microliths in level 6A. Dating of the faunal remains by C-14 was given to be $10,620 \pm 210$ BP. According to Chaix (2000: 49) several dog remains were found in level 6A. To ensure an accurate date on the dog skeletal material, Chaix had an AMS date made on the dog skull. Dating of the skull resulted in an estimated age of $10,050 \pm 100$ years BP.

The skeletal material consisted of the skull, right and left mandible, atlas, axis, left humerus and left femur. All teeth in the maxilla were missing except for two fragments of the P4 and I3. Only three teeth were present in the left mandible (P3, M1, M2). The skull lacks a pronounced sagittal crest and is well rounded. Chaix (2000: 54) states that the relation between the condylobasal length and the median palatal length is very similar to Neolithic dogs of Switzerland. Chaix observed that the facial length was not reduced and the alveoli of the missing teeth exhibit no evidence of crowding. Chaix also reported that measurements of the carnassial (M1), were equivalent to dimensions taken from late Mesolithic dogs.

Measurements of the distal breadth of the humerus showed that the Saint-Thibaud dog was much smaller than Holocene wolves, 24.6 mm versus 42.1. Height estimates were done using the length of the femur and reported as 40 cm. Chaix (2000: 50) states that this individual was small sized when compared to dogs of the early and late Mesolithic of northern Europe, which have a range of 49 - 54.1 cm.

Chaix concluded that based on the skull proportions, dentition and estimated size the Saint-Thibaud animal is an early domesticated dog. Dating of the skull at 10,000 BP puts the Saint-Thibaud dog in the category of being one of the oldest domestic dog finds in the world.

Ireland

The oldest reported dog remains in Ireland date to the Neolithic period. Sites that have exhibited evidence of dog skeletal material are: 1) Doeys Cairn, Co. Antrim, 2) Fourknocks, Co. Meath, 3) Keenoge, Co. Meath, 4) Ballyeelish, Co. Tipperary, 5) Palmerstown, Co. Dublin, 6) Carrowglass, Co. Dublin, 7) Chapelizod, Co. Dublin, 8) Aghanskeagh A, Co. Louth, 9) Carrowmore/Knocknerea, Co. Sligo, 10) Screedagh, Co. Sligo, 11) Coolatore, Co. Westmeath, and 12) Pollacorragune I, Co. Galway. In Europe, the Neolithic period spanned from 8000 – 4000 BP (Lillios, 2001). McCormick (1985/6: 37) reported that not only are the stratigraphic associations with the Neolithic material questionable because of excavation methods that would be unacceptable by modern standards, but also the stratigraphical contexts of the faunal remains were frequently not critically examined making the archaeological deposition of some species debatable.

Dog remains reported by McCormick were found in association with Neolithic tombs. McCormick (1985/6: 40) states that in most cases the deposits seemed to be representative of "token" animals that were a part of the food supply. The dog skeletal material was frequently mixed with pig, cattle and sheep/goat. In many cases the faunal list from the tomb excavations simply list canid remains as dog/wolf.

Sweden and Denmark

There is scant evidence of ancient remains of domestic dogs in Nordic countries. Olsen (1985: 72) reports the presence of canine crania from the Mesolithic in both Sweden and Denmark; however, the material has been dated at 8,800 to 7,000 BP. The best known skeletal material of the domestic dog are the Danish finds from the Maglemosian settlements from the bogs at Mullerup, Svaerdborg, Holmegaard, Lundby and Aamosen near Halleby River, all in Zealand (Degerbøl 1961: 35). At present, there have not been any domestic dog remains that have approached the antiquity of the prehistoric dogs found in England, France and Germany.

The dogs of Sweden and Denmark were observed by Olsen to be small in size with relatively short limbs with similarities to the physical size to the Star Carr dog. Olsen further observed that many of the bones displayed evidence of cut marks, a possible indication of butchering.

Degerbøl (1961: 35) states that these Danish finds were very fragmentary with relatively few bones found although tens of thousands of bones of other faunal remains were excavated at the same site. Degerbøl attributes the dog remains as evidence from early kitchen middens of the fisher and hunter people.

Hungary

A large number of domesticated dog remains were recovered at Vlasac, located on the Iron Gate gorge of the Danube. Bökönyi (1975:168, 178) reports that C-14 dating places the age of the site at 8,000 BP, preceding the pottery-Neolithic. Over 1900 dog remains were excavated which represented about 6.5% of the total faunal remains recovered. Only 103 wolf remains were recovered (.0035% of total). Bökönyi describes the dog material as fragmented except for two almost complete skulls, numerous complete and almost complete mandibles, several large maxilla fragments, a few fragmented long bones and over 170 lower carnassials (M1). Bökönyi (1975: 168) states that based on the broken condition of the bones, dogs were certainly eaten although it represented only a small portion of the diet, which was, dominated by fish (60%) and red deer (23%).

Bökönyi observed that the dog remains exhibited extremely shortened premolar regions of the mandible. The overall size of the mandible was reduced with a decreased tooth size. Several samples had premolars that were obliquely positioned or turned crosswise, another characteristic of domestication. The cranium is slightly arched with a high median crest. The long bones are long and slender which leads Bökönyi to believe that the Vlasac dogs are representative of a running type dog. The overall sizes of the Vlasac dogs are reported by Bökönyi to be much smaller than the local wolf population.

An interesting aspect of the Vlasac site was the discovery of "transitional" individuals. For the most part the Vlasac dogs were clearly different than the wolf material when comparative measurements were taken of the canid mandibles (Bökönyi 1975: 172). Although Bökönyi reported that there appeared to be considerable differences between the dog and wolf skeletal remains, Bökönyi also discovered several individuals that bridged the two populations. Bökönyi (1975: 172,178) hypothesizes that possibly these individuals could represent wolf/dog crosses or the transitional forms could be the earliest attempts of local domestication.

Iraq

At Jarmo, Iraq in the Zagras Mountains of Iraqi Kurdistan, over 50 cranial and mandibular fragments of domestic dogs were discovered. The mound was dated from 8500 to 9000 BP. Lawrence and Reed (1983) examined the skeletal fragments and did a comparative study to *Canis lupus pallipes* as well as Eskimo dogs, Kurdish dog and the prehistoric dog from Jaguar Cave, Idaho.

The Jarmo site was of particular importance since it is one of the oldest known agricultural communities to be excavated. The site displayed evidence of permanent stone and mud-walled houses and numerous artifacts, which have been interpreted to indicate that the community relied on farming and herding for subsistence. The discover of dogs at this site was considered to be significant archaeological evidence of dog domestication since it coincided with the numerous pig, sheep and goat remains that were found.

Lawrence and Reed (1983: 486) observed that the fragments appeared to be unusually massive. Tooth measurements revealed that the Jarmo dogs were more similar to the Eskimo dogs and fell at or below the lowest range for *C.l. pallipes*. The authors further reported that the sagittal and occipital crests had a pronounced downward curve that matched the Eskimo dogs. The maxillary teeth were slightly small in size with a curvature of the tooth row, which suggested a domestic dog. The most pronounced characteristic of the Jarmo samples is the mandible, which Lawrence and Reed state is very close in size to the big-toothed, massive-skulled breeds such as mastiff or Eskimo dog.

The authors (Lawrence and Reed 1983: 488) concluded that the Jarmo sample may be evidence of hybridization or an extreme form of *lupus*. However, they also hypothesize that the Jarmo dogs may be derived from a local race of wolves, which may explain some of the differences seen in this sample which is not typically seen in other domestic dog samples.

Russia

The Eliseevichi I site, located in the central Russian Plain of the Bryansk Region, has had one of the most important archaeological finds of early dog to date. Excavations of the alluvial terrace of Eliseevichi I produced a variety of faunal material dated to the Upper Paleolithic. The site has been periodically excavated during 1930-1940, 1960 and 1970-1980. Occupation of the site has been distinguished by mammoth-bone dwellings, hearth deposits and large quantities of cultural material such as animal and human figurines, ornaments, bone carvings and worked mammoth tusks (Sablin and Khlopachev 2002). Skeletal remains of two dogs were found in and around hearth deposits. Dating of the cultural deposits have yielded six dates that range between $17,340 \pm 170$ and $12,630 \pm 360$ years BP. Potentially the Eliseevichi site may contain the oldest known domestic dog find in the world.

The dog remains consisted of two adult crania that were found in conjunction with a cultural layer and hearth deposit. Sablin and Khlopachev observed that the skulls had broad, flat frontals and a strongly pronounced crista mediana. The zygomatic breadths measured 145.7 in one animal and approximately 148.0 in the second, which according to the authors is quite large. Examination of the teeth revealed that the teeth were very similar to wolves but the authors conclude that size reduction of the teeth cannot be used as evidence of domestication because ice Age dogs were the same size as wolves. Unusual findings of the Eliseevichi dogs were the measurements taken of the greatest palatal breadth to the condylobasal length. The researchers found that the Eliseevichi dogs had an extremely large palate but a dramatically shortened rostrum. Based upon these measurements, Sablin and Khlopachev stated that the Ice Age dogs from Eliseevichi differed from all recent wolves and have much shorter muzzles than Siberian Huskies and Great Danes. For example, the ratio of the palatal breadth to the condylobasal length in Great Danes is $0.377 - 0.380$, Siberian Huskies $0.328 - 0.384$, and wolves $0.309-0.369$. However the Eliseevichi dogs measured 0.386 and 0.387 respectively. Sablin and Khlopachev estimated that the reconstructed withers height was approximately 70 cm, which is representative of a large, heavy breed.

Sablin and Khlopachev (2002) conclude that the Eliseevichi dogs may have represented a new development in human hunting strategy where humans and wolves were competing for food. The Eliseevichi dogs are an important link in the history of dog domestication not only because of the $13,000 - 17,000$ BP date, but also they may represent an early attempt of domestication *in situ* from local wolves.

Armenia

According to Manaserian and Antonian (2000:227), no dog remains have been recovered from the early Paleolithic in Armenia. However numerous dog skeletal remains have been found dating from the Neolithic to the Middle Ages. Neolithic sites containing dog remains are Shengavit, Mokhrablur and Metsamor. Bronze Age and Iron Age sites are Tsamakaberd, Sevan, Lehashen, Arteek, Ketee, Gilli and Shirakavan. Middle Age sites with dog remains include Artashat and Beniamin.

Twelve archaeological sites contained intact dog skulls. Dog skulls dated at approximately 6000 BP have shown remarkable preservation so that osteometric analysis has been possible. Manaserian and Antonian assert that because so many complete dog skulls were found at the various sites, this would indicate that the animals were not being used as a dietary source, since animal brains were a common food source.

Manaserian and Antonian (2000: 227) observed that there were insignificant differences between the dogs found at the different sites, leading the authors to believe that the regional population was restricted. The cranial characteristic, which did exhibit variation, was the sagittal crest (*crista sagittalis*), which varied from poorly developed to pronounced. They further observed that the nasal bones were shortened, while the muzzle was long. Unfortunately no measurements of the dentition were taken.

Comparative analysis of the Armenian dogs to wolves and jackals showed that the temporal index of dogs was 27-41 % in the Armenian dogs, 23-32% in modern dogs, 22-43 % in wolves and 15 % in jackals (p.227). Further comparison in wolf-dog hybrids and jackal-dog hybrids revealed 22-28% and 11-20%, respectively. This evidence points to a closer association to wolves and dog than jackals.

An interesting aspect of the Armenian finds was the large numbers of bronze zoomorphic statuettes, pendants and pictographs found at the site, many of these depicting dogs. One unique piece was a bronze statuette of a dog with a collar and leash.

Israel

The first find in Israel of a possible domestic dog was reported by Davis and Valla (1978). Located at Mallaha, near the Huleh Lake in the Upper Jordan Valley, this much cited archaeological discovery was viewed as distinctive not only because of its antiquity, but also because of its association with a human skeleton. The finds were dated at 11,310 ± 880 and 11,740 ± 570 BP, falling within the Natufian period. Two specimens of canid remains were excavated, a mandible and a puppy that was approximately 3-5 months in age. Buried within the tomb in association with the puppy, was an elderly adult human. The human was buried in a flexed position with its hand cupping the thorax of the puppy. Although the authors (Davis and Valla 1978: 610) hypothesize that the burial is unique because it "offers proof that an affectionate rather than gastronomic relationship existed between it and the buried person", they overlook the possibility that the burial of the dog had a ceremonial or a symbolic purpose.

Examination of the deciduous lower fourth molar (dm_4) produced a measurement of 13.3 mm for the maximum crown length. When comparisons of the same tooth were done with the jackal, Israeli and Turkish wolves and modern dogs, the puppy was more similar to a wolf or dog but fell outside the range for jackals. The adult mandible exhibited poorly developed metaconids, with a slight degree of tooth crowding frequently seen in dogs and wolves but not jackals. The lower first molar to alveolar length index also fell within the range of wolf and dog.

Davis and Valla (1978: 609) compared the amount of dental overlap of the lower forth premolar and the lower first molar of the Mallaha specimens to a collection of recent dogs from Israel and Egypt and to recent wolves. The dogs gave values of 0.65 to 0.70 with the wolves ranging from 0.62 to 0.67. The Mallaha canid produced a value of 0.67. The authors concluded that dental overlap criterion was not an efficient method of separating dogs and wolves.

Canid remains have also been excavated from two submerged prehistoric sites, Atlit-Yam and Kfar-Galim, in the Mediterranean Sea off the Carmel coast of Israel (Dayan and Galili 2000). The sites were designated as Pre-Pottery and Ceramic Neolithic, respectively. Atlit-Yam was dated at 7,500 – 8,100 BP and the Ceramic settlement, Kfar-Galim, was dated at 6,500 – 7,000 BP. Preservation of the remains was very good due to the layer of sand covering the skeletal material that hampered damage from marine erosion. The Atlit-Yam dog remains consisted of a mandible, several individual teeth and a braincase with rostrum fragments. The Kfar-Galim specimen was constituted by a nearly complete cranium.

Measurements of both specimens indicated that the older Atlit-Yam canid was smaller than the modern Israeli wolf but not significantly. The Kfar-Galim dog was also slightly smaller in toothrow length, bullar length, and upper carnassial length than Israeli wolves. However the Kfar-Galim dog exhibits the most dramatic difference in skull length measurements when compared to Israeli wolves (183.60 mm vs. 172.20 mm). The Kfar-Galim dog also exhibited the characteristic flattening of the tympanic bullae typically seen in domesticated dogs.

Dayan and Galili (2000: 32) conclude that the minor changes seen in the skull measurements of the Atlit-Yam canids may be resultant of a slower rate of morphological change during the early stages of domestication. Dayan (1994) in an earlier study related size in different species to climatic conditions. In his study of carnivores in Israel, he tested Bergmann's rule, which states that species from colder climates tend to be larger than those of warmer climates. However the results seen in the Israeli sample were contradictory to Bergman's rule and didn't exhibit the expected increase in size seen during the cooler periods. Therefore the slight differences seen in the Israeli wolves and the Kfar-Galim and Atlit-Yam dogs is not unusual, according to Dayan who considers domestication to play a more important roll in size reduction than environmental factors. However, Tchernov and Horwitz (1991) hypothesize that cultural shifts from nomadic to sedentism can create a microevolutinary response that would be reflected in the slight metric morphological changes as seen in the Israel specimens. If Dayan is correct, the slight metric changes seen in the Carmel Coast dogs and Israeli wolves may be indicative of the earliest attempts at canine domestication.

An interesting side note on the history of the dog in Israel can also be derived from Biblical sources. Vesey-Fitzgerald (1957:34-35) states that according to the Bible, the Israelites disliked dogs and they regarded them as "unclean" lowly creatures. Of some thirty passages of references to dogs in the Scriptures almost all are derogatory. Vesey-Fitzgerald suggests that, while the Ancient Hebrews may have found dogs to be useful for guarding flocks, they never considered them to be pets or companions.

Africa

Except for Egypt, according to Clutton-Brock (1995:14), there is no archaeological evidence of domestic dogs has yet to be discovered from sub-Saharan Africa before AD 500. Although some scholars have speculated that dogs could have evolved from Ethiopian wolves, there is not archaeological confirmation to support this theory. Tribal groups in Africa, such as the !Kung San bushmen, have only recently adopted dogs for hunting and the archaeological record is devoid of any evidence of dogs prior to the historic period. Although Europe, Asia and North America have all shown evidence of domestic dogs dated back to antiquity, at present Africa has yet to produce the same archaeological findings.

Egypt

Although it is known that the ancient Egyptians, Babylonians and Assyrians all were known to be avid dog breeders, Egypt is devoid of any archaeological evidence of domestic dog as ancient as the sites in Israel. One of the earliest forms of dogs represented in art is seen on green tablets found in Egypt dated to 6000 – 6400 BP (Vesey-Fitzgerald 1957: 53-54). There are also dogs depicted on the Egyptian monuments that are dated to about 5000 BP. At least three different types of dogs are represented in the tombs, a mastiff-type, a sleek Greyhound type, and a curl-tailed Spitz type (Vesey-Fitzgerald 1957:54). Dogs were also embalmed and mummified although the Egyptians didn't hold them in the same regard as their idol worship of cats. However any archaeological evidence that domestic dogs existed in this region during the prehistoric has yet to be found.

Kazakhstan

One of the largest Eneolithic settlement sites on the southern part of the West Siberian Plain in northern Kazakhstan is Botai. The Eneolithic culture, which is contemporaneous with the Copper Age but lacking copper, is dated in this region ranging from 5600 BP and ending with the arrival of bronze at 4500 BP. However, Olsen (2000:72) asserts that dating for the Mesolithic and Neolithic in this region has not been clearly defined. The area is rich with pithouses of which 158 have been documented. In addition to Bronze Age artifacts, the site has produced an abundance of faunal remains totaling more than 300,000 bones (Olsen 2000:74). An estimated 99% of these bones have been identified as horse, with dog being the second most abundant remains found. Olsen has identified at least 13 separate canine deposits consisting of at least 18 individuals. Of these 18, Olsen has been able to ascertain that 15 individuals are dogs and 3 are wolves. Using horse and human remains for dating, the site has been dated at 5650 BP.

In a comparative analysis to modern dogs, the Botai dogs are most similar to the Samoyed breed (Olsen 2000: 82-83). Olsen concludes that the similarity to the Samoyed breed is not unexpected since the Samoyed people that are associated with the development of the Samoyed breed originated on the west side of the Ural Mountains. Measurements of the Botai dogs indicated that all the specimens were similar. Olsen could not find any discernible difference between the Botai dogs and modern Samoyed breed except for a slight increase in skeletal robustness in the Botai sample, possibly an environmental adaptation to cold. Estimated shoulder height of the 15 samples revealed that the Botai dogs fell between the height measurements of male and female Samoyeds.

Olsen (2000: 86-87) concluded that although the horse remains displayed evidence of butchering and ritual use, the dog skeletal remains don't exhibit any signs that they were being consumed by humans. However Olsen does acknowledge that the discovery of only partial dog skeletons or skulls does indicate that they were dismembered. But Olsen infers that this does not represent disarticulation for consumption, but rather some kind of ritual activity. Her support for this theory is supported by the lack of evidence of fractured bones that would indicate marrow extraction. Olsen suggests that, since the dog burials are located near house thresholds and foundations they were very likely regarded as "guardian animals" watching over the household. Olsen states that the only faunal remains to be found in association with human remains were horses. Therefore if the dogs at Botai were sacrifices, Olsen asserts that they would have been found in context with human interments. Although the Botai dogs are not ancient, their discovery is nevertheless important. The lack of cutmarks indicating butchering coupled with the location of the burials in relationship to the households suggests that they had a sacred or mythological place in Botai culture. Although such a hypothesis had yet to be proven, Olsen hypothesizes that there are strong factors that imply such a relationship.

Thailand

The discovery of canid bones at four prehistoric sites in Thailand, dating between 5500 BP to the present, has yielded important information on the domestication of dog in Southeast Asia. In the Ban Chiang prehistoric settlement site in the Udon Thani Province, canid remains dating to 5500 BP were examined by Higham et al. (1980). The site was comprised of series of burial and occupational layer ascribed to six prehistoric phases (Higham et al. 1980). The mound contained over 60 species of faunal remains including cattle, shellfish, pigs, small mammals and wild ungulates. The authors' focus was to determine if the canid remains found at the site had any biological affinity to cuon (*Cuon alpinus*), golden jackal (*Canis aureus)*, Chinese wolf (*Canis lupus chanco*), Indian wolf (*Canis lupus pallipes*) or Thai village dog. Measurements taken of the skull were analyzed by using a computer program, which compiled the data and compared by multivariate means.

Based on their analysis, Higham et al. (1980: 150, 154-155, 159) concluded that the Ban Chiang canids were more closely related to the modern village dog of Ban Chiang and the Chinese wolf than any other species. Examination of the dentition showed that there was a clear distinction between the cuon and jackal. The researchers also performed nine mandibular measurements that indicated that the prehistoric remains fell within the discriminate function distribution for the modern dog. Higham et al. further state that the prehistoric specimens had a significantly broader rostrum and a deeper, thicker jaw relative to jaw length, all characteristics of the modern dog. The Ban Chiang specimens also exhibited markedly smaller auditory bullae, another feature of a domesticated canid. Higham et al. concludes that the overwhelming majority of canid bones from Ban Chiang sites come from a domesticated dog. Their support of this conclusion was based on close similarities of skull shape, mandibular characteristics and jugular process shape that is all morphologically equivalent to the domestic dog and wolf. Additionally, the overall body size of the Ban Chiang dogs was comparable to the modern village dog but smaller than the Australian dingo.

The Ban Chiang dog specimens showed clear evidence of cutting, breakage and charring of the prehistoric remains (Higham et al. 1980: 159). These features indicate that dogs were consumed as a part of the diet, a tradition that still occurs today.

Higham et al. (1980: 159, 161) propose that the morphological similarities of the Ban Chiang dogs to the Chinese wolf points to an origin of China for these southeast Asia canids. The researchers believe that the domestic dogs seen at the Ban Chiang prehistoric settlement sites were probably introduced from China by the first lowland rice agriculturalist in Thailand. However, they also infer that by the time these animals were introduced in this region, they had already been domesticated from Chinese wolves long enough that many of the wolf-like characteristics had already been altered through selective breeding.

Australia

At present, there is no archaeological evidence that domesticated dogs existed in Australia before 5,000 years ago. The dingo, the only known aboriginal dog to the region, was thought to be derived from an Asian dog that originated from either the Arabian or Indian wolf (Wilton et al. 1999:108). It is believed that the dingo was brought to Australia by sea by the first inhabitants, possibly as a food source, where they thrived and spread.

According to Olsen (1985: 87) the best evidence of archaeological remains of a dingo has been derived by the discovery of a mummified dingo found in a cave on the Nullarbor Plain. Identification of the remains as dingo was based on physical characteristics such as skull proportions, size, coat color and dentition. Dating of the remains was done on soft tissue and yielded a date of 2200 BP. Additional dingo remains have been found, but none had produced dates older than 3000 BP (Olsen 1985: 87). Although meager numbers of isolated teeth have been recovered that are possibly more ancient, provenience and dating of these finds are tentative, at best.

Japan

At the Natsushima Shell Mound in Kanagawa Prefecture in Japan, the oldest dog remains found are dated to 9,300 BP (Shigehara and Hongo 2000: 62). A second site, Kamikuroiwa Cave in Ehime Prefecture, yielded dog remains that had been intentionally buried sometime between 8,000 – 8,500 BP. Additionally, a rockshelter in Tocibara was reported to contain skeletal remains of both the extinct Japanese wolf and domestic dog (Clutton-

Brock 1995:14). These remains were dated at 8,000 BP. After the introduction of rice agriculture, the native people placed less reliance on hunting and there was a decrease on the utilitarian use of dogs as hunting companions. This is reflected in the sharp decline in the number of archaeological sites that contain dog remains in later periods (Shigehara and Hongo 2000: 62).

According to Shigehara and Hongo (2000: 61) native Japanese wolves are not considered to be the wild progenitors of Japanese dogs. It is believed that dogs were brought over from the Asian mainland where they disseminated into the surrounding Japanese islands. After their introduction, the Japanese dogs did not undergo any drastic morphological changes maintaining similar body and cranial proportions as the mainland dogs. Shigehara and Hongo (2000: 63, 65) believe that Jomon dogs of Japan remained unchanged until about 300 years ago when the Japanese started to practice selective breeding. Until that time the traditional thinking had been to accept nature as it was and not alter what occurs naturally.

The authors conclude that the ancient Jomon dogs of Japan were not native to the region but were derived from an Asiatic breed. The archaeological evidence indicates that these early dogs were most likely descended from a single origin. This theory seems to have substantial validity since the Jomon dogs remained unchanged for thousands of years. Given that the Yayoi people, who migrated from the Asian mainland, probably brought them over from the mainland when they migrated to Japan. Additional evidence for support of this theory is also supplied by molecular analysis of the ancient Japanese dogs done by Ishigiro et al. (2000: 291). In their study they concluded that the Jomon dogs contained haplotypes seen in Southeast Asia but no haplotype clusters indicative of the native Japanese wolf. These molecular results also supported Tanabe's (1991: 648) earlier study of blood polymorphisms and cranial observations that suggested that the Jomon dogs were most similar to dogs from south China or East Asia probably brought to Japan 10,000 – 12,000 years ago.

Siberia

Obviously Siberia may be abundant in archaeological finds, however many of the early reports were sketchy in details concerning faunal remains. Some reports simply include the dog as a list of "culinary debris" (Olsen 1985: 66). Another problem is that much of the canid skeletal material cannot be reliably determined to a specific stratigraphic horizon, making accurate dating debatable. Siberia may be able to provide some important information on dog domestication and its spread into North America. However with the collapse of the Soviet government and the continuing crisis of the Russian economy, funding for research has become extremely difficult making future archaeological research questionable.

Ovodov (1998) examined the mummified remains of a Late Pleistocene Altaic dog recovered in Razboinichiya Cave located in the Altai region of southern Siberia. The dog was found in association with numerous skeletal remains of extinct species including bear, wolf and birds. Dating of the stratum, but not the remains themselves, produced a date of 14,850 ± 700 years BP. This site had previously been excavated in the 1880's and the 1920's with both excavations recovering dog remains. However given the limited resources for dating such material at that time, estimates of the antiquity of the dogs could only be inferred by geological context. The Altai dog was identified as domestic dog based on morphometric cranial characteristics. According to Ovodov, the Altaic dog possessed pronounced signs of domestication such as reduced basal and palatal lengths and snout. Although the dog featured characteristics typical of *Canis familiaris,* it still retained the large teeth distinctive to wolves. Ovodov further reported that split dog bones found at the Afontova Gora-2 site would indicate that dogs were not only used as possible hunting companions but also a food source.

At Lake Baikal, an early Neolithic cemetery consisting of hundreds of human burials as well as one grave that contained the skeletal remains of a Tundra wolf (Bazaliiskiy and Savelyev 2003). Radiocarbon dating of the wolf produced a date of 7230 ± 40 BP. Unfortunately Bazaliiskiy and Savelyev did not report any skeletal description of the remains that led them to conclude that the animal was indeed a wolf. However the authors have no explanation on how a cold-climate animal found itself in the south area of Siberia, which was known to have been a region of high humidity and warm climate during the Mesolithic period. They do however, hypothesize that the appearance of the wolf in a specially created grave would not only indicate that it was very important to the ancient society but also most likely was transported to the Lake Baikal region as the result of human intervention.

Olsen (1985) made an interesting observation that might apply to the Lake Baikal wolf. In Olsen's research of Siberian canid fossil evidence, he points out that archaeology of Siberia prior to the 1980's is poorly defined. In many of the early archaeological reports, Olsen states that enigmatic remains of large canids are often interchangeably referred to as dogs or domesticated wolves, leaving their taxonomic status unclear. Other dog burials in Siberia, such as the Ushki I site, also have questionable dates. A domestic dog at Ushki I was reported to be 10,360-10,760 years BP. Olsen believes that these dates could be in error since the site is in an area of volcanic activity producing a skewed C14 date. Another site Ust´-Belaia, which has also produced domestic dog remains, also has problematical dating. Although previously reported to be dated at 9000 years old, a later study stated that it was only 3000 years BP.

China

It has been suggested by Vila et al. (1997) and Savolainen et al. (2002) that the origin of the domestic dog may have taken place in China, or at the very least in Asia. It has also been suggested that early wolves were tamed which became the ancestral stock for the domestic dog. These theories have been strongly supported by Pleistocene and Neolithic assemblages found in China. Since jackals and coyotes do not exist in China but yet there are abundant wolf and dog deposits, it has given archaeological support to the theory that the dog was descended from the wolf.

At Chouk'outien near Beijing, human skeletal remains have been dated to between 460,000 and 230,000 years BP (Olsen and Olsen 1977: 534; Dickson and Carlson 2004: 180). The site, which consisted of a cave, held multiple layers of occupation as well as assemblages of wolf. The wolf differed from the common wolf of the area in that it was smaller and had a slender snout region and weak sagittal crest. Although this site holds importance because of the association of man and wolf, it can not be determined if the cave simultaneously housed both humans and wolves or if both species occupied the site at different times. Olsen (1985:12) also reports that a small wolf *(Canis lupus variabilis)* has also been found in several early to late Pleistocene sites in China in association with both *Homo erectus* and *Homo sapiens*.

One of the oldest sites to yield domestic dog remains is at the Neolithic village of Pan p'o in Shensi Province (Olsen and Olsen 1977: 534). Dated at almost 7000 years old, the dogs exhibited all the classic signs of domestication. The authors also reported that these dog remains were very similar in size to the Puebloan dogs seen in North America. Another interesting feature that Olsen and Olsen described was the "turned-back" apex of the coronoid process typically seen in domestic dogs, was also present in the small modern Chinese wolf but not in larger subspecies of wolves.

Another site that has produced dog remains is the site of Cishan in Hebei Province (Olsen 1985: 48). Skeletal remains consisted of five crania and two mandibles, which were compared to *Canis lupus* osteological material. Radiocarbon dating of the remains yielded a date of 7355 ± 100 and 7235 ± 105 BP. The remains were later concluded to be a domestic dog based upon the cranial morphology.

A second site at Peiligang in Henan, has also a domestic dog mandible as well as lithic and ceramics (Olsen 1985: 50). The age of the assemblage based on C14 ranges from 9300 ± 1000 BP, 7885 ± 480 BP, 7185 ± 200 BP and 6435 ± 200 BP.

In the Zhejiang Province, the village of Hemudu contains the archaeological remains of six dogs (Olsen 1985: 50). The dogs exhibited morphological changes attributed to domestication such as a shortened snout, small physical size and crowded dentition. Reported date of the site has been described as 6310 ± 100 BP and 6065 ± 120 BP.

One of the largest deposits of domestic dog remains has been associated with the Yangshao culture in northern China (Olsen 1985: 52-53). At Banpo, a Yangshao cultural site, at least five domestic dogs have been uncovered. Comparison of the dog remains was done to *Canis lupus* using morphometric techniques. The canid remains were determined to be domestic dog based upon the curved inferior margin of the mandible, small carnassials, protruding rostrum and small skull size. Many of the dog remains have been found in refuse areas with other food debris leading to speculation that the dogs were used for consumption, although no analysis of butchery marks has been done. An estimated age of the site has been suggested at 6200 to 5600 BP.

Throughout China dozens of sites have yielded domestic canid remains. However, specific details about the canids are often scant and lacking in description of morphological features, comparative study and multivariate analysis. This problem is not unique to China but is probably the most disappointing given that China may very well be the region where dogs were first domesticated. Excavations often placed more emphasis on human remains, lithic and ceramic artifacts with only a brief mention of associated faunal material. During the 1970's and 1980's archaeologists began to see the importance of faunal remains and began to do a more careful inventory and analysis of faunal assemblages. Although many of the canid remains collected at earlier excavations have been reexamined, a sizable number of such finds were later discarded after the initial listing on the site report. Canids buried in conjunction with humans were more likely to be better documented than those found in trash middens. For instance at the Bronze Age site (3384 to 3100 BP) of Anyang, hundreds of tombs contained dog burials, many associated with people. Special attention was focused on these animals since they appeared to be sacrificial because they were adorned with bells, jade and bronze artifacts (Olsen 1985: 61). Documentation of these sacrificial dogs was quite thorough, perhaps because of the wealth of artifacts discovered with their association or their relationship with human burial customs. Dog remains discovered at less auspicious sites frequently were not deemed to be of importance and therefore not recognized as having historical value. With recent interest in the origins of the domestic dog being focused in the molecular genetics field, as well as archaeology, it is hopeful that more importance will be placed on the analysis of canid remains in China.

CHAPTER V

Discussion

Mitochondrial DNA sequences have been used as molecular clocks to determine the earliest domestication of the dog. Vila et al. (1997) suggests that using such clocks indicates that dogs were domesticated over 100,000 years ago. However existing archaeological data contains no evidence of domestic dog before 15,000 years ago, at the outside. The incommensurability of these two data sets is further complicated by animal behaviorists casting doubt on the likelihood that dogs were domesticated from wolves, which suggested that their behavior was too complex. In this chapter I critically examine these three disparate research approaches in order to suggest the most probable date of dog domestication based on the current understanding of all three types of evidence.

Problems with mtDNA inheritance

Advances in molecular genetics have made it possible to amplify regions of mtDNA and do comparative analysis between different individuals or species. However, with the claim of Vila et al. (1997) that the separation of the dog from the wolf occurred over 100,000 years ago, many archaeologists, zoologists, biologists and even some molecular geneticists have viewed these controversial assertions with considerable skepticism. The most critical feature of Vila et al. hypothesis is that since wolves and dogs differ by 12 substitutions in the control region of the mtDNA, that the date of divergence can be calculated based on the premise that mutations occur at a fixed rate, often referred to as the "molecular clock". Vila et al. further conclude that given the number of substitutions seen, the origin of the dog as a separate species would be far older than previously speculated. However, zoo-archaeologists maintain that the dog has a more recent origin of not more than 15,000 years based upon the fossil evidence. Vila et al. (1997: 1687) also imply that the separation of dog from wolf is a "domestication event" initiated by selective breeding by Pleistocene humans. This argument is also deemed by archaeologists as debatable, since it is believed that early man was far too primitive to engage in selective breeding of wild animals with the specific goal of creating progeny with distinctive characteristics. Although Vila's et al. research is concise and thorough, many of the conclusions reached by the researchers are unsubstantiated by solid, multidisciplinary scientific evidence.

The current molecular approach to determine the origin of the domestic dog has been the analysis of mtDNA, specifically the D-loop control region. Mitochondrial DNA has been the favored tool for evolutionary and forensic studies since their sequences were unraveled in 1981 (Gibbons 1998:28). Unlike nuclear DNA, which contains the mixture of genes from both parents, mtDNA was believed to be only inherited from the maternal line. It was observed that mitochondria that were abundant in the tail structures of sperm failed to gain access of the interior of the oocyte and any paternal mtDNA molecules that did enter the oocyte would be greatly diluted by the greater abundance of oocyte mtDNA or eliminated entirely (Williams 2002:610). Recent research in human genetics has proven that this is not true. In 1992, DNA testing was done on the suspected remains of the last Russian tsar, Nicholas II (Gibbons 1998:28-29). Much to the surprise of researchers, it was found that Nicholas II had inherited two different sequences of mtDNA. Suspecting that the researchers could have made an error, they exhumed the body of Nicholas' II brother and it was found that he too had inherited two mtDNA sequences, a condition known as heteroplasmy. In another study an individual with a hereditary optic neuropathy, a disease caused by a mtDNA gene mutation, was DNA tested (Gibbons 1998: 29). Even more surprising was that this individual contained three different mtDNA sequences in his cells, a condition known as triplasmy. Since it has long been believed that humans only carried one copy of maternally inherited mtDNA, the discovery of an individual that carried three copies was not believed to be possible. The researchers were able to trace the mutations back to a woman born in 1861, which meant that the overall divergence rate was predicted to be one mutation every 25 to 40 generations. The researchers concluded that phylogenetic studies have substantially underestimated the rate of mtDNA divergence. These new findings will have serious ramifications on future evolutionary studies.

Although paternal inheritance of mtDNA had been detected in mice, it was believed that this event was extremely rare and was only induced after several generations of interspecific backcrosses (Gyllensten et al. 1991: 255-257). However as genetic testing has become more routinely done in humans with diseases of suspected genetic origins, it has been found that paternal mtDNA inheritance may possibly occur in at least 10% up to 20% in humans. In studies done by Schwartz and Vissing (2002: 576-580) and Williams (2002: 609-612), it has been discovered that defective forms of mtDNA may accumulate preferentially in different tissues within a single person (Fig. 24). In one case study, Schwartz and Vissing (2002: 577) genetically screened a man who had a history of severe fatigue after exceptionally mild exercise exertion. Upon sequencing it was found that the patient's muscle tissue mtDNA was identical to that of his father and uncle's blood. However the patient's blood was identical to that of his mother.

These cases of heteroplasmy inheritance of paternal mtDNA has led researchers to speculate on how often this condition occurs as this rate has implications for assessing the dates of divergence events as this type of mutation could distort the "molecular clock". It is assumed by evolutionists that mutations occur every 300 to 600 generations in humans. If it is assumed that a generation consists of 20 years, then a mutation would be expected to be seen once every 6,000 to 12,000 years. However when researchers sequenced mtDNA in the studies done on MIA soldier families, it was discovered that a mutation occurred once every 40 generations, or approximately every 800 years (Gibbons 1998:28). These results have made evolutionists reassess dating estimates based on mtDNA.

Certain areas on the DNA may also mutate faster than at others (Gibbons 1998:29). These areas, denoted as "hot spots", have been known to mutate so quickly that after several thousand years it would be possible for the mutated areas to revert back to their original sequences. Therefore, when this type of mutation occurs in the mtDNA, it would give the impression that very few mutations occurred over tens of thousands of years when, in actuality, multiple mutation events may happen in a few generations.

If mtDNA does mutate this rapidly, as preliminary studies indicate, this will change timeline estimates of evolutionary relationships. Evolutionary divergence rates are based on the premise that those species' lineages with the fewest number of mutations have diverged more recently and are more closely related. Yet, since it is now known that maternal and paternal mtDNA can combine, the fundamental assumption that mtDNA is always maternally inherited must be rejected.

In 1997 a surprising study was published by Janke et al. (1997) which confounded paleontologists. It has been commonly acknowledged that based on the fossil record, there existed three types of mammalian groups: eutherians (humans, dogs, pigs, whales, etc.); marsupials (kangaroos, wallabies, koalas, etc.); and monotremes (platypus, echidna). Paleontologists believed that eutherians and marsupials were derived from a common ancestor whereas monotremes evolved independently in a different geographic landmass. However some biologists believed that marsupials and monotremes were linked together by a common ancestor. Janke et al. compared coding regions in the mtDNA of the wallaroo, platypus, opossum and various other mammals, including humans. They (1997: 1280) concluded that marsupials and monotremes have a common evolutionary ancestry but that eutherians evolved separately. The researchers further concluded that based on the new findings, the proposed dating of mammalian divergences needed to be revised to reflect the molecular data. Yet, evolutionary biologists were perplexed by Janke's et al. findings since the fossil record did not support their conclusions.

A new study conducted by Killian et al. (2001) disputed Janke et al. research findings. Killian and colleagues believed that the use of mtDNA to classify (1997) mammalian evolution was so flawed that it might have erroneously linked the monotremes and marsupials (Duke University Medical Center 2001). Using a section of nuclear DNA that codes for the M6P/IGF2R gene, which has proven to have a long and well-established evolutionary history in the animal kingdom, the researchers compared 15 different mammals (Killian et al. 2001: 513-515). After determining the nuclear traits of each species, the researchers constructed a minimum evolutionary tree and split decomposition networks based on log Determinant distances. They concluded that eutherians and marsupials did in fact have a common evolutionary ancestry with monotremes evolving

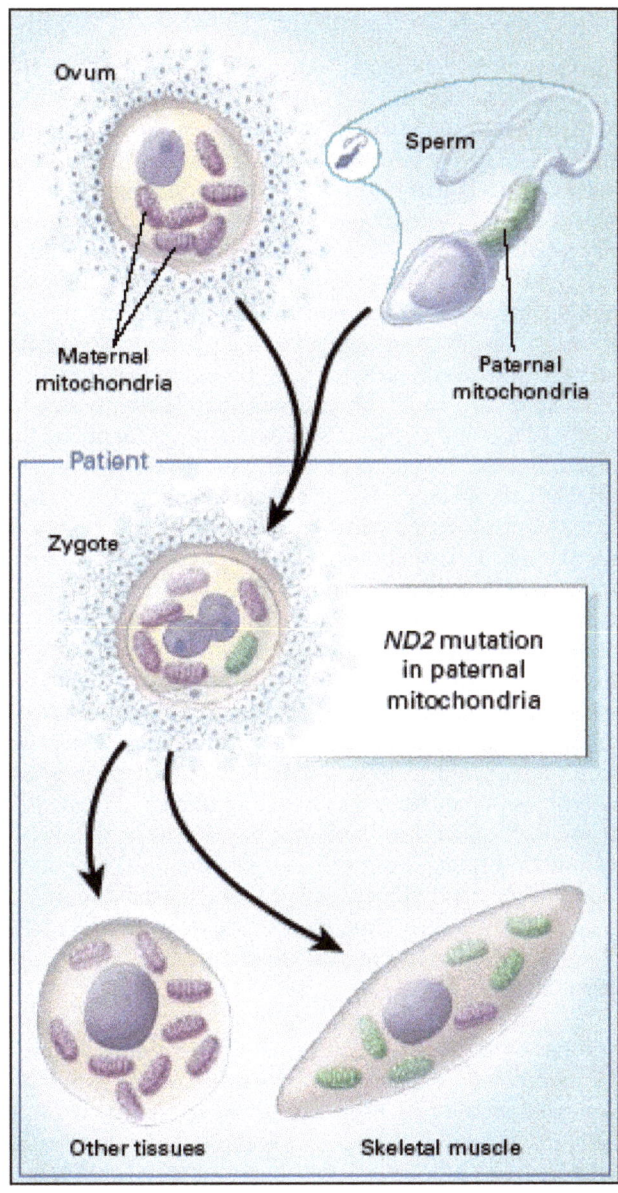

Fig. 24. A mitochondrial mutation may have led to selective replication of paternally derived DNA (green) in muscle. In contrast, mitochondria in the other tissues were inherited from the mother (purple) (Williams 2002: 611).

separately, a clear contradiction to the work done by Janke et al. (1997). Killian et al. performed a bootstrap analysis to measure the relatedness of the genes analyzed. This study revealed that the accuracy of the nuclear DNA study measured 97-100%, whereas 9 out of 15 coding regions of the mtDNA in the Janke et al. study fell below the 95% confidence interval (Killian et al. 2001: 515; Janke et al. 1997:1279). Killian et al. surmised that the Janke et al. study had incorrectly assumed equal substitution rates among sites, an assumption that is known to seriously bias tests of phylogenetic hypotheses. Killian stated (Duke University Medical Center 2001): "This is the first molecular evolutionary study that seriously and powerfully says the paleontologists have been right all along in grouping mammals the way they did. It turns out that common sense is correct."

The stability of ancient mtDNA has been further tested by Gilbert et al. (2003) from whole teeth on 37 archaeological human specimens to determine if control sites commonly used genetic analysis, were susceptible to postmortem damage. The archaeological samples ranged from 675 AD to 1700 AD and were recovered from various sites in Greenland, Britain and Denmark, with the Greenland samples identified as Viking. The researchers took extra precautions to eliminate the possibility of contaminate DNA. What the researchers discovered could possibly have serious ramifications on all future evolutionary studies using mtDNA. Gilbert et al. found that certain regions within the control sequence were "hotspots" for mutation or contamination resulting from postmortem decay indicating that DNA molecules can be modified at the same point. These hotspots or damaged areas affect the same genetic positions as evolutionary change. The researchers found that at key areas in the sequence that separates European sequences from Middle Eastern, the postmortem damage made the Viking skeletons to appear to have originated in the Levant. The authors concluded (Gilbert et al. 2003: 41) that after repeated extractions, and amplifications, that mtDNA heteroplasmy, nuclear copies of mitochondrial genes, or polymerase misincorporations did not contribute to the mutations seen within the control region. The researchers hypothesized that certain areas within the non-coding control region are susceptible to mutation whereas coding regions were not prone to mutation because there may have been some type of selection to constrain mutation rates within critical regions which is lacking in the non-coding areas. They also theorize that some form of protection at the non-coding regions may be removed or degraded after death, which would contribute to the elevated mutation rates. They suggest that postmortem damage may explain many unusual results obtained from ancient human remains. If these results are found to be consistent within other groups, this new discovery could also cast doubt on the genetic analyses and evolutionary relationships of dogs as proposed by the molecular studies of canids. What is also very pivotal about this study is that it highlights how unstable and prone to mutation the non-coding control region is. Additionally it also raises questions about the speed of degradation within the DNA. In the studies done on the evolutionary origins of canines, for the most part, researchers used heparinized blood taken from living canines to be used for sequencing. However, since it is known that postmortem decay occurs immediately upon death, it would be reasonable to infer that fresh blood would also begin this degradation process once it is withdrawn from the body. Although refrigeration would slow this process, it would not stop it. Therefore, it is reasonable to hypothesize that the relatively small amount of mutational change seen in the control regions used for evolutionary studies could be the result of the same type of postmortem damage as seen in the ancient samples.

Far more advances have been made in mtDNA research quite simply because of its relatively small size in comparison to nuclear DNA. It has been much easier for researchers to use the noncoding regions of mtDNA for study that trying to glean to same information out of the three billion base pair nuclear DNA. This is not to say that mtDNA research is erroneous, but rather it should be recognized that extreme caution needs to be used when making broad based generalizations. This same amount of caution needs to be applied to the wolf/dog divergence studies. As noted earlier, most research that has been conducted on canid divergence has been based on mtDNA. Again the researchers made the assumptions that mtDNA was maternally inherited, mutations in the mtDNA occurred at a fixed rate, the number of mutations in the control region can be used to extrapolate data on the dating of evolutionary events, and that mutations occur in all areas of the mtDNA at the same speed. Human genetics research has proven these assumptions to be erroneous and canid phylogenic studies must deal with this new understanding. Until molecular geneticists inadvertently discovered that humans could possess both paternal and maternal mtDNA, paternal inheritance was never considered to be a possibility. However, now that heteroplasmy has been discovered in mice and humans, it is prudent to assume heteroplasmy exists in canids as well since canines exhibit many physiological conditions found in humans. Therefore since molecular biologists so strongly believed in maternal inheritance, the possibility of canids exhibiting paternal inheritance has never been researched.

Another concern is the consistency of sampling. Some of the canid studies have used hair to extract mtDNA and have compared those results to blood samples taken from different breeds. Since it has been shown that heteroplasmy individuals can have maternal mtDNA in the blood and paternal mtDNA in other tissues, it behooves researchers to compare "like" to "like", or rather blood to blood, or hair to hair. This is not to say that paternal mtDNA in the blood might not yet be discovered in some future study, but until that time it would be presumptive not to suspect that canines could not carry the same anomaly.

Thus, there are at least two concerns regarding the use of the rate of mutation seen in mtDNA as a way of estimating evolutionary events. First, molecular biologists interested in canid genetics generally assume that canids exhibit the same rate of mutation as in humans. It has not been addressed in canid genetic research if there are specific areas within the control region that mutate at a faster rate. It this is found to be true in canines as it has in humans, this could complicate or invalidate the use of the molecular genetics in dating canid divergence. Second, if mutation rates are not stable, artificial selection, a chief characteristic of domestication in canids, may increase the frequency of mutation. If mutation rates do increase with domestication, this would also invalidate the mitochondrial clock by making some post domestication evolutionary events appear much older than they actually are.

The use of mtDNA to date evolutionary events is a relatively new development. It is not surprising that as molecular techniques become refined and as technology advances that previously assumed genetic theories are starting to be questioned. This is particularly true of PCR. The PCR machines that are heavily relied on in molecular research ten years ago, are now considered quite primitive. Tremendous advances continue to be made as the microchip industry becomes perfected.

Potential limitations of DNA sequencing

As previously stated, molecular research relies heavily on PCR reactions to provide the gene sequence of the control regions being examined. During a PCR run, fragments of purified DNA are combined with oligonucleotides to initiate DNA synthesis. The oligonucleotide primers are designed to facilitate amplification of the targeted DNA sequence but also suppress unwanted sequences from being produced. Synthesis of the DNA is catalyzed by *Taq* polymerase, a heat stable enzyme that aids in producing new strands of DNA. During the PCR run, the temperature is raised and lowered many times causing the DNA strands to uncoil for replication and recoil. Each new strand of DNA can act as a template for a new strand of DNA to be produced. PCR reactions are run in instruments call thermocyclers which automatically repeats the heating/cooling cycles numerous times and thereby increases the amount of DNA in the reaction at an exponential rate.

In several of the molecular studies discussed, DNA from museum collections was used for comparison to modern canine specimens to provide insight into the evolutionary history of canids. However, unless many precautions are taken, based upon the Panck Institute study, results may be ambiguous leading to inaccurate conclusions being made.

In a comprehensive study done by the Max Planck Institute for Evolutionary Anthropology, researchers provided a thorough review on the technical pitfalls and the stringent criteria needed to ensure the reliability of results when sequencing ancient DNA in human and faunal specimens (Hofreiter et al. 2001: 353-359). One of the biggest problems in sequencing reactions is contamination (Audic and Bérand-Columb 1997). According to Hofreiter et al. (2001: 353-354) when sequencing ancient DNA and modern DNA, the extraction and preparation of the DNA must be done in a laboratory that is rigorously separated from working involving modern DNA. Hofreiter et al. also maintains that as a routine precaution, the laboratory needs to be bleached, UV irradiated with protective clothing used on all laboratory personnel to ensure that no contamination can occur. Hofreiter et al. contends that contamination can simply occur by the mere fact that modern DNA can be pervasive both inside and outside that laboratory and therefore can not be easily distinguished from ancient DNA.

Hofreiter et al. (2001: 353-354) further warns the PCR reactions may not be totally reliable if the ancient DNA template contains very few or a single DNA strand (single-strand DNA was used in the Vila et al. 1997 study), which is common in museum specimens. Upon death, DNA starts to degrade, which causes incorrect bases to be inserted during the PCR run. This is due to the deamination products of cytosine. According to Hofreiter et al., under the proper conditions, this destruction could be so complete that no useful molecules would remain. If degradation has occurred and incorrect bases have been inserted into the ancient DNA sequence, during the PCR the errors in the first cycles will become incorporated into all molecules in the final PCR product. Therefore, if the original ancient DNA has undergone extensive degradation, the resulting PCR sequence will contain a large member of incorrect bases inserted into the amplified ancient DNA sequence.

In a study conducted on horses, both contemporary and from horses discovered in the Alaskan permafrost dated to 12,000 – 28,000 years old as well as equine remains discovered at archaeological sites in Europe, researchers were able to compare mtDNA sequences to determine a phylogenetic relationship (Hofreiter et al. 2001: 353-355). It was concluded that the mtDNA sequences of the Pleistocene horses, as well as all the mtDNA sequences from the horses from the archaeological sites in Europe, were found to fall within the variation of modern horses. This led researchers to believe that the mtDNA diversity is not the result of accelerated evolution or the introduction of wild horse mtDNA's into the domestic gene pool but rather the mtDNA of wild horses entered modern horses at the earliest stage of domestication.

Phylogenetic analysis of nuclear DNA is infrequently done due to the complexity of the structure, with most studies relying on mtDNA to derive sequences for evolutionary studies. However, Hofreiter et al. (2001: 354) adds a precautionary comment when molecular studies use mtDNA to reconstruct the phylogenetic relationship of populations. The researchers state that for species that are not very closely related to each other, mtDNA sequencing is an acceptable method of analysis since enough time has passed between speciation events so that all parts of the genome from each species will show the same phylogeny. The scientists warn however, that when closely related species or population genetic questions are studied, it is important to remember that the mtDNA represents only a single genetic locus that might or might not reflect the overall history of the genome. If the researchers' suspicions are true, then the mere fact that wolves and dogs are linked together so closely may unintentionally compromise any interpretation of the mtDNA sequencing and assumptions pertaining to the evolutionary history.

It is important to note that given the long history of the researchers doing molecular dog genetics, that as trained molecular biologists they would be aware of the possibility of contamination and the effects of DNA degradation upon death, and would act appropriately to ensure the accuracy of their research. However in the comparative studies done with museum samples, there is no discussion in the material and methods sections as to how the museum specimens or the modern samples were prepared to guarantee that there was no possibility of cross-contamination. In future studies these facts should be clearly stated in the scientific reports since it pertains to the accuracy of retrieving DNA from ancient samples as well as ensuring that there is no extraneous DNA in the PCR product.

The use of PCR and thermocyclers to sequence DNA has greatly enhanced the field of molecular genetics. Since its introduction in 1986 by Kary Mullis (1990), the technology has continued to advance and improve with each advancing year. Although PCR has revolutionized DNA sequencing and is now the cornerstone of molecular analyses, it is not without technical pitfalls. Numerous articles have been written on protocol and parameters that are needed to optimize sequencing research. A discussion of some of the more important aspects of DNA amplification that can make PCR ineffectual will be highlighted and reviewed.

Before amplification even begins, the most important issue to be addressed is those surrounding laboratory facilities and research technique. As previously discussed in the pitfalls concerning the use of museum specimens, all laboratories are a potential source to contaminate DNA. Therefore it has been recommended in molecular protocols that assembly of PCR's are best carried out in laminar flow hoods equipped with UV lights. The lights should be continually on when the hood is not in use in order to destroy possible contaminants as well as other potential sources of extraneous DNA. All supplies necessary for PCR need to be kept in the hood also. When pipetting of samples, special types of tips need to be used that have a fiber plug in the end to prevent aerosol contamination in other samples. It is also standard laboratory procedure that all instruments, microcentrifuge tubes, pipette tips, gloves, etc. need to be disposable and sterile. Researchers extracting DNA and doing PCR reactions need to wear protective clothing and gloves, the latter which needs to be changed frequently during the course of the procedure. Protective clothing should also include facemasks and head caps to prevent contamination by skin or hair cells. Work surfaces in the lab area need to be routinely decontaminated with weak solutions of bleach.

Another technical pitfall can arise during the process of assembling the different products needed for amplification. As essential component of amplification is the design of the oligonucleotide primers. The primers are critical in that they are imperative to the successful obtainment of products in high yield as well as the suppression of unwanted sequences. Primers are designed by researchers to target specific segments in the template DNA. In order that primers are compatible to the targeted DNA, numerous computerized programs are available that enable a researcher to optimize primer function. However it must be noted that primer selection is totally dependent upon the researcher.

Other factors which can hinder the success of sequencing are magnesium concentrations in buffer solutions, buffer pH, potassium chloride concentration and *Taq* polymerase. It is also commonly known that different manufacturers brand of *Taq* performs differently so it is imperative to use the same brand of *Taq* in all samples that are being used for comparative studies. An additional problem with *Taq* is that it needs to be stored at -20°C. During the process of thawing and refreezing *Taq* will become damaged. Therefore most researchers store small aliquots of *Taq* that can be discarded after two cycles of freezing and thawing.

The thermocycler in which the PCR reaction takes place is also critical to the successful sequencing of DNA. The reaction taking place in the thermocycler consists of three steps. During the first phase the temperature of the thermocycler raises to 95°C which causes the template DNA strand to separate. During cycle two, the temperature drops anywhere from 37°C to 55°C which allows the primers to attach to the appropriate regions on the single strands of DNA. During the third phase, new DNA is created by the *Taq* when the temperature is raised to 72°C. The *Taq* enzyme extends the ends of the primers and thereby produces two new strands of complimentary DNA. The three phases described above are referred to as denaturation, hybridization and DNa synthesis. Thermocyclers work remarkably efficiently and fast, however the successful synthesis of template DNA is reliant upon the researcher who programs the temperature and length of time for each run, as well as the number of cycles.

Some new alternative methods

In the last few years, there have been attempts to find other types of analyses that can either verify or disprove mtDNA sequencing research. One method that has proven to be highly accurate is the measuring of amino acid racemization, although it is highly susceptible to environmental conditions. In a study done by Krings et al. (1997) on Neanderthal DNA sequences, amino acid racemization was able to pinpoint those ancient samples that contained DNA sufficient for analysis.

In Pääbo's (1989) study of ancient DNA, it was concluded that fossil remains are highly affected by hydrolytic as well as oxidative damage that can adversely affect DNA recovery. Analysis of Miocene specimens for viable DNA proved to be unsuccessful and it was concluded that retrieval of DNA sequences older than 100,000 years is not possible (Pääbo and Wilson 1991:46). Molecular analysis of Neanderthals has been especially useful in helping to pinpoint problem areas in DNA sequencing results. In studies done by Krings et al. (1997) and Ovchinnikov et al. (2000) on Neanderthals it was proven that it was possible to retrieve DNA from Neanderthal specimens since they fall within age range that DNA can survive. However it was further discovered that even in those specimens younger than the 100,000-year cut-off, it was rare that the specimens provided any DNA which could be amplified, which highlights the instability of ancient DNA. Krings et al. (1997) noted that there were several identifiable problems surrounding the chemical stability when using fossil DNA. In Krings et al.'s (1997:26) opinion, because of the ancient nature of fossil samples, any retrievable DNA may be damaged. If damage and degradation occurs in the DNA template, misincorporations by the DNA polymerase during the initial cycles of PCR amplification will be represented in the final PCR product Krings et al. (1997: 20-22) also found evidence of heteroplasmy in the mitochondria which further complicated the consistency of the results. It was also determined by Krings et al. that sequencing differences was due to variation in the efficiency of individual primers, which had the affect of misincorporating nucleotides into the template DNA. In order to identify these mistakes in the coding regions, Krings et al. state that all PCR reactions need to be substantiated by at least two independent PCR reactions. An additional discovery also revealed that in some cases the incorporating of the wrong nucleotide insertion can actually be favored by a primer and make the sequencing more efficient (although it will be the wrong sequence). In the Neanderthal analysis, Krings et al. (1997: 26) found that if the template DNA is damaged, misincorporations at these sites are more likely to occur. This problem was especially evident in Neanderthal extracts that were proven to contain modern human DNA sequences in the ancient mtDNA. It was theorized that the modern DNA was introduced after the specimen was handled during excavation and while being curated. For this to occur, the damaged areas of DNA allow the introduction of exogenous molecules that combine themselves into the damaged sequence and become amplified during the PCR reaction. Krings et al. found that the misincorporations are very common in Neanderthal specimens and contributes greatly to the amount of DNA variation seen in sequences.

Based upon the complications seen in the recovery of DNA in ancient samples, amino acid racemization has become an important rapid method of screening old specimens. This method has become a great timesaver in that it identifies those samples with no recoverable DNA so that no needless expensive sequencing will be attempted. Hofreiter et al. (2001:354) explain that when determining the degree of preservation, amino-acid analyses takes into account the total amount of amino acids preserved in a specimen. According to Hofreiter et al., the amino acid composition and the extent of racemization of several amino acids have proven to be a useful screening method. Racemization can be identified as the partial conversion of one enantiomer into another. To further explain, amino acids share a common structure of a carbon center, surrounded by a hydrogen, carboxyl group, amino group and a side chain. During racemization the amino group can "flip" sides so that the new structure is a mirror image of the original structure. Therefore an L-amino acid can convert into a D-amino acid. Hofreiter et al. states that whenever excessive amounts of racemization occur that it has been proven that DNA extractions are futile. However the researchers also note that the measurement of amino acid racemization can also prove the authenticity of DNA sequences retrieved from a specimen by showing that retrieval of macromolecules is conceivable. In Krings et al.'s study (1997:19-20), Neanderthal bone samples were hydrolyzed with acid based solutions and examined by high-powered liquid chromatography (HPLC) and fluorescent detection. Both techniques provide very rapid results and can therefore immediately identify if viable DNA exists.

Currently other methods of screening are being developed to further substantiate the presence of ancient DNA. Hofreiter et al. (2001: 354) suggest that pyrolysis (the rate of decomposition by heat) measured by gas chromatography/mass spectrometry (GC/MS) may have some future application but has not been currently used on ancient bone. However, further testing will have to be implemented to determine if pyrolysis analysis will be as effective as amino acid racemization for screening purposes.

It is important to comment at this time that the majority of the molecular studies done on dogs have not used ancient fossilized samples but rather tissue samples taken from various wild and domestic populations. Primarily the usage of ancient DNA has been to identify if the red wolf is a separate species or if it is a hybridized gray wolf/coyote (Brownlow 1996; Nowak 1992; Roy et al. 1996; Roy et al. 1999) However, in the case of the Jaguar Cave dog (Clutton-Brock 1995:13) or Seamer Carr dog it would be possible to further confirm previous analysis that these animals are truly the oldest specimens of domesticated dogs by DNA sequencing. If amino acid racemization proves that these samples have viable DNA and if sequencing can be run, then it would be possible to determine if these animals have the same number of mutations as modern dogs or if they are more closely related to wolves. However it would be doubtful if such studies would be done since any molecular or chemical analysis would involve the destruction of a portion of a valuable archaeological specimen.

In Vila et al. 1997 study it states in the research notes that DNA was extracted from blood, tissue, or hair. Blood and hair were also used in Vila et al. (1999a) study. In those sequences derived from blood extractions it would be interesting to know what type of blood was used (whole, heparized, EDTA). If EDTA blood was used, this could have ramifications on the outcome of the amplified PCR product. It is known that EDTA (ethylenediaminetetraacetic acid) can sequester the activity of magnesium, a necessary component of DNA polymerase, which catalyzes template synthesis of DNA in the PCR reaction. Although it may be assumed that Vila and colleagues are aware of the effects of EDTA on DNA sequencing, since it is not clearly stated in the articles, it can not be excluded as a possible factor influencing the amplification process and thereby causing misincorporations by the DNA polymerase during PCR. It is these small details which Vila and collaborators fail to address in their studies done on the canine that makes it extremely difficult to critique the conclusions made in their research.

Limitations of current molecular studies

An additional concern in the canine evolution studies is the small size of control regions of mtDNA used for comparative analysis. In all studies, less than 800 base pair sequences were used. In Vila et al. 1997 and 1999 studies, the region of mtDNA selected for its high mutation rate consisted of 261 base pairs. In Leonard's (2002) study done in collaboration with Vila and others, a 257 base pair fragment was used for comparison. Wayne (1993:220) states that the dog differs from the wolf by at most 0.2% in its mtDNA sequence. Vila, Maldonado and Wayne (1999:73) reported that dog and wolf sequences differed by 0-12 substitutions in the control region. Based upon the number of substitutions seen in the control region, the researchers concluded the evolutionary rate of divergence. However it can be argued that using such small sections of mtDNA is not suitable for drawing conclusions about evolutionary relationships. The 261 base pair region represents less than 1.7% of the total mtDNA genome. To put this in an anthropological perspective, since the adult human body contains 206 bones, this would be akin to making evolutionary comparisons and conclusions based upon 3 bones per skeleton. And if Vila and colleagues use a 1000 base pair region to assume an evolutionary rate, this would represent only 6% of the total mtDNA. Granted, as previously stated, much of the mitochondrial genome encodes for certain metabolic proteins and cellular activity within the mitochondria itself with only a small proportion of the mtDNA consisting of areas that are non-coding. However this is specifically the reason that so many molecular geneticists are enamored with mitochondrial research. The limited number and small size of the non-coding regions are much easier for the geneticists to analyze versus the huge size of nuclear DNA. However, is too much information lost in the mitochondria that skews conclusions on evolutionary rates?

Although geneticists may argue that the non-coding regions represent the essential elements for inferring evolutionary history, is that statement truly accurate? For example, when viewing the human skeleton can you make an evolutionary inference based on three phalanges or on three other bone fragments? It might be argued that this would be possible if the bones in question were from the skull however, has mtDNA research been so refined so that there is absolute certainty that only one region is more diagnostic than others? Also, Morell (1997:1647-1648) states that the sequences used in the studies of Wayne, Vila and others are known to have notoriously high and uneven rates of change making divergence dates undependable. Stephen O'Brien at the Laboratory of Genomic Diversity states to Morell that although the genetic study led by Wayne is "first-rate", he cautions that the dating concluded in the study is very "dubious – it's 135,000 years plus or minus 300%". This statement is further supported by Koop and Crockford's study (2000:279-280) of fox, coyote, dog and wolf sequences that showed that when a simple rate test was calculated on the divergence percentages between the different species, it would appear that the mtDNA mutation in wolves and dogs is changing at a faster rate than mtDNA in coyotes. According to Koop and Crockford, mtDNA time estimates may be overestimated by a factor of two.

In Vila et al.'s (1997) study, it was proposed that the wolf and dog sequences were representative of four clades. However in Koop and Crockford's (2000: 280) paper it was found that at least eight ancestral mitochondrial lineages existed. In Savolainen et al.'s (2002) study, the researchers reported that they discovered six different phylogenetic lineages. This is an example of how different researchers can examine the same molecular haplotypes but yet they all envision separate patterns of variation delineating the clades. As previously stated, scientific research is not an exact science. Conclusions reached are the result of interpretations made by individuals, and are dependent on the accuracy and experience of the scientist. Therefore, if there is confusion concerning the number of phylogenetic groups in the domestic dog and wolf lines, interpretation of the mean genetic distance between the different clades which predicts evolutionary divergence could be as equally uncertain.

Another troublesome area concerning assumptions made about canine mitochondrial evolution is that researchers fail to address the effects of hybridization events on the amount of genetic variation seen in the mtDNA. Dowling and DeMarais (1993) showed that in a morphologically diverse group of minnows, hybridization had a pervasive influence throughout their evolutionary history. The authors found in their analysis that relationships based on mtDNA do not reflect an organisms phylogeny. Dowling and DeMarais (1993: 445) also speculate that during the Pleistocene and Holocene transitional stage, that the affects of a changing environment might have altered habitats so dramatically that it may have promoted hybridization to produce mosaics. They conclude that hybridization can create genetic diversity by providing genetic variation for selection and drift to translate into new phenotypes.

Hybridization has also been found to have an effect on mtDNA variation seen in North American deer (Carr and Hughes 1993), caribou and reindeer (Cronin et al. 1995). The authors found that upon sequencing, reindeer and caribou shared several alleles, which the authors concluded were the result of ancestral alleles or genetic introgression. Similar results were also obtained in Polziehn et al. (1995) study of bovine and bison populations. It was discovered by the authors that a few bison in the Custer State Park contained bovine mtDNA. The researchers postulated that the introduction of the bovine DNA most likely occurred by a single female who was the offspring of a first generation of hybrid female backcrossed to a bison bull. What is of importance in this study is that it shows evidence for hybridization between a domestic and wild species. The offspring of backcrosses would not be indistinguishable phenotypically from the other wild individuals. The bison containing the bovine mtDNA were found to exhibit no physical characteristics of bovine and were imperceptible from other wild bison in the herd. Polziehn et al (1995: 642) makes an important point concerning the implication of hybridization. They state that as a population decreases the impact of hybridization increases, which simply put means that large populations will be least affected whereas small populations will be the most affected.

Unfortunately the detection of hybridization between wolves and dogs can be much more difficult given that there is genetic fragmentation of dogs into breeds (Vila et al. 2003: 22). Wolves and dogs throughout history have occupied the same geographic areas, which would allow hybridization to occur. The detrimental effects of hybridization has been witnessed in multiple wild wolf populations whose numbers have dwindled but have had increasing contact with domestic dogs so that now many wild wolf populations are composed mainly of hybrids (Vila et al. 2003:17-18). Although it is possible to use genetic markers to identify some species, it is difficult to find distinguishing genetic markers in closely related species such as in the dog and wolf (Vila et al. 2003:17).

Koop and Crockford (2000: 280-282) state that hybridization presents a confounding factor in domestication models. The authors surmise that the use of maternally inherited mtDNA to study dog origins limits observations to only the female lineage of any hybridization event. They further observe that morphologically distinct female dogs or wolves can contain several different mtDNA lineages making it difficult to explain the validity of any specific domestication model. Although the differences seen in the various clade sequences could be due to the normal amount of mutation that would be expected in the mitochondria, Koop and Crockford believe that this variation could also be explained by hybridization events that have occurred throughout history and have contributed to the overall genetic diversity. This diversity, according to Koop and Crockford, could have been the result of multiple founding events or the interbreeding of dogs with wolves. Therefore the authors conclude that different DNA lineages can not be used to estimate when dogs were derived from wolves. In their opinion only ancient samples should be used for evolutionary analysis since modern breeds have been culturally modified through intentional hybridization or have been induced by environmental factors that would facilitate hybridization.

An interesting finding of the mtDNA sequencing studies is that the scientist can not differentiate between the different breeds of dogs based upon their haplotypes, although it is possible to use genomic DNA to assign individual dogs to specific dog breeds (Parker et al. 2004). Genetically the mtDNA from a poodle looks the same as the mtDNA from a St. Bernard. Wayne and Ostrander (1999:250) speculate that the genealogic relationship between breeds is not apparent probably because most breeds originated too recently for unique sequences to be identified. The authors hypothesize that the high genetic diversity of dogs can be explained that they originated from a diverse founding gene pool. Therefore, it can be questioned that if dogs are so genetically diverse, how can diversity be used to make evolutionary assumptions since you would expect diversity to already exist? As most forensic scientists know, DNA fingerprinting is very individual specific, however when used for evolutionary comparisons it is of little use since the sequences mutate too rapidly. It can therefore be deducted that drawing comparisons between the diversity of dogs and wolves through sequencing would be inconclusive.

Within the last year, scientists have made interesting discoveries concerning 'junk' DNA sequences. These particular areas within the DNA sequence were thought to be nonessential nucleotides that did not code for proteins. Often thought of as genetic 'parasites', the junk DNA is believed to accumulate in mammalian genomes over millions of years being copied into new genomic locations (Dennis 2002:458). According to Dennis, most of the junk are retrotransposers, which reproduce through an RNA intermediate and use reverse transcriptase to restore their original DNA sequence so that they can jump back into the genome. However, in a study of mice, researchers found that retrotranspons can have a tremendous amount of affect on how characteristics are expressed. Scientists have found that if a retrotranspon lands in a host gene it can alter the gene's function. In mice, according to Dennis, many retrotrasnposons are active and thought to be responsible for about 10% of naturally occurring mutations that cause a noticeable change in characteristics. It was demonstrated that just one piece of junk DNA can produce several colors of genetically identical mice. Therefore another possibility of the diversity of canines is that naturally occurring mutations could be the result of retrotransposon insertions rather than any intentional manipulation by humans, breeding for new domesticated traits.

In Vila et al. (1997; 1999a), Tsuda et al. (1997), Wayne (1993), Wayne and Ostrander (1999), and Savolainen et al. (2002), there is an interesting consistency in their method of calibrating the mitochondrial clock. In all studies, a date of one million years since the divergence of wolves and coyotes is used to estimate the amount of time it would take to obtain the exhibited substitution rates. This divergence is based upon the fossil record. So, a question can be raised, is if the fossil record is the gold standard for estimating divergence between wolves and coyotes, why do the researchers dispute the validity of the fossil record when estimating the divergence between dogs and wolves? Clearly the researchers are using only those parts of the archaeological record which proves their assumptions about molecular substitution rates while ignoring the bigger picture. The research of Savolainen at al. (2002) shows that molecular genetics and archaeology are not necessarily in conflict, but can in conjunction explain evolutionary relationships.

The study of Savolainen and colleagues (2002) has been discussed previously but certain conclusions are worthy of further discussion and in the opinion of this author, the most plausible. Savolainen et al. were able to ascertain the dog populations consisted of six phylogenetic groups (Clades A, B, C, D, E, and F). This conclusion is similar to Vila et al. (1997) research but Savolainen and researchers found evidence of two additional clades not discovered in Vila et al. study. The researchers discovered that clades A, B, and C were found in all geographical regions of the world except in North America. They further discovered that the frequencies of the three clades were also in the same amounts worldwide. Clades D, E, and F were found regionally in: Turkey; Spain; Scandinavia; Japan and Korea; and Japan and Siberia, respectively. The scientists surmised that given the worldwide distribution of clades A, B and C that the founding population for dogs had come from a gene pool which contained those three clades and is therefore the clades of the greatest antiquity.

Savolainen and colleagues (2002: 1611-1612) additionally examined the number of haplotypes seen in East Asia and Europe. The researchers hypothesized that there would be far greater haplotype diversity in the ancestral population then in more recently derived populations. They found that clades A exhibited the greatest amount of diversity with the largest number of diverse nucleotides found in East Asia. It was reported that those haplotypes found west of the Himalayas, 28.1% were unique whereas those haplotypes from the East were composed of 51.5% specifically unique to that region. The same type of pattern was seen in clade B with the East exhibiting 41.2% unique haplotypes with the West exhibiting only 6.8%. Clade C was shown to have less variation but still exhibited a higher percentage of unique haplotypes in the East. Therefore, the scientist concluded that the haplotype frequencies indicated that dogs were derived from a common gene pool that was composed of the three phylogenetic clades A, B and C. It was further proposed that because the greatest amount of diversity was found in the East, that there was a greater probability that dogs had an East Asia origin.

To add further support to their study, Savolainen et al. (2002: 1612-1613) plotted the haplotypes into a minimum-spanning network, which produces a star-like pattern. In the center is the founder haplotype with new haplotypes distributed radially. It was discovered that the dog haplotypes of clade B and C had very symmetrical starlike patterns with an easily discernable central core indicating a single wolf haplotype origin. The authors speculate that these subclusters suggest that clade A could have originated from several different wolf haplotypes. Using clade A to determine the age since this was speculated to be the oldest clade, and assuming a *single* origin from one wolf and by making a comparison to the calculated mean between East Asian sequences, a prediction of the antiquity of clade A was determined. Based upon the 3.39 substitutions clade A was judged to be 41,000 ± 4,000 years old. However when Savolainen et al. did the same calculations but assumed *multiple* origins from three subclusters, the age approximation of clade A dramatically changed. In the multiple subcluster scenario, the substitution rate of the three subclusters was determined to be 0.45, 0.65 and 1.07. Given these mutation rates it was determined that the subclusters could be dated at 11,000 ± 400 years, 16,000 ± 3,000 years and 26,000 ± 8,000 years. The age of clades B and C was estimated to be 13,000 ± 3,000 years and 17,000 ± 3,000 years.

Savolainen et al. concluded that dogs originated either ~ 40,000 years ago assuming a single origin from a wolf forming clade A, or ~ 15,000 years if a multiple origin involving forming clades A, B and C. In order to try to pinpoint a more exact date, the researchers reexamined data that was gathered on haplotypes in Europe. Upon analysis, the oldest clade A subcluster in Europe was determined to be 9,000 ± 3,000 years old.

To further add support, Savolainen et al. examined dates gathered from archaeological finds worldwide. In China the oldest finds are approximately 9,500 years old, however the archaeological evidence is very scant and the authors concede that they do not preclude that something more ancient may be discovered in the future. Southeast Asia yielded dates of 14,000 B.P. based upon questionable canid remains, or 9,000 B.P. when dating remains with typical canid morphology. In Europe, the oldest find based upon a single jaw fragment is found in Germany and is dated to 14,000 yrs B.P. However the authors point-out that there is a tremendous age gap between the German specimen and other European finds which are dated at approximately 9,000 yrs B.P. In North America the oldest canid specimens have been dated at 8,500 yrs B.P. Therefore the authors conclude that based upon the molecular dates of 40,000 yrs B.P. or 15,000 yrs B.P. and the oldest archaeological date of 14,000 yrs B.P., that the most likely date for the origin of the dog is ~ 15,000 yrs B.P. Savolainen et al. make a very important point when drawing their conclusion about the dating of canine origins which other researchers have failed to recognize. They infer that molecular and archeological dating should be used in conjunction when estimating the evolutionary record. Although both methods seem to be in contradiction to each other, it is important to use both together when drawing conclusions. This author is in agreement with the conclusions reached by Savolainen and fellow researchers that the incorporation of genetic data with the fossil record is the best method to resolve issues of evolutionary history.

The use of molecular genetics and its usage to infer evolutionary history is simply a theory, but to validate such theory it needs to be substantiated by physical evidence to make it credible. This fact was proven in Killian et al. (2001: 513-515) study of marsupials and eutherians. Killian and colleagues were concerned that the value and accuracy of decades of morphological study had been discounted by mtDNA inference and reexamined molecular methodology to try to resolve the conflicting issues. They found that the use of nucleotide substitution models assumed an equal rate of substitution within the different molecular regions, and was known to seriously bias tests of phylogenetic hypotheses in many situations. This conclusion had also been previously reported by Janke et al. (1997: 1280) in which the authors cautioned about the usage of the application of mtDNA sequencing to date evolutionary divergences. The authors state that if molecular dating is based upon the dating of ancient divergences (such as the one million year split between wolf and coyote) that the efficiency of such an approach is illusory, because too distant references will not permit proper resolution of more recent divergences (i.e. wolf and dog). This clearly shows how important fossil evidence is in making evolutionary inferences. The use of mitochondrial DNA should not be used exclusive of archaeological evidence. Although mtDNA can show genetic similarities between species, it is statistically unreliable when it is applied to evolutionary genetics. I believe that the Savolainen et al. approach, which uses both the fossil record and the molecular data, is a more effective approach. It is also my belief that molecular geneticists may be unintentionally biased in their conclusions about dogs, cattle, goats, etc. because they are known domesticated animals and any changes seen in the sequencing are attributed to a domestication event administered by intentional human manipulation rather than natural selection. However when the same type of mtDNA changes occur in non-domesticated species, the geneticists attribute those changes as the result of the natural process of evolution.

Contributions of animal behavior studies to the understanding of dog domestication

In the molecular studies it is inferred that the process of domestication began with humans capturing wild wolves, preferably as young pups, and became indoctrinated into the human social structure as a valued hunting companion. Clutton-Brock (1995:10) proposes that those captured pups that became aggressive would have been killed or driven away. However Clutton-Brock maintains that those tame wolves that remained with the human group would have bred with other tamed wolves that scavenged around the settlement. This hypothesis, however, does not take into account some of the innate behavioral aspects of wolves that would make such a transition difficult.

Some researchers have suggested that a possible origin of dogs was the small Indian wolf, *Canis lupus pallipes.* Dingoes specifically have been speculated to be the direct descendant of this particular species of wolf. There has also been some speculation that Indian wolves are less aggressive and would be easier to tame. This assumption however may be erroneous. For many years there have been reports that the Indian wolf is not the submissive species it was once believed. In one year alone, 45 children were alleged to have been killed by wolves in a 250 square-mile area (Mech 1996:16), whereas in 1996 wolves were reported to have killed or seriously injured 64 children in India (Mech 1998: 11). Typically the children that are attacked live in remote villages and are either left unattended in a field to defecate or play (Mech 1996: 16). The human habitation areas are usually located in regions where wolf contact occurs regularly given the wild environmental habitat. According to Mech the wolves have been known to travel among human habitations and into the huts, themselves. Almost all the children that were attacked were under the age of ten. Mech believes that wolves in India have begun to lose their fear of humans and with a combination of living in close proximity to humans, and the presence of children in heavy vegetative cover, may promote boldness in wolf behavior (Mech 1998: 11). This type of behavior becomes continually reinforced as the wolves succeed in grabbing children, which Mech ascertains would propagate the trait in the local population. Mech compares the conduct to behavior similarly seen in bears frequenting campsites. As the bears become less fearful of humans, they have been known to pillage campsites, garbage cans, automobiles and dumping areas. Wolves, like other carnivores, are also opportunistic feeders, scavenging kills from other animals, preying on weak or injured animals or eating the refuse left by humans.

Given the wolf's tendency for attacking vulnerable animals, a question that needs to addressed is what would the advantage be fore early man to bring a dangerous carnivore into its camp and condition it to have no fear of humans? Certainly infants and small children would be easy prey for such an animal. Early humans with their primitive weaponry would be at a disadvantage trying to fend off a wolf pack. Modern wolves in most instances have an innate fear of humans because of hundreds of years of persecution and only have been know to attack humans in remote areas. However, ancient wolves would have known no such fear and would have possibly been even more aggressive in their contacts with human beings. If early man relied upon tamed wolves to be companions in hunting, would the advantage of having an unpredictable animal in the camp outweigh the disadvantage of it possibly attacking and killing infants and children?

Another issue that needs to be addressed is what would be the caloric requirement for maintaining a tamed wolf in human camps. In studies done on Arctic peoples who have maintained dogs as a feature of their traditional lifestyle, it was found that of the total food supply generated annually, dogs consumed in the range of 20-30% with an average of 28% (Morey and Aaris-Sorensen 2002:45). The minimum requirement for maintaining a dog is approximately 1000 pounds of meat and fat per dog per year. The caloric requirement to maintain a tamed wolf would not only place a greater demand on food supply used to sustain the human community but would also place the humans in direct competition with the wolves for food. The maintenance of an adequate food supply is essential for human survival even in abundant periods. Therefore having a tamed wolf presents the additional liability of increased demand on food supplies possibly causing a depletion that would hinder human survival. Given that Vila et al. (1997) believe that dogs were domesticated 135,000 ya, the environmental constraints at that time would make it unlikely that there would have been any economic advantage in maintaining a wolf.

Another theory, which has been postulated by both molecular geneticists and archaeologists, is that wolves were initially domesticated by capturing young pups, which were taken back to camp and tamed. This scenario is also very problematic given the basic behavioral characteristics of the wolf, which predisposes them to avoidance and flight when approached by humans. In order to discuss this theory of how early wolves were tamed, it will be necessary to briefly review some of the behavioral aspects of wolf development, which have been discussed in Chapter III.

As previously addressed, wolf behavior is dramatically different than behavior seen in domesticated dogs. Upon birth the wolf mother remains with the pups during their first month of life (Packard 2003: 51) depending upon the wolf fathers to provision the lactating female (Packard 2003: 50). Wolf pups nurse for up to ten weeks and begin to eat regurgitated food at three weeks. Between five to ten weeks wolf pups begin to venture outside the den but when the den is approached, the pups will retreat or will be picked up and carried back to the den by the female. By the age of six weeks wolf pups are fast enough to avoid humans with locomotor skills comparable to a small dog (Frank and Frank 1982: 509). At the age of two years wolves are sexually mature and usually disperse from the pack.

In comparative studies done on wolf and canine social development and behavior it has been demonstrated the difficulty of raising wolf pups. It has been reported that by the time the wolf pups reached 21 says old, they were already displaying fear/flight behavior. The researchers found that if wolf pups were older than 15 days, it was difficult to socialize the pups to humans. It was also observed that wolf pups were extremely sensitive to dietary changes and tended to loose weight and responded poorly to any modification from mother's milk and regurgitated food. Unless the pups were slowly transitioned over several weeks with new foods wile maintaining to nurse and feed with the mother, it was found that compounded with gastrointestinal upsets, growth rate decline, and appetite suppression, the pups failed to thrive. Researchers also reported that in handraised pups it was necessary for the humans to spend approximately 12 hours a day with their caregivers for them to become socialized with humans. Even in those pups that were handraised, they still showed a marked preference for canine social partners over human caregivers, and when given the opportunity they would hide behind adults when approached by humans. Additional studies have also shown that continuous human contact has to be maintained for the social behavior toward humans to be preserved and lasting. Researchers have therefore concluded that in order for a strong social bond to be successful, pups need to be human raised prior to fear/flight responses being developed and if they had no other interaction with other wolves.

Behaviorally it has also been reported that by the time the pups are 3-4 months old, they begin to exhibit predatory behavior and will kill small animals. By the time the wolves reach one year of age, they become more aggressive and will stalk and kill larger animals with success. As these juvenile animals start reaching adulthood, they begin to show increasing independence and become restless in captivity. Once these animals reach sexual maturity around two years of age, it has been observe that become more fixated on small children (Fentress 1967: 347). Several researchers have also reported that even in "tame" wolves, if given free run, they would spend considerable amount of time trying to avoid humans, although they would appear to be friendly and wag their tail when approached. Even in those young animals which have been socialized as young pups, when deprived of human contact for as little as six weeks, they would not retain the socialization and become fearful of humans (Woolpy and Ginsberg 1967: 361). Although adult socialized wolves would retain friendliness towards humans after long separations. According to Woolpy and Ginsberg wolves never exhibit the one-mannishness that is seen in domestic dogs possibly because wolves are quite gregarious in a pack.

Another attribute of wolf behavior is that even in socialized animals, the natural instinct predisposes it towards wariness. Woolpy and Ginsberg (1967: 361) found that if a wolf was presented with any intense environmental novelty, that even in the most socialized animal, the fear response was so innate the animal would revert to their wild-type behavior.

It has also been observed that in some wolves, as they became socialized, many animals become bold and assertive in their behavior. In experiments conduced by Woolpy and Ginsberg (1967: 360), in animals that have a reduced fear response they would bite, tug and tear at clothes. If any attempt were made to restrain the animal, a full-blown attack would occur. In some instances it was necessary for the experimenters to work in teams to make sue that the aggression didn't escalate further.

Given the complexity of wolf behavior, the question that needs to be asked is, would early man in an uncontrolled environment without the benefit of fences, cages, nutritional supplements and an enormous amount of free time be able to tame and domesticate wild wolves 15,000-135,000 yrs? Also, would the advantages of such an endeavor outweigh the disadvantage of the time investment required for these efforts to be successful?

As previously discussed, for wolves to socialize towards humans they have to be captured at approximately two weeks old. Research has shown that the older the animal, the less likely it is to be adaptive with humans, therefore it is necessary to integrate wolf pups with humans prior to 21 days old when the fear/flight response is initiated. To capture such young animals it would be necessary to take them from a den within two weeks of being born. However is known that wolf mothers do not leave the den during the first month of life and are dependent on the fathers to bring back food. Would it be possible for early man to successfully crawl into a den to grab a puppy while face-to-face with a protective mother? Although it might be probable, it would be immensely dangerous and life threatening. A more likely scenario is that it would be safer to drive the mother out of the den, possibly by fire, and either kill her or keep her driven away while the puppies were seized. Most animals will not defend their young to the death, but will eventually flee when faced with insurmountable odds, which makes stealing of young easier.

Once the pups had been captured it would have been necessary to supply them with nourishment in the form of milk for up to ten weeks of age. The only possible way that this could be done would require a lactating human female to nurse the pups. This is not an unlikely concept since Simoons and Baldwin (1982: 422) reported that Australian Aboriginal women nurse dingo pups, including Polynesians who nurse both dogs and pigs. Simoons and Baldwin ascertain that breast feeding young animals is ideal when domesticating animals since newborns will imprint without much difficulty. However both dogs and wolves require almost hourly feedings during the first few weeks of life. It has been observed in canids that pups will fall asleep while continuing to suckle and periodically will wake up and start nursing again. This would require a human female to constantly have a pup carried to her breast. Also puppies tend to lose body heat very easily so to would be necessary for them to be blanketed and carried close to the human body in order to be kept warm. Additionally puppies need to be stimulated to urinate and defecate which is done when the mother is licking them in the inguinal area. In a captive pup, a human would have to rub them so that puppy could eliminate. Around three weeks of age the pups would need to be introduced to solid food. In a wild pup this is supplied by the mother regurgitating her food. In a captive neonate, a human would have to chew the food for the pup. Consumption of masticated food has been observed to last several months, at least until the pups acquire their permanent dentition which begins around the age of four months. Plus as previously discussed, wolf pups are exceptionally sensitive to dietary changes that can result in gastrointestinal upsets such as diarrhea. Even today, uncontrolled diarrhea can result in death in young animals unless medical intervention is obtained.

As discussed above, the care of a neonate wolf would be very time consuming and physically demanding to a human female, not unlike caring for a newborn human infant. Although some researchers speculate that he nurturing of young animals was possibly done by women whose own infants had died, and thereby provided some sort of emotional release. Nevertheless, early humans would be presented with a multitude of obstacles to overcome from the time of the initial capture to the point where the pup is self-sufficient enough to not require constant human care.

An additional difficulty is how can a wolf be contained within a camp so that socialization can be maintained. In all studies done on wolf socialization researchers had to house the pups in kennels or enclosed facilities in order to be able to interact effectively with the animals. Even in older juvenile wolves that had undergone socialization, if given open space unrestricted with fencing, the wolves would attempt to avoid capture. Zimen (1987: 291) also found that pups born to socialized adults were just as fearful as those born to wild wolves. In fact, Zimen states that even highly socialized wolves would prevent the socialization of pups'. Therefore in order to overcome the innate flight tendencies it is necessary to contain the animals in such a way that they cannot avoid human contact. Even if early humans had constructed some type of enclosure, the jaws of wolves are powerful enough to crush the skull of a moose and would be able to chew their way out of almost any enclosure. Also, wolves are master diggers, and it was found that even in modern facilities they could dig under most fencing and escape. It is highly unlikely that early humans would have been able to provide the necessary type of confinement required while maintaining the constant interaction in order to tame captive wolves. Not only would the construction of a pen be labor intensive, it is also doubtful that any pen that could have been constructed would also be escape-proof.

Another problem with "man domesticating wolf" theory is the assumption by both molecular biologists and archaeologists that initially female wolves were the first to be domesticated. It has been postulated that tamed wolf females bred with wild males would whelp their pups at the human campsites with the puppies being integrated into the human social unit. This theory assumes that the creation of a domesticated species can only be successfully done if the offspring are under human control. However, these types of assumptions fail to take into account the reproductive behavior or cycle of wolves. It is taken for granted that only female wolves were first domesticated, females would not become reproductively mature and second, third or fourth winters, with delivery of their first litter at 2-5 years of age (Packard 2003: 38). At the very minimum with optimal nutrition during its lifetime of a tame wolf, humans would recognize some economic, emotional or physiological benefit in keeping an animal for possibly several years before offspring are produced. Upon reproductive maturity a female would have to be allowed into the camp or the female would have to be tethered in some fashion away from the campsite, although this last scenario seems very unlikely. However does it seem rational, or even safe, that humans would want to attract more predators into their campsites for up to a month in order to acquire offspring? And if humans did encourage this activity, how would a pregnant female be contained so that her pups would be delivered at the camp? Any pet owner who has had a litter of kittens in a closet knows that even in domesticated animals, most females will attempt to deliver in a secluded area away from the intrusion of humans and other animals.

Theories of domestication fail to take into account basic, innate behavioral characteristics that either predispose or make an animal unsuitable for domestication. In order for domestication to be successful, wild behavioral characteristics need to be modified so that an animal can be tamed and controlled. Wolf behavior cannot be overlooked when considering domestication theories; rather it is critical to understanding how this process evolved.

Limitations of the archaeological record

In context of the archaeological evidence, there is a striking difference between the dates of the oldest dog find and the conclusions reached in the molecular research. In North America, one of the oldest reported dog remains found at Jaguar Cave, Idaho has been dated at approximately 10,000 years ago (Lawrence 1967, 1968; Lawrence and Bossert 1967, 1969). However there has been some conflicting evidence that the original dating of this material may have been over estimated by as much as 6,000-9,000 years (Clutton-Brock 1995: 13). In the Yukon Territory, the Old Crow site has produced dog remains dated at approximately 12,000 years ago (Beebe 1980). Great Britain has also yielded ancient dog remains at the Star Carr site (Degerbol 1961). Based upon C-14 dating, the Star Carr dog was estimated to be 9488 ± 350 BP. In Germany, several sites containing dog remains have generated dates ranging from 14,000-10,990 BP. These finds have much significance in that a small wolf with slight morphological modifications might e one of the first indications of an intermediate-type of canine bridging the gap from wolf to dog. The oldest dog finds in France has been dated at 10,000 years old, and exhibit the typical morphological modifications associated with domestication (Chaix 2000). Dog remains from an archaeological site in Iraq suggests a date of 9,000 years old (Lawrence and Reed 1983). The earliest archaeological find of a suspected domestic dog in Israel is unique in that it was associated with a human burial (Davis and Valla 1978). Its age has been estimated at 11,000 BP. Japan has also uncovered dog remains believed to have been brought over from the Asian mainland. Dating of this material is believed to be approximately 9,000 years old (Shigehara and Hongo 2000). The earliest Siberian finds are dated at 14,850 ± 700 BP, however the dating has only been inferred by geological estimates (Ovodov 1998). The cranial morphology displayed distinctive characteristics typical of dogs. Although the Siberian find is exciting, it had been excavated in the 1880's and only reexamined recently which may put this find in question since prior to the 1980's archaeology done in this region was poorly documented. China has yielded one site dated at around 9,000 BP (Olsen 1985) and could probably produce additional sites of greater antiquity. However many faunal remains have been discarded and are poorly researched.

Based upon the oldest evidence yielded at sites worldwide the earliest domestic dog is dated at 14,000 yr BP. However these early remains are based upon a few jaw fragments with limited dentition. The skeletal material that has produced the most information is Star Carr. It is especially significant in that it is an almost complete skeleton of a mature dog. Its diminutive cranial size and the robustness of the long bones leaves little doubt that the skeleton is representative of a dog and not a wolf. The Israeli find, although exciting because of its association with a human and its great antiquity, is more

Fig. 25. Egyptian artists often depicted dogs resembling the present day Pharaoh hound (photo K. Durr).

questionable in the opinion of this author. The Israeli remains consisted of a 3-5 month old puppy and an adult mandible. However analysis of both remains indicated that the skeletal material fell within the range of dog and wolf and outside the range of jackal. Therefore, the remains cannot be definitively classified as dog. Equally as exciting is the discovery mad in Siberia. The 14,850 ± 700 yr BP date would certainly make it the oldest dog find, however it too is questionable given that the dating was not done by C-14 but by geological stratigraphy.

However if the archaeological record is more accurate and the oldest finds range at the 14,000 yr BP date, it can be estimated when there had been enough endocrine alterations in dogs to have them exhibit greater adaptability to contact with humans. In Belyaev's (1978; 1981) study of foxes, it was documented that the foxes started exhibiting noticeable morphological changes in the eighth to tenth generation. However the foxes in Belyaev's study were continuously selected for one particular behavioral trait in a controlled environment with intense contact with humans. Like wolves, foxes are strict seasonal breeders, mating only once a year in response to changes in the day length (Trut 1999: 167). The early dogs would have most likely had a similar reproductive cycle as wolves. Foxes however, reach sexual maturity at eight months of age whereas wolves are mature at two years. In the wild, wolves may not successfully produce a litter until their third, fourth or fifth year. If is assumed that a generation represents six years in wolves, and if no artificial selection is involved, Crockford (2000b:16) suggests that behaviorally, reproductively and morphologically different descendants from the ancestral wolf population in 200 years. Crockford's hypothesis seems probable if the breedings are controlled and not random. However, I believe that in free-ranging primitive wild dogs that are neophobic and without any external environmental pressure, it would be much harder and take much longer to induce these changes. In Belyaev's study, basal levels of corticosteroids dropped to half the level seen in the control group after 12 generations of intensive selective breeding (Trut 1999: 166). This type of artificial selection would not be possible in a natural environment, and if attempted would take much longer to precipitate, if at all.

The problem with the fossil record is based upon the earliest canine remains dated at 14,800 yrs. These remains are questionable, either because the skeletal material is poorly preserved and fragmentary or because the remains cannot be definitively identified as a true dog. However, by 9000 BP, there are enough morphological changes in canids that wolves and dogs can be clearly identified. This 9,000 year time line is particularly significant since it has been postulated that goat, sheep, cattle, and pig were also domesticated at approximately around this time. By, 5000 BP, there are indications that a few distinctive looking breeds had been developed. Egyptian artists during this time period depict both a Greyhound type of dog as well as a mastiff-type of breed (Vesey-Fitzgerald 1957: 54-55). From 4000-2800 BP, the number of different types of dogs portrayed by artists dramatically increases and dogs resembling modern-day Spitz, Wolfhound, Great Dane, Saluki, and short-legged terrier are frequently represented (Fig. 25).

CHAPTER VI

Conclusion

Domestication of the Dog: An Alternative Hypothesis

The review of research presented above indicates that the early dates for the origin of the dog (15,000-135,000 years ago) are based upon a number of assumptions which leave the time of origin of the dog and its domestication in question. More critical to this model is the assumption that molecular changes in the mtDNA directly reflect human domestication of the dog. After years of wolf behavioral studies by various researchers, it is unlikely that early humans 15,000-135,000 years ago would have had any success in capturing, taming or most importantly, controlling wild wolves. Therefore, I support an alternative theory of canine domestication that takes into account behavioral studies, molecular genetics and the archaeological record. It is difficult to make the transition from bones to behavior, especially when attempting to contrast the behavior of prehistoric wolves to present-day wolves. Unfortunately, behavioral patterns are usually not directly recorded in the fossil record. In spite of this limitation, lines of evidence other than the fossil record support such conjectures.

The work of Vila et al. (1997) is accurate in its sequencing of the mtDNA however the researchers assumed that changes in the mtDNA was evidence of domestication when the mutations could have been naturally occurring events that are seen in the continuing process of evolution. These mutations signaled the beginnings of the separation of dogs from wolves, but do not document intentional selection by humans. Similar changes have been noted in other domesticated species such as horses, goats and pigs. Furthermore, as these mutations accumulated over thousands of years and as dogs evolved into a separate species, certain behavioral modifications as well as endocrine alterations may have occurred that reduced the fear/flight behavior and resulted in some intermediate dogs to better tolerate a human's presence. These genetically different animals however, were not the product of domestication, but rather a new adaptation to a changing environment. This process involved multiple lineages' originating in East Asia that eventually spread westward. At approximately 15,000 years ago, some dogs had sufficiently evolved that some especially adaptive animals could be assimilated into human culture. Eventually future generations of offspring began to exhibit the morphological changes typically seen in domesticates. Regional pressures tended to accelerate or slow this process which is reflected in the diversity of dates found worldwide in the archaeological record.

There are several points which support an alternative exploration of the origins and domestication of dogs. As previously reviewed in the previous chapter, scientists are becoming less convinced that the composition and mutations seen in mtDNA accurately reflect evolutionary relationships. As research continually broadens, as technology improves, and with the development of better, faster molecular techniques, previous assumptions about mitochondria are being disproved. The theory that mtDNA is only maternally inherited has now been shown to be incorrect, with estimates that possibly up to 20% of humans exhibiting heteroplasmy. What is lacking in canine studies is research documenting whether or not this same type of condition is as prevalent in dogs as it is in humans. Because it has been reported in both mice and humans, other mammalian species may also display paternally inherited mitochondria as well.

It has also been disproven that mtDNA mutates at a fixed rate. Now researchers know that not only is mtDNA not the molecular clock it was originally believed, clicking off a mutation every 6,000 to 12,000 years, but it also may be acquiring mutations as well as repairing those sites at a greater speed than expected. Both nuclear DNA and mtDNA have programmed within their structure, innate repair mechanisms so that errors committed during replication do not get passed on to future generations. It was once believed that DNA repair systems were only necessary to restore function to those sites that coded for specific proteins, however it has been found that repair also happens within the non-coding regions as well. A perfect example of this has been witnessed in studies done with ancient DNA. In some cases it has been found that DNA extracted from fossil remains, when sequenced, will contain modern DNA. What researchers have found that as fossil DNA becomes degraded, contaminant DNA from other species or from the human researchers themselves will get incorporated into the sequence. This shows that DNA will try to repair these deteriorated regions even if it means inserting foreign DNA from another source.

Therefore in Vila et al. (1997) study, the assumption that mutations occur at a fixed rate, mtDNA is maternally inherited and repair of non-coding regions does not occur, has now been shown to be in question. This is not to infer that molecular sequencing done in the study is wrong, but rather as the science of molecular genetics has become more refined, the presumption that these long-held beliefs were correct has now been shown to be misleading. What is pivotal about Vila and fellow colleagues study, is it focused interest on canine genetics and evolutionary theory. This in turn led to other scientists expanding on the original research which has also encompassed other species as well. I ascertain that this additional knowledge about mtDNA is now reflected in Vila et al. (2001) research of domestic horses. In this study, the researchers do not state that mutations seen in the mitochondria are the result of domestication. What the authors do imply is that the diversity in mtDNA was not due to an ancient domestication event but that it *preceded* domestication.

I propose that as the spontaneous mutations arose in the canid genome, it consequently had an effect on the function of the endocrine system. This belief has been strongly influenced by the work of Belyaev (1978; Belyaev et al. 1981) and Trut (1999), who have studied for over forty years the ramifications of the selection for tame behavior and physiological changes. Belyaev argued that during the course of domestication, behavior not size or reproductive capacity was the key factor that was consistently selected for. Belyaev and Trut proved this theory by selecting foxes for tameness and began a breeding program based upon that trait alone. After only seven years, the researchers not only witnessed distinct behavioral changes but physiological changes as well in some of the foxes. Belyaev called this effect *destabilizing selection* (Belyaev 1978: 307-308). According to Belyaev, if a species is operating under stabilizing selection, the environment is stable, mutations that disrupt the phenotype or ontogeny are eliminated, new variations do not exist, and the unfit are discarded. However with destabilization, the selection affects, directly or indirectly, the systems of neuroendocrine control of ontogenesis. With this type of selection normal patterns of gene activation and inhibition are altered which leads to an increase in the range and rate of hereditary variation. Belyaev asserted that destabilization occurs when new stress factors were added to the environment, such as domestication. Belyaev hypothesized that a balance between neurotransmitters and hormone levels (Trut 1999: 162) regulated behavioral responses. He also reasoned that because mammals from different taxonomic groups shared similar regulatory mechanisms for hormones and neurochemistry, this would explain why domesticated animals have undergone the same basic morphological and physiological changes (Trut 1999: 162).

Belyaev to prove his theory that behavior is related to hormonal changes that regulated gene function, measured changes in the adrenal system, specifically plasma levels of cortiosteriods which regulate an animal's adaptation to stress (Belyaev 1978: 306; Trut 1999: 164). He found that in tame fox females the level of serotonin and its metabolite 5-hydroxyindoleacetic acid was higher than levels measured in wild females (Belyaev 1978: 306). Belyaev asserted since serotonin is known to inhibit some forms of aggression, that the high levels seen in the tame animals was linked to behavioral change. Belyaev also found that after 20 generations of foxes, the females had gradually starting having twice a year heat cycles which differed from the normal wild-type cycle of one reproductive period per year (Crockford 2000b: 14). In addition, the tame foxes began exhibiting neonate type features such as a shortening muzzle, droopy ears, curled tail, unusual color markings, and "dog-like" behavior (Crockford 2000b: 14).

In a later study, Crockford (2000b: 14-15) expanded on Belyaev's original work by hypothesizing that the thyroid hormone may be affecting serotonin levels. According to Crockford, since thyroid hormone induces functioning of growth hormone (GH), melanocycte stimulating hormone (MSH), as well as adrenal steroids, that the behavioral, reproductive and physical differences witnessed in the tame animals was due to influences of the thyroid hormone. Therefore, Crockford suggests that due to the stress of human-dominated environments, wolves that were more stress-tolerant would have been better adapted and would have past this adaptation on to their offspring. She also states that this change could have occurred relatively rapidly (i.e. 200 years) which would explain the lack of "intermediate" forms of canids in the archaeological record. Although Crockford does not provide any controlled studies to support her theory and in this authors opinion other factors contributing from the adrenal system may be the cause rather than the thyroid.

Belyaev and Crockford both provide convincing arguments. Crockford's theory that endocrine changes induced by stress and human encroachment into dog/wolf habitats seems especially plausible. Belyaev's (1978: 306-308) fifty year tameness study on foxes is pivotal in that it clearly demonstrates that when only a behavioral characteristic is selected for, it causes a multitude of physiological and morphological changes that is typical of all domesticated species. Belyaev stated that these changes were likely due to alterations in the central and peripheral mechanisms of the neuro-endocrine control of ontogeny, which affect the timing and amount of gene expression.

The farm-fox experiment is especially important in the development of domestication theories because of its depth and meticulous attention to detail. Belyaev's research clearly shows that tame behavior, or rather tolerance to human contact, can have a profound affect by rapidly modifying skeletal structure as well as hormonal mechanisms within a few generations. Therefore, this author believes that naturally occurring behavioral changes that were indirectly influenced by the expansion of human populations caused the morphological changes seen in archaeological remains of canids. These initial changes were not the result of a domestication event and not initiated by human selection until much later when man had converted from a hunter/gatherer to an agricultural existence, as supported by the archaeological record.

Savolainen et al. (2002: 1611) have produced strong evidence that the large genetic variation of dog haplotypes seen in East Asia is indicative that dogs originated in that geographic area. According to the researches clade A included three wolf haplotypes found in China and Mongolia whereas clade B contained wolf haplotypes seen in East Europe and one in Afghanistan. Therefore the researchers believed that clade A had origins in East Asia and clade B in Europe or Southwest Asia. They also found that 71.3% dogs had haplotype clade A with clade A represented in all geographic areas. When the researchers compared haplotypes, they found greater diversity in haplotype numbers in East Asia, with 44 types identified and 30 being unique to that region.

Savolainen et al. (2002: 1612) also reported that more than 95% of all sequences in dogs belonged to the three phylogenetic clades A, B and C, which was interpreted to e representative of an origin from a common gene pool. The complexity of clade A with its numerous subsets of haplotypes, which is in direct contrast to the simplistic star-like pattern of clade B and C, would indicate that several wolf haplotypes were involved in producing clade A. Additionally the authors found that the genetic distance from the central core to the subclusters was much greater than those seen in clades B and C which would indicate that clade A is much older.

What is both unique and outstanding in Savolainen and colleagues approach to their molecular research is that they recognize the importance of the archaeological record.

Rather than ignore fossil evidence, they incorporate the archaeological history when attempting to interpret the complex molecular results, which on their own could have multiple conclusions, all perfectly plausible. Yet the researchers acknowledge that to comprehensively analyze the mitochondrial DNA method used for evolutionary studies, it is essential to integrate the observations taken from the fossil record in order to be able to generate an accurate picture of evolution. Savolainen and researchers found that the molecular data could be analyzed by two possible methods. One method assumed a single origin from wolf, and when calculated, it generated a date of 41,000 ± 4,000 years for dog origins. However when they recalculated data assuming several origins, an averaged date of approximately 15,000 years was generated. In order to determine which date was the most possible, they examined the evidence gleaned from the archaeological record and concluded that the 15,000-year date was more plausible.

The work of Savolainen and fellow researchers has been exemplary in that it has fill-in some important gaps in the archaeological record. The authors pointed out that one failure of the archaeological record is that it cannot define the number of geographical origins or the location of when or where a species originated. However molecular genetics can provide meaningful data to indicate where speciation events most likely occurred. In this study, the researchers recognized that the East Asia region represented a large genetic reservoir of numerous unique haplotypes and nucleotide diversity that is expected in an ancestral population. They also surmised that the haplotypes seen in Europe and Southwest Asia were derived from a subset of the East Asian types.

I am in agreement with Savolainen et al. that the genetic diversity seen in East Asia is typical of a founding population. The research thoroughly documents the haplotype substitutions seen in dogs from Europe, Asia, Africa, and Arctic America as well as Eurasian wolves and is convincing in its conclusion that the beginnings of dogs began with multiple lines of wolves originating in East Asia. The geographic distribution of the haplotypes clearly shows that East Asian wolves provided the genetic structure for canines from which types unique to the West later developed.

In summary, the molecular data has been interpreted that around 15,000-135,000 years ago, a change in the mtDNA sequence indicates that dog separated from wolves. The researchers surmise that this wolf-to-dog transformation is evidence of domestication. Other researchers hypothesize that humans managed to capture and tame wolves to make them useful for hunting and as companions. From these tamed wolves the researchers imply that, early man selectively bred them and eventually developed them into the domesticated dogs we see today. I propose however, an alternate wolf/dog domestication model. I suggest that the mutations seen in the sequencing data are not evidence of domestication, but rather evidence of natural evolutionary divergence that occurred without human intervention. During the course of this evolution a separate species of canid, *Canis familiaris,* developed. I suggest that dogs were dogs long before man even considered the possibility of exploiting these animals through selective breeding to produce an animal with characteristics tailored to human needs.

This hypothesis has been suggested in part by Wayne and Ostrander (1999), and hypothesized by Koler-Matznick (2002, 2003b, 2003c) based upon her work studying the behavior of New Guinea singing dogs. Koler-Matznick has emphasized the importance of examining not only behavioral characteristics of wolves that would make them difficult to integrate into human culture, but has also suggested that some type of canine other than wolf were the first domestic dog. According to Koler-Matznick this canid was a medium-sized generalist species of canid, a "wild *Canis familiaris*" that possibly evolved from an extinct ancestor that was the progenitor to both the wolf and dog. Koler-Matznick's proposal is an interesting hypothesis, which can not be rejected. However in light of the current findings of the molecular genetics which indicates that wolves and dogs are closely linked, this author asserts that the data currently supports a wolf ancestry of dogs. This author proposes that as early humans encroached into wolf habitats, this had an influence on the balance of hormonal levels and neurochemistry that altered the rate of hereditary variation. This resulted in the morphological changes seen in the archaeological remains of canids, such as the retention of neonate features that is typically seen in all domesticated animals. I further propose that these new transitional animals were smaller and less aggressive, and posed less danger to humans. As these animals scavenged around camps, some of these early canids produced offspring better adaptive to stress and having reduced fear/flight behavior. These animals, more tolerant of humans may have developed a commensal relationship with humans; scavenging the human sites and preying upon other species that were attracted to the refuse accumulating around human occupation sites. These animals could be some of the first identified in the archaeological record at around 14,000 yrs BP. Eventually this new type of canine began to exhibit extreme morphological changes making them easier to recognize as dogs in the fossil record. I further suggest that "true" domestication of dogs occurred between 12,000-10,000 yrs BP when selection pressure from humans developed a modified animal distinguishable from its wild-type ancestor.

It has also been suggested that the Indian wolf, *Canis lupus pallipes,* was possibly the wolf that was initially tamed since it is smaller in size and is believed to lack heightened aggressive behavior that is typically seen in gray wolves or timber wolves. Although the child-grabbing behavior seen in present day clearly indicates that these animals do have aggressive tendencies, it does provide support that wolves can live in close proximity to humans. These animals provide a model that plainly shows how a species when faced with changes in its environment from the encroachment of human populations can adapt and develop a less enhanced fear/flight behavior.

Genetic analysis provides scientific evidence of divergence of ancestral forms, it can not however provide evidence of knowing the "intent" of prehistoric people, or how and why certain events occurred. Morey (1994: 338) best sums up domestication theories by stating: "For early domestication, the data required to evaluate scenarios based on human intention are, by definition, unattainable. In other words, models that explain domestication this way can not be empirically challenged, and on this basis alone, they are not scientific models."

This is one of the continuing problems of the "genes vs. morphology" debate. Frequently geneticists equate facts presented in the sequencing of the mtDNA as evidence of domestication. Archaeologists also follow the same path, by viewing morphological changes in the fossil record as evidence of domestication. Both approaches provide an alternate view of domestication that not only stimulates future research but also demonstrates the complexity of domestication models. This seems to be especially true in canine domestication research, perhaps because dogs have become one of the most important facets of our human existence. Based upon the hundreds of different canine breeds seen today, it is hard to imagine that the earliest canines could have evolved naturally. Both geneticists and archaeologists provide valuable insights from the prospective of their respective fields when postulating domestication theories. However, is it possible that there is some form of unintentional bias when hypothesizing about domesticated animals versus non-domesticated species? For instance, when morphological changes are seen in non-domesticated species as evidenced in the fossil record, other circumstances such as climatic changes, dietary adaptations or new ecological niches are frequently suggested as contributing factors that have accelerated such modifications. When such changes are seen in domesticated species however, the general assumption is that humans have selectively bred isolated individuals to produce desirable traits or eliminate undesirable ones, and continued to perpetuate the changes. This tendency may inadvertently influence hypotheses drawn in molecular studies when it is suggested that mutational change may correspond to domestication events. Although both fields of study provide well-documented evidence for their theories, there is an inclination to rely on a particular data set that supports one specific interpretation. This is not unexpected since molecular biologists and archaeologists would naturally be more familiar with research done in their respective fields and would not be as well-versed in theories outside their field of expertise.

Additionally, little attention has been given to behavioral aspects of wolf behavior that would make it highly improbable that prehistoric man would have adopted wild wolves and selectively bred them to be hunting companions. This assumption is questionable given the complexity of wolf social structure and behavior. Wolves are highly efficient predators that are extremely dangerous even under controlled conditions. Wolf hybrids have not been found to be easier to train and still exhibit unpredictable behavior. Can the behavior of modern wolves be a good analogy for primitive wolf behavior? Logically, it can be hypothesized that wolves living 15,000 to 135,000 years ago could have been even more bold and dangerous given that humans posed little or if any threat to them given that he lacked speed and was physically weaker. Even with his primitive weapons it still would have been difficult to defend oneself from a wolf pack if attacked. However an equally plausible hypothesis is that wolves today are more dangerous given hundreds of years of persecution. It is entirely possible that there has been an unintentional selection for ferocity because humans have eliminated those animals that are weaker and less fearful. Neither hypothesis can be categorically rejected. However for the purposes of this study, I have made comparative analogies using present day wolf behavior as a model for prehistoric wolves.

Throughout history there has been documented evidence of the disastrous consequences of supplying food to wild predators. This is especially true of bears, mountain lions, giant cats, and even dingoes, that once they equate humans with food, they loose all their fear of humans and become much more dangerous and impossible to control. Would wolves have been any different? Additionally, wolves and humans competed for the same prey and food resources. As competitive species there would have been no advantage for humans to incorporate wolves into their social structure since they would have been vying for the same food resources.

In studies where wolves have been reportedly socialized, the researchers had to sit passively in an enclosure for days on end until the wolves showed no fear at human movement. But is this truly socialization? Although researchers have found that very young wolf pups can be more easily receptive to human's interaction, it still takes an enormous amount of time to accomplish true socialization. In all cases the socialization aspect is accomplished through restraint, usually by confining the animals in a kennel or pen. However there has been no research that shows that free-ranging wolves can be truly socialized, conditioned to tolerate a human presence within a narrow range of parameters determined by the animal perhaps, but tolerance is not tameness.

Many hypotheses infer that prehistoric humans could adopt and tame wolf pups rather easily and trained like any dog. This assumption may also be in question. In studies done by Hare et al. (2002) and Miklosi et al. (2003) it was clearly demonstrated that socialized wolves failed to respond to human cueing to solve simple tasks. Dogs on the other hand, out-performed wolves in all areas where it required communicative signals from the human. Therefore, there may be some sort of basic cognitive difference between dogs and wolves that makes wolves so difficult to train. From my own personal experience, in all the years that I have been involved in training dogs and participating in dog training classes I have never seen a wolf that was trained to "come", "heel" or "fetch". Even in wolf hybrids, it has been found that the animals can only be trained if the percentage of wolf is extremely low, less than one-third (Hope 1994: 38).

Wolf hybrids are known for having unpredictable behavior, typical of their wild ancestry. Pure wolves would be no less unpredictable or dangerous to their human caregivers. Even in wolves that have been raised by owners sophisticated in wolf behavior and communication, it has been noted that even if the wolves have been around their human caregivers for years, the animals can attack without provocation, especially children. I question if prehistoric humans would have had more control and would have been no less vulnerable to attack.

Therefore I suggest that prehistoric humans did not tame wild wolves that became the precursors to domesticated dogs. Wolf behavior clearly indicates that this would have been unlikely in a free-ranging population. A more probable scenario is that dogs had already evolved into dogs before man considered the possibilities of domestication.

In addressing the data compiled from the archaeological record, I ascertain that the earliest fossil dog finds are questionable in the identification of the animal. The fossils are too fragmentary to be certain that it is a dog or a short-nosed wolf. And it is also questionable that these animals, if dogs, are domesticated or simply refuse from a meal, religious sacrifice or some other unknown association which can not be gleaned from examination of the bones alone. True domesticated species are not seen until 12,000-10,000 years ago and I hypothesize that domesticated dogs also fall within this time period as well.

There are numerous possibilities for future research that would test my hypothesis of dog domestication. First, to determine the accuracy of mtDNA in predicting evolutionary events, comparisons need to be made using nuclear DNA. It could then be determined if the rate of mutation is the same in both mitochondria and nuclear, or if mtDNA has a higher mutation rate, which skews the evolutionary time line. Additionally, it might also be found that once man became involved with domesticating animals that mutations started occurring at a faster rate. If this does occur, it might be determined that evolutionary predictions may be erroneous since it is assumed that mutations occur at a fixed rate and therefore hypotheses of canine domestication based on molecular sequencing may also be inaccurate.

Secondly, another significant area of research would be the analysis of mtDNA extracted from mummified dog remains in Egypt. Comparisons could be done between this ancient DNA and modern breeds in order to determine what the mutation rate actually is. It might be learned that mutations are accumulating at a faster rate, as artificial selection in breeding becomes prevalent. This would add more clarity on the accuracy of using mutations in the mitochondria to determine canine evolutionary history.

Thirdly, another possible area to explore for future research would be to analyze the mtDNA from canine female relatives to test the maternal inheritance of mtDNA. For instance, in some Toy breeds of dogs that live up to 18 years or more, samples could be taken from great grandmother, grandmother, granddaughter and so on, to test the notion if maternal inheritance is accurate. Some male offspring could also be added as well. It might be found that dogs also exhibit heteroplasmy, a condition that has been reported in humans and mice.

Fourth, it would also be of interest to test the fossil remains of some of the earliest suspected dog finds and conduct a comparative analysis to modern samples. Not only would it possible to compare the mutation rates but also determine how different the fossil sequences are from current modern breeds. However, the ancient samples may present some problems given the possibility of contamination. Therefore if future fossil remains are discovered, care must be taken in their handling. Because molecular testing has become an important aspect of archaeology, some samples should be collected on-site and kept isolated from further handling. All remains should be handled with gloves, and in some cases the excavators should wear facemasks, to insure that contaminant DNA is not transferred.

Fifth, a study done using the same methods as Belyaev and Trut's fox study may prove to be insightful if conducted on the African wild dog (*Lycaon pictus*). Previous studies done on African wild dogs have shown that the wild dogs have been excellent subjects for studies of cooperation, hunting behavior, social behavior and interspecfic competition (Creel and Creel 2002). Although the African wild dog is neither a dog nor a member of the *Canis* family, it is a wolf-like carnivore with the same number of chromosomes as the domestic dog and similar neuroanatomy. A study done on captive animals specifically selected for tame behavior would be enlightening if it showed the same results as Belyaev's fox research.

Finally, given that there have been studies on how postmortem decay adversely affects mtDNA causing mutations in key regions used for evolutionary studies, it would be interesting to test if this is also of true blood. Since most molecular studies on canines use fresh blood, it would be of interest to find out how quickly blood degrades where mutational changes in the sequence are evident and if mutational changes increase over the period of time from collected to stored, or if lengthy storage contributes to mutation. These studies would have to use a range of samples left at room temperature, refrigerated and frozen that have been stored at a variety of time periods.

In conclusion, I suggest that care must be exercised using the term "domestic" dog. Frequently this term is used as a description of a generic canine when instead; it can be interpreted as a description of an event. Domestication infers a particular action taken by humans, basically that an animal's breeding is under human control. It is a term that is used too informally and should only be used to describe an intentional action taken by ancient people. I believe that the earliest fossil remains of dogs were not representative of domestication. Rather they were the products of evolution driven by natural selection and were not truly domesticated until the late Pleistocene and early Holocene. This view does not infer knowing the intentions of prehistoric people, which can not be scientifically proven. However I do conclude that the fossil evidence can not simply be ignored in light of the new molecular research. It is also important that in the future geneticists should not use anthropological terms to describe molecular events. Future molecular research should not only include scholars from genetics but archaeology as well, to get a more complete view of evolution.

Literature Cited

Acland GM, Blanton SH, Hershfield B, Aguirre GD. 1994. XLPRA: A Canine Retinal Degeneration Inherited as an X-linked Trait. *Am J Med Genet* 52: 27-33.

Aquirre GD, Ray K, Acland GM. 1999. Overview of the International Workshop on Canine Genetics. *J Heredity* 90 (1): 1-2.

Archer J. 1997. Why Do People Love Their Pets? *Evol Human Behav* 18:237-259.

Audic S, Bérand-Columb E. 1997. Ancient DNA is Thirteen Years Old. *Nat Biotech* 15:855-858.

Avise JC. 1989. A Role for Molecular Genetics in the Recognition and Conservation of Endangered Species. *Trends in Ecology and Evolution* 4: 279-281.

Avise JC, Neigel JE, Arnold J. 1984. Demographic Influences on Mitochondrial DNA Lineage Survivorship in Animal Populations. *J Mol Evol* 20: 99-105.

Ballard WB, Ayers LA, Gardner CL, Foster JW.1991. Den Site Activity Patterns of Gray Wolves, *Canis lupus* in South Central Alaska. *Can Field-Nat* 105: 497-504.

Ballard WB, Ayers LA, Krausman PR, Reed DJ, Faney SG.1997. Ecology of Wolves in Relation to a Migratory Caribou Herd in Northwest Alaska. *Widl Monogr* 135: 1-47.

Bazaliiskiy VI, Savelyev NA. 2003. The Wolf of Barkal: The "Lokomotiv" Early Neolithic Cemetery in Siberia. *Antiquity* 77 (295): 20-30.

Beebe BF. 1980. A Domestic Dog (*Canis familiaris linn.*) of Probable Pleistocene Age From Old Crow, Yukon Territory, Canada. *Canadian J Archaeology* 4: 161-168.

Bekoff M. 1977. Social Communication in Canids: Evidence for the Evolution of a Stereotyped Mammalians Display. *Science* 197: 1097-1099.

Belyaev DK. 1978. Destablizing Selection as a Factor in Domestication. *J Heredity* 70:301-308.

Belyaev DK, Ruvinsky AO, Trut LN. 1981. Inherited Activation-Inactivation of the Star Gene in Foxes. *J Heredity* 72: 267-274.

Benecke N. 1987. Studies on Early Dog Remains From Northern Europe. *J Archaeol Sci* 14: 31-49.

Bergman C. 1847. Uber Die Verhaltnisse Der Narmekonomie Der Thiere Zu Ihrer Grosse. *Gottingen Studien* 3:595-708.

Bökönyi S. 1969. Archaeological Problems and Methods of Recognizing Animal Domestication. In: P.J. Ucko and G. Dimbleby, (editors.) *Domestication and Exploitation of Plants and Animals*. London: Duckworth. pp. 219-229.

Bökönyi S. 1975. Vlasac: An Early Site of Dog Domestication. In: A.T. Clason (editor) *Archaeozoological Studies*. Amsterdam: North Holland Publishing Company. pp. 167-178.

Boyer R. 2002. *Concepts of Biochemistry*. Second Edition. M. Boggs and J. Huber (editors.) Pacific Grove, CA: Brooks/Cole Publishing Company.

Breen M, Langford CF, Dickens HF, Holmes NG, Carter NP, Thomas R, Suter N, Binns MM. 1998.Canine FISH Cytogenics. *Canine Practice* 23 (1): 37.

Brisbin Jr. IL. 1976 The Domestication of the Dog. *Amer Kennel Club Gazette* 93:22-27.

Brisbin Jr. IL, Risch TS. 1997. Primitive Dogs, Their Ecology and Behavior: Conservation Concerns of Unique Opportunities to Study the Early Development of the Human – Canine Bond. *JAVMA* 210 (8): 1122-1126.

Brothwell DR. 1975. Salvaging the Term "Domestication" for Certain Types of Man-Animal Relationships: The Possible Value of an Eight-Point Scoring System. *J Archaeol Sci* 2:397-400.

Brown WM, George Jr. M, Wilson AC. 1979. Rapid Evolution of Animal Mitochondrial DNA. *Proc Natl Acad Sci USA* 76: 1967-1971.

Brownlow CA. 1996. Molecular Taxonomy and the Conservation of the Red Wolf and Other Endangered Carnivores. *Conserv Biol* 10 (2): 390-396.

Carr SM, Hughes GA. 1993. Direction of Introgressive Hybridization Between Species of North American Deer (*Odocoileus*) as Inferred From Mitochondrial-Cytochrome-B Sequence. *J Mamm* 74 (2):331-342.

Clark KM. 1995. The Later Prehistoric and Protohistoric Dog: The Emergence of Canine Diversity. *Archaeozoological* 7: 9-32.

Clark KM. 1996. Neolithic Dogs: A Reappraisal Based on Evidence From the Remains of a Large Canid Deposited in a Ritual Feature. *Inter J Osteoarchaeol* 6: 211-219.

Clark KM. 2000. Dogged Persistence: The Phenomenon of Canine Skeletal Uniformity in British Prehistory. In: S.J. Crockford, (editor.) *Dogs Through Time: An Archaeological Perspective*. Oxford: BAR Publishing, BAR International Series 889. pp. 163-180.

Chaix L. 2000. A Preboreal Dog From the Northern Alps (Savoie, France) In: S.J. Crockford, (editor.) *Dogs Through Time: An Archaeological Perspective*. Oxford: BAR Publishing, BAR International Series 889. pp. 49-59.

Clayton DA. 2000. Transcription and Replication of Mitochondrial DNA. *Human Reprod* 15: Suppl 2: 11-17.

Clutton-Brock J. 1995. Origins of the Dog: Domestication and Early History. In: J. Serpell, (editor) *The Domestic Dog, its Evolution, Behavior and Interactions with People*. Cambridge: Cambridge University Press. pp. 7-20.

Clutton-Brock J, Noe-Nygaard N. 1990. New Osteological and C-Isotope Evidence on Mesolithic Dogs: Companions to Hunters and Fishers at Star Carr, Seamen Carr and Kongemose. *J Archaeol Science* 17:643-653.

Cole SR, Bauerstock PR, Green B. 1977. Lack of Genetic Differentiation Between Domestic Dogs and Dingoes at a Further 16 Loci. *Aust J Exp Biol Med Sci* 55: (2): 229-232.

Coppinger R, Schneider R. 1995. Evolution of Working Dogs. In: J. Serpell, (editor.) *The Domestic Dog, its Evolution, Behavior and Interactions with People.* Cambridge: Cambridge University Press. pp. 21-47.

Corbett LK. 1995. *The Dingo in Australia and Asia.* Sydney: University of New South Wales Press.

Cordy-Collins A. 1994. An Unshaggy Dog History. *Nat Hist* 2:34-40.

Creel S, Creel NM. 2002. *The African Wild Dog: Behavior, Ecology, and Conservation.* Princeton and Oxford: Princeton University Press.

Crockford SY. 2000a. A Commentary on Dog Evolution: Regional Variation, Breed Development and Hybridization With Wolves. In: S.J. Crockford, (editor). *Dogs Through Time: An Archaeological Perspective.* Oxford: BAR Publishing, BAR International Series 889. pp. 295-312.

Crockford SY. 2000b. A Role for Thyroid Hormone Physiology in Domestication. In: S.J. Crockford, (editor). *Dogs Through Time: An Archaeological Perspective.* Oxford: BAR Publishing, BAR International Series 889. pp. 11-20.

Cronin MA, Renecher L, Pierson BJ, Patton JC. 1995. Genetic Variation in Domestic Reindeer and Wild Caribou in Alaska. *Anim Genet* 26:427-434.

Cummings JM, Wakayama T, Yanagimachi R. 1997. Fate of Microinjected Sperm Components in the Moose Oocyte and Embryo. *Zygote* 6: 213 – 222.

Darwin C. 1859. *Origin of Species* (First Ed.). London: John Murray.

Darwin C. 1860. *On the Origin of Species by Means of Natural Selection, or the Preservation of Favoured Races in the Struggle for Life.* New York: Appleton.

Darwin C. 1871. *The Descent of Man and Selection in Relation to Sex.* London: Murray.

Davis SJM. 1981. The Effects of Temperature Change and Domestication on Body Size of Late Pleistocene to Holocene Mammals in Israel. *Paleobiology* 7: 101-114.

Davis SJM, Valla FR. 1978. Evidence for Domestication of the Dog 12,000 Years Ago in the Natufran of Israel. *Nature* 276: 608-610.

Dayan T. 1994 .Early Domesticated Dogs of the Near East. *J Archaeol Sci* 21: 633-640.

Dayan T, Galili E. 2000. A Preliminary Look at Some New Domesticated Dogs From Submerged Neolithic Sites off the Carmel Coast. In: S.J. Crockford, (editor.) *Dogs Through Time: An Archaeological Perspective.* Oxford: BAR Publishing, BAR International Series 889. pp. 29-33.

Dayan T, Simberloff D, Tchernor E, Yom-Tov Y. 1991. Calibrating the Paleothermometer: Climate Communities, and the Evolution of Size. *Paleobiology* 17 (2) 189-199.

Dayan T, Simberloff D, Tchernor E, Yom-Tov Y. 1992a. Canine Carnassials: Character Displacement in Wolves, Jackals and Foxes of Israel. *Biol J Linnean Soc* 45: 315-331.

Dayan T, Tchernor E, Simberloff D, Yom-Tov Y. 1992b. Tooth Size: Function and Coevalution in Carnivore Guilds. In: *Structure, Function and Evolution of Teeth.* London: Freud Publishing House. pp. 215-222.

Dayton L. 2003. On the Trail of the First Dingo. *Science* 302: 555-556.

Degerbøl M. 1961. On a Find of a Preboreal Domestic Dog (*Canis familiaris L.*) From Star Carr, Yorkshire, With Remarks on Other Mesolithic Dogs. *Prehistoric Society Proceedings.* London. 27: 35-55.

Dennis C. 2002. A Forage in the Junkyard. *Nature* 420: 458-459.

Deville P, Van Leeuwen IS, Voesten A, Rutteman GR, Vos JH, Cornelisse CJ. 1994. The Canine p53 Gene is Subject to Somatic Mutations in the Thyroid Carcinoma. *Anticancer Res* 14: 2039-2046.

Diamond J. 2002. Evolution, Consequences and Future of Plant and Animal Domestication. *Nature* 418: 700-707.

Dickson DB, Carlson DL. 2004. Hominid Evolution in the Pliocene and Pleistocene Epochs. In: *Ancient Preludes.* Third Edition. Peosta, Iowa: Eddie Bowers Publishing Co. pp. 13-32.

Dowling TE, DeMarais BD. 1993. Evolutionary Significance of Introgressive Hybridization in Cyprinid Fishes. *Nature* 362: 444-446.

Dowling TE, DeMarais BD, Minckley WL, Douglas ME, Marsh PC. 1992. Use of Genetic Characters in Conservation Biology. *Conserv Biol* 6: 7-8.

Duke University Medical Center. 2001. *Kangaroo, Platypus Are Not Related After All; Duke Scientists Refute Current Molecular Method of Classifying Mammals.* Science Daily. http://www.mc.duke.edu/

Enloe J. 2001. Magdalenian. In: P.N. Peregrine and M. Ember, (editors.) *Encyclopedia of Prehistory. Volume 4: Europe.* New York: Kluwer Academic/ Plenum Publishers. pp. 198-209.

Evans JP, Brinkhous KM, Brayer GD, Reisner HM, High KA. 1989. Canine Hemophilla B Resulting From a Post Mutation With Unusual Consequences. *Proc Natl Acad Sci USA* 86: 10095-10099.

Fentress JC. 1967. Observations on the Behavioral Development of a Hand-Reared Male Timber Wolf. *Am Zoologist* 7:339-351.

Fox MW. 1965. *Canine Behavior.* Charles W. Thomas (editor.) Springfield, Ill: Thomas.

Fox MW. 1969. The Anatomy of Aggression and its Ritualization in *Canidae:* A Developmental and Comparative Study. *Behaviour* 35: 242-258.

Fox MW. 1970. A Comparative Study of the Development of Facial Expressions in Canids, Wolf, Coyote and Foxes. *Behaviour* 36: 49-73.

Fox MW. 1972. Behavior of Wolves and Dogs. *Auburn Veterinarian* 28 (2): 59-61.

Frank H. 1980. Evolution of Canine Information Processing Under Conditions of Natural and Artificial Selection. *Z Tierpsychol* 53: 389-399.

Frank H, Frank MG. 1982a. On the Effects of Domestication on Canine Social Development and Behavior. *Appl Anim Ethology* 8: 507-525.

Frank H, Frank MG. 1982b. Comparison of Problem – Solving Performance in Six-Week-Old Wolves and Dogs. *Anim Behav* 30: 95-98.

Frank H, Frank MG. 1983. Inhibition Training in Wolves and Dogs. *Behav Processes* 8: 363-377.

Frank H, Frank MG. 1984. Information Processing in Wolves and Dogs. *Acta Zool Fennica* 171: 225-228.

Fuller TK. 1989. Denning Behavior of Wolves in North Central Minnesota. *Am Mid Nat* 121: 184-188.

Gergits WF, Casna NJ. 1998. DNA Profile Testing of Vizslas: Breed Purity and Registry Identifications. *Canine Practice* 23 (1): 36-37.

Gibbons A. 1998. Calibrating the Mitochondrial Clock. *Science* 279:28-29.

Gilbert T P, Willerslev E, Hansen AJ, Barnes I, Rudbeck L, Lynnerup N, Cooper A. 2003. Distributing Patterns of Postmortem Damage in Human Mitochondrial DNA. *Am J Hum Genet* 72: 32-47.

Girman DJ, Vila C, Geffen E, Creel S, Mills MGL, McNutt JW, Ginsberg J, Kat PW, Mamiya KH, Wayne RK. 2001. Patterns of Population Subdivision, Gene Flow and Genetic Variability in the African Wild Dog (*Lycan pictus*). *Mol Ecology* 10: 1703-1723.

Gollan K. 1980. *Prehistoric Dingo*. Ph.D. Thesis. Australian National University, Canberra.

Gordon D, Corwin MB, Mellersh CS, Ostrander EA, Ott J. 2003. Establishing Appropriate Genome – Wide Significance Levels for Canine Linkage Analysis. *J Heredity* 94 (1): 1-7.

Gottelli D, Sillero-Zubiri C, Applebaum GD, Roy MS, Girman DJ, Garcia-Moreno J, Ostrander EA, Wayne RK. 1994. Molecular Genetics of the Most Endangered Canid: The Ethiopian Wolf *Canis simensis*. *Molecular Ecology* 3:301-312.

Gray AP. 1954. *Mammalian Hybrids*. Bucks, UK: Farnham Royal.

Gray MW, Burger G, Lang BF. 1999 Mitochondrial Evolution. *Science* 283: 1476 – 1481.

Gupta PK, Balyan HS, Sharma PC, Ramesh R. 1996. Microsatellites in Plants: A New Class of Molecular Markers. *Current Science* 70 (1): 45-54.

Gyllensten U, Wharton D, Josefsson A, Wilson AC. 1991. Paternal Inheritance of Mitochondrial DNA in Mice. *Nature* 352:255-257.

Haag WG. 1970. Dog Remains From Hogup Cave. *Univ. Utah Anthrop. Papers.* 84: 273-274.

Handley BM. 2000. Preliminary Results in Determining Dog Types From Prehistoric Sites in the Northeastern United States. In: S.J. Crockford, (editor.) *Dogs Through Time: An Archaeological Perspective.* Oxford: BAR Publishing, BAR International Series 889. pp. 205-214.

Harcourt RA. 1974. The Dog in Prehistoric and Early Historic Britain. *J Archaeol Sci* 1: 151-175.

Hare B, Brown M, Williamson C, Tomasello M. 2002. The Domestication of Social Cognition in Dogs. *Science* 298: 1634-1636.

Harrison DL. 1973. Some Comparative Features of the Skull of Wolves. (*Canis lupus linn.*) and Pariah Dogs (*Canis familiaris linn.*) From the Arabian Peninsula and the Neighboring Lands. *Bonner Zodogische Beiträge* 24 (3): 185-191.

Higham CFW, Kijngam A, Manly BFJ. 1980. In Analysis of Prehistoric Canid Remains From Thailand. *J Archaeol Sci* 7: 149-165.

Hodges S. 2002. T*he Pleistocene: Dog Domestication* http://www.powow.com/sandyhodges/paleo/dog.html.

Hofreiter M, Sere D, Pioneer HAN, Ouch M, Pääbo S. 2001. Ancient DNA. *Nature* 2:353-359.

Hope J. 1994. Wolves and Wolf Hybrids as Pets are Big Business – But a Bad Idea. *Smithsonian* 25 (3): 34-45.

Iljin NA. 1941. Wolf-Dog Genetics. J Genet 42: 359-435.

Ishiguro N, Okumura N, Matsui A, Shigehara N. 2000. Molecular Genetic Analysis of Ancient Japanese Dogs. In: S.J. Crockford, (editor.) *Dogs Through Time: An Archaeological Perspective.* Oxford: BAR Publishing, BAR International Series 889. pp. 287-292.

Janke A, Xu X, Arnason U. 1997. The Complete Mitochondrial Genome of the Wallaroo (*Macropus robustus*) and the Phylogenetic Relationship Among Monothematic, Marsupial, and Eutheria. *Proc Natl Acad Sci USA* 94:1276-1281.

Jenks SM, Wayne RK. 1992. Problems and Policy for Species Threatened by Hybridization: The Red Wolf As a Case Study. In: D.R. McCullogh and R.H. Barrett, (editors.) *Wildlife 2001*. New York: Elsevier Applied Science. pp. 237-251.

Jezyk PF, Felsburg PJ, Haskins ME, Patterson DF. 1989. X-Linked Severe Combined Immunodeficiency in the Dog. *Clin Immunol Immunopathol* 52: 173-189.

Kettlewell B. 1973. *The Evolution of Melanism: The Study of a Recurring Necessity, With Special Reference to Industrial Melanism in the* Lepidoptera. Oxford: Clarendon Press.

Killian JK, Buckley TR, Stewart N, Munday BL, Jirtle RL. 2001. Marsupial and Etherians Reunited: Genetic Evidence for the Theria Hypothesis of Mammalian Evolution. *Mammalian Genome* 12:513-517.

Kleiman DG. 1967. Some Aspects of Social Behavior in the Canidae. *Am Zoologist* 7: 365-372.

Koler-Matznick J. 2002. The Origin of the Dog Revisited. *Anthrozoös* 15: 98-118.

Koler-Matznick J. 2003a. *The New Guinea Singing Dog Conservation Society.* http://www.rarebreed.com/breeds/ngsd_club.html.

Koler-Matznick J. 2003b. Personal communication: Authors residence, College Station, TX.

Koler-Matznick J. 2003c. An Updated Description of the New Guinea Singing Dog *Canis Hallstromi Troughton* 1957. *J Zoology*, London 261:1-10.

Koop BF, Crockford SJ. 2000. Ancient DNA Evidence of a Separate Origin for North American Indigenous Dogs. In: Crockford SJ, (editor.) *Dogs Through Time: An Archaeological Perspective.* Oxford: BAR Publishing, BAR International Series 889, 2000. pp. 271-284.

Krings M, Stone A, Schmitz RW, Krainitzki H, Stoneking M, Pääbo S. 1997. Neanderthal DNA Sequence and the Origin of Modern Humans. *Cell* 90:19-30.

Langford CF, Breen M, Dickins HF, Holmes NG, Binns MM, Carter NP. 1998. Chromosome Paints and Their Uses. *Canine Practice* 23 (1): 38.

Lawrence B. 1967. Early Domestication of Dogs. *Zeitschrift Für Säugetierkunde* 32: (1) 44-59.

Lawrence B. 1968. Antiquity of Large Dogs in North America. TEBIWA. *The Journal of the Idaho State University Museum.* 11 (2): 43-49.

Lawrence B, Bossert WH. 1967. Multiple Character Analysis of *Canis lupus, latrans,* and *familiaris*, With a Discussion of Their Relationships of *Canis niger. Am Zoologist* 7: 223-232.

Lawrence B, Bossert WH. 1969. The Cranial Evidence for Hybridization in New England *Canis breviora. Museum of Comparative Zoology* 330: 1-13.

Lawrence B, Bossert WH. 1975. Relationships of North American *Canis* Shown by a Multiple Character Analysis of Selected Populations. In: Fox MW, (editor.) *The Wild Canids: Their Systematics, Behavioral Ecology and Evolution.* New York: Van Norstrand Reinhold. pp. 73-86.

Lawrence B, Reed CA. 1983. The Dogs of Jarmo. In: Braidwood LS, Braidwood RJ, Howe B, Reed CA, Watson PJ, (editors.) *Prehistoric Archeology Along the Zagros Flanks.* Chicago: University of Chicago Oriental Institute. pp. 485-489.

Leach HM. 2003. Human Domestication Reconsidered. *Curr Anthrop* 44 (3): 349-368.

Lehman N, Wayne RK. 1991. Analysis of Coyote Mitochondrial DNA Genotype Frequencies: Estimation of the Effective Number of Alleles. *Genetics* 128: 405-416.

Leonard JA, Wayne RK, Wheeler J, Valdez R, Guillen S, Vila C. 2002. Ancient DNA Evidence for Old World Origin of New World Dogs. *Science* 298: 1613-1616.

Lewin B. 2000. *Genes VII.* New York: Oxford University Press, Inc.

Lillios K. 2001. European Megalithic: Western European Late Neolithic, Western European pre-Baker Chalcolithic, Western European pre-Beaker Eneolithic, Western European pre-Beaker Copper Age. In: Peregrine PN, Ember M, (editors.) *Encyclopedia of Prehistory. Volume 4: Europe.* New York: Kluwer Academic/ Plenum Publishers. pp. 157-184.

Lin L, Faraco J, Li R, Kadotani, Rogers HW, Lin X, Qui X, de Jong PJ, Nishino S, Mignot E. 1999. The Sleep Disorder Canine Narcolepsy is Caused by a Mutation in the Hypocretin (Orexin) Receptor 2 Gene. *Cell* 98: 365-376.

Lingaas F, Aarskavg T, Sundgren PE. 1998. Within and Between Genetic Variation in 16 Dog Breeds. *Canine Practice* 23 (1): 37.

Lorenz K. 1954. Man Meets Dog. London: Methuen.

MacEwer EG. 1990. Spontaneous Tumors in Dogs and Cats. Models for the Study of Cancer Biology and Treatment. *Cancer Matastasis.* 9: 125-126.

Manaserian NH, Antonian L. 2000. Dogs of Armenia. In: Crockford SJ, (editor.) *Dogs Through Time: An Archaeological Perspective.* Oxford: BAR Publishing, BAR International Series 889. pp. 227-234.

Manwell C, Baker CMA. 1984. Domestication of the Dog: Hunter, Food, Bed-Warmer, or Emotional Object. *J An Breeding and Genet* 101 (4): 241-256.

McCormick F. 1985/6. Faunal Remains From Prehistoric Irish Burials. J Irish Archaeol 3: 37-46.

McKern SS, McKern TW. 1974. *Living Prehistory: An Introduction to Physical Anthropology and Archaeology.* Menlo Park, CA: Cummings Publishing Co.

McMillan RB. 1970. Early Canid Burial From the Western Ozark Highland. *Science* 167: 1246-1247.

Meadows RH. 2000. The Contributions of Barbara Lawrence to the Study of Dogs With a Comprehensive Listing of Her Measurement Definitions. In: Crockford SJ, (editor.) *Dogs Through Time: An Archaeological Perspective.* Oxford: BAR Publishing, BAR International Series 889. pp. 35-48.

Mech LD. 1970. *The Wolf.* New York: Doubleday Publishing Co.

Mech LD. 1988. *The Arctic Wolf: Living With the Pack.* Stillwater, MN:Voyageur Press.

Mech LD. 1996. Wolves and "Child Lifting" in India. *International Wolf:* 6(4): 16.

Mech LD. 1998. "Who's Afraid of the Big Bad Wolf?" Revisited. *International Wolf:* 8 (1): 8-11.

Mech LD, Wolfe P, Packard JM. 1999. The Role of Regurgitation in Food Transfer Within an Arctic Pack of Wolves. *Can J Zool* 77: 1192-1195.

Mech LD, Adams LG, Meier TJ, Burch, JW, Dale BW. 1998. *The Wolves of Denali.* Minneapolis: University of Minnesota Press.

Mellersh CS, Ostrander EA. 1997. The Canine Genome. *Adv Veter Med* 40:191-215.

Mellersh CS, Langston AA, Acland GM, Fleming MA, Ray K, Weigand NA, Francisco LV, Gibbs M, Aguirre GD, Ostrander EA. 1998. The Evolving Canine Map. *Canine Practice* 23 (1): 38.

Miklosi A, Kubinyi E, Topal J, Gacsi M, Viranyi Z, Csanyi V. 2003. A Simple Reason for a Big Difference: Wolves Do Not Look Back at Humans But Dogs Do. *Curr Biol* 13: 763-766.

Møhl J. 1986. Dog Remains From a Paleoeskimo Settlement in West Greenland. *Arctic Anthrop* 23 (1&2): 81-89.

Morey DF. 1992. Size, Shape and Development in the Evolution of the Domestic Dog. *J Archaeol Sci* 19:181-204.

Morey DF. 1994. The Early Evolution of the Domestic Dog. *Amer Scient* 82: 336-347.

Morey DF, Wiant MD. 1992. Early Holocene Domestic Dog Burials From the North American Midwest. *Curr Anthrop* 33: 224-229.

Morey DF, Saris-Sørensen K. 2002. Paleoeskimo Dogs of the Eastern Artic. *Artic* 55 (1): 44-56.

Mullally LB. 1994. The Dingo: Natural Treasure or Feral Pest? *Dog World,* May : 22-27.

Mullis K. 1990. The Unusual Origin of the Polymerase Chain Reaction. *Sci Am* 263(4):56-65.

Musil R. 2000. Evidence for the Domestication of Wolves in Central European Magdalenian Sites. In: S.J. Crockford SJ, (editor.) *Dogs Through Time: An Archaeological Perspective.* Oxford: BAR Publishing, BAR International Series 889. pp. 21-28.

Newsome AE, Corbett LK. 1982. The Identity of the Dingo II. Hybridization With Domestic Dogs in Captivity and in the Wild. Aust *J Zool* 30: 365-374.

Newsome AE, Corbett LK. 1985. The Identity of the Dingo II. The Incidence of Hybrids and Their Coat Colours in Remote and Settled Regions of Australia. *Aust J Zool* 33: 363-375.

Newsome AE, Corbett LK, Carpenter SM. 1980. The Identity of the Dingo I. Morphological Discriminants of Dingo and Dog Skulls. *Aust J Zool* 28:615-625.

Nobis G. 1979. Der Älteste Haushund Lebte Var 14,000 Jahren. *UMSHAU* 19: 610.

Nobis G. 1981. *Aus Bonn: Das Älteste Haustier Des Menschen. Unterkiefer Eines Hundes Aus Dem Magdaleniengrab Von Bonn-Oberkassel.* Das Reinische Landesmuseum Bonn. pp. 49-50.

Nowak RM. 1979. *North American Quaternary* Canis. Monogr Mus Nat Hist, Univ Kansas No. 6. pp.1-154.

Nowak RM. 1992. The Red Wolf is Not a Hybrid. *Conserv Biol* 6: 593-595.

Nowak RM. 1995. *Hybridization: The Double-Edge Threat.* http://www.canids.org/PUBLICAT/CNDNEWS/hybridiz.html

Nowak RM. 1999. *Walker's Mammals of the World.* Sixth Edition, Vol. 1. Baltimore and London: The John Hopkins University Press. pp. 676-678.

O'Connor TP. 1997. Working at Relationships: Another look at Animal Domestication. *Antiquity* 71: 149-156.

Okumura N, Ishiguro N, Nakano M, Matsui A, Sahara M. 1996. Intra- and Interbreed Genetic Variations of Mitochondrial DNA Major Non-coding Regions in Japanese Native Dog Breeds (*Canis familiaris*). *Anim Genet* 27: 397- 405.

Olsen SJ. 1985. *Origins of the Domestic Dog: The Fossil Record.* Tucson, Arizona: The University of Arizona Press.

Olsen SJ, Olsen JW. 1977. The Chinese Wolf, Ancestor of the New World Dogs. *Science* 197: (4303) 533-535.

Olsen SL. 2000. The Secular and Sacred Roles of Dogs at Botai, North Kazakhstan. In: Crockford SJ, (editor.) *Dogs Through Time: An Archaeological Perspective.* Oxford: BAR Publishing, BAR International Series 889. pp. 71-92.

Onar V, Sözcan, Pazant G. 2001. Skull Typology of Adult Male Kangal Dogs. *Anat Histol Embryol* 30: 41-48.

Ostrander EA, Kruglyak L. 2000. Unleashing the Canine Genome. *Genome Research* 10 (9): 1271 – 1274.

Ostrander EA, Gilbert F,. Patterson DF. 2000. Canine Genetics Comes of Age. *Trends in Science* 16 (3): 117:124.

Ovchinnikov IV, Götherströms A, Romanova GP, Kitaritonov VM, Lidéns K, Goodwin W. 2000. Molecular Analysis of Neanderthal DNA From Northern Caucasus. *Nature* 404: 490-493.

Ovodov ND. 1998. The Ancient Dogs of Siberia. In: *ICAZ Abstracts.* August 23-29, p 223.

Pääbo S. 1989. Ancient DNA: Extraction, Characterization, Molecular Cloning and Enzymatic Amplification. *Proc Natl Acad Sci USA* 86:1939-1943.

Pääbo S, Wison AC. 1991. Miocene DNA Sequences – A Dream Come True? *Curr Biol* 1:45-46.

Packard JM. 2003. Wolf Behavior: Reproductive, Social, and Intelligent. In: Mech LD, Boitani L, (editors.) *Wolves: Behavior, Ecology and Conservation.* Chicago: Chicago University Press.

Packard JM, Mech LD, Ream RR. 1992. Weaning in an Artic Wolf Pack: Behavioral Mechanisms. *Can J Zool* 70: 1269-1275.

Parker HG, Kim LV, Sutter NB, Carlson S, Lorentzen TD, Malek TB, Johnson GS, DeFrance HB, Ostrander EA, Kruglyak L. 2004. Genetic Structure of the Purebred Domestic Dog. *Science* 304: 1160-1164.

Patterson DF. 2000. Companion Animal Medicine in the Age of Medical Genetics. *J Vet Intern Med* 14: 1-9.

Patterson DF. 2001. *Canine Genetic Disease Information System: A Computerized Knowledge Base of Genetic Diseases in the Dog.* St. Louis, Mo: Mosby-Harcourt.

Pennisi E. 2002. A Shaggy Dog History. *Science* 298: 1540-1542.

Petersen-Jones SM, Sohal AK, Sargan DR. 1994. Nucleotide Sequence of the Canine Rod-Opsin-Encoding Gene. *Gene* 143: 281-284.

Phillips MK, Henry VG. 1992. Comments on Red Wolf Taxonomy. *Conserv Biol* 6: 596-599.

Polziehn RO, Strobeck C, Sheraton J, Beech R. 1995. Bovine mtDNA Discovered in North American Bison Population. *Conser Biol* 9:1638-1643.

Reich DE, Wayne RK, Goldstein DB. 1999. Genetic Evidence for a Recent Origin by Hybridization of Red Wolves. *Mol Ecol* 8: 139-144.

Risenhoover KL, Bailey JA. 1988. Growth Rates and Birthing Period of Bighorn Sheep in Low-Elevation Environments in Colorado. *J Mammalogy* 69:592-597.

Roy MS, Geffen E, Smith D, Ostrander EA, Wayne RK. 1994a. Patterns of Differentiation and Hybridization in North American Wolflike Canids, Revealed by

Analysis of Microsatellite Loci. *Mol Biol Evol* 11 (4): 553-570.

Roy MS, Girman DJ, Taylor AC, Wayne RK. 1994b. The Use of Museum Specimens to Reconstruct the Genetic Variability and Relationships of Extinct Populations. *Experientia* 50: 551-557.

Roy MS, Geffen E, Smith D, Wayne RK. 1996. Molecular Genetics of Pre-1940 Red Wolves. *Conserv Biol* 10 (5): 1413-1424.

Russell N. 2002. The Wild Side of Animal Domestication. *Soc & Anim* 10 (3): 287-302.

Russell PJ. 1992. *Genetics*. Third edition. In: Davies G, Dolan K, (editors.) New York: Harper Collins Publishers.

Ryon CJ. 1977. Den Digging and Related Behavior in a Captive Timber Wolf Pack. *J Mammal* 58: 87-89.

Sablin MV, Khlopachev GA. 2002. The Earliest Ice Age Dogs: Evidence From Eliseevichi I. *Current Anthrop* 43 (5): 795-799.

Savolainen P, Zhang Y, Luo J, Lundeberg J, Leitner T. 2002. Genetic Evidence for an East Asian Origin of Domestic Dogs. *Science* 298: 1610-1613.

Schenkel R. 1967. Submission: Its Features and Function in the Wolf and Dog. *Am Zoologist* 7:319-329.

Schwartz M. 1997. *A History of Dogs in the Early Americas.* New Haven: Yale University Press.

Schwartz M, Vessing J. 2002. Paternal Inheritance of Mitochondrial DNA. *N Engl J Med* 347(8): 576-580.

Scott JP. 1954. The Effects of Selection and Domestication Upon the Behavior of the Dog. *J Natl Cancer Instit* 15 (3): 739-758.

Scott JP. 1968. Evolution and Domestication of the Dog. *Evolutionary Biol* 2: 243-275.

Seddon JM, Ellegren H. 2002. MHC Class II Genes in European Wolves: A Comparison With Dogs. *Immunogenetics* 54: 490-500.

Simonsen V. 1976. Electrophoresis Studies on the Blood Proteins of Domestic Dogs and Other *Canidea*. *Hereditas* 82: 7-28.

Shigehara N, Hongo H. 2000. Ancient Remains of Jomon Dogs From Neolithic Sites in Japan. In: Crockford SJ, (editor.) *Dogs Through Time: An Archaeological Perspective.* Oxford: BAR Publishing, BAR International Series 889. pp. 61-67.

Snow CJ. 1967. Some Observations on the Behavioral and Morphological Development of Coyote Pups. *Am Zoologist* 7: 353-355.

Stallings RL, Ford AF, Nelson D, Torney DC, Hildebrand CE, Moyzis R. 1991. Evolution and Distribution of (GT)n Repetitive Sequences in Mammalian Genomes. *Genomics* 10: 807-815.

Stewart D, Baker AJ. 1994. Patterns of Sequence Variations in the Mitochondrial D-loop Region of Shrews. *Mol Biol Evol* 11: 9-21.

Sundqvist A-K, Ellegren H, Olivier M, Vila C. 2001. Y Chromosome Haplotyping in Scandinavian Wolves (*Canis lupus*) Based on Microsatellite Markers. *Mol Ecology* 10: 1959- 1966.

Sutton MD, Holmes NG, Brennan FB, Kelly EP, Duke EJ. 1998. Genetic Analysis of the Irish Greyhound Population for Parentage Determination by Multilocus DNA Fingerprinting, Canine Single Locus Probes and Canine Microsatellite Analysis. *Canine Practice* 23 (1): 37.

Tanabe Y. 1991. The Origin of Japanese Dogs and Their Association With Japanese People. *Zool Sci* 8: 639-651.

Tautz D, Renz M. 1984. Simple Sequences are Ubiquitous Repetitive Components of Eukaryotic Genomes. *Nucleic Acids Res* 12: 4127-4137.

Tchernov E, Horwitz LK. 1991. Body Size Diminution Under Domestication: Unconscious Selection in Primeval Domesticates. *JAnthropol Archaeol* 10: 54-75.

Tchernov E, Valla FF. 1997. Two New Dogs, and Other Natafrain Dogs, From the Southern Levant. *J Archeol Sci* 24: 65-95.

Thiel RP, Hall WH, Schultz RN. 1997. Early Den Digging by Wolves *Canis lupus* in Wisconsin. *Can Field-Nat* 111: 481-482.

Tomasello M, Call J, Hare B. 1998. Five Primate Species Follow the Visual Gaze of Conspecfics. *Anim Behav* 55: 1063 – 1069.

Trut LN. 1999. Early Canid Domestication: The Farm-Fox Experiment. *Am Scien* 87:160-169.

Tsuda K, Kikkawa Y, Yonekawa H, Tanabe Y. 1997. Extensive Interbreeding Occurred Among Multiple Matriarchal Ancestors During the Domestication of Dogs: Evidence From Inter and Intraspecies Polymorphisms in the D - Loop Region of the Mitochondrial DNA Between Dogs and Wolves. *Genes Genet Syst* 72: 229-238.

U.S. Fish and Wildlife Service. 1994. Untitled. *Endangered Species Technical Bulletin* XIX: 7.

Valdez R. 1995. *El Perro Mexicano*. Mexico: Instituto De Investigactiones Antropologicas, Universidad Nacional Autonoma De Mexico.

Vesey-Fitzgerald B. 1957. *The Domestic Dog: An Introduction to its History.* In: Routledge and Kegan Paul, (editors.) London: Routledge and Kegan Paul Limited/ Hazell Watson and Viney Limited.

Vila C, Wayne RK. 1999. Hybridization Between Wolves and Dogs. *Conserv Biol* 13: 195-198.

Vila C, Maldonado JE, Wayne RK. 1999a. Phylogenetic Relationships, Evolution, and Genetic Diversity of the Domestic Dog. *J Heredity* 90 (1): 71-77.

Vila C, Savolainen P, Maldonado JE, Amorin IR, Rice JE, Honeycutt RL, Crandell KA, Lundeberg J, Wayne RK. 1997. Multiple and Ancient Origins of the Domestic Dog. *Science* 276: 1687-1689.

Vila C, Amorim IR,. Leonard JA, Posada D, Castroviejo G, Petrucci-Fonseca F, Crandall KA, Ellegren H, Wayne RK. 1999b. Mitochondrial DNA Phylogeography and Population History of the Grey Wolf *Canis lupus. Mol Ecol* 8: 2089-2103.

Vila C, Walker C, Sundquist A-K, Flagstad Ø, Andersone Z, Casulli A, Kojola I, Valdmana H, Halverson J, Ellegren H. 2003. Combined Use of Maternal, Paternal and Biparental Genetic Markers for the

Identification of Wolf-Dog Hybrids. *Heredity* 90:17-24.

Walker DN, Frison GC. 1982. Studies on Amerindian Dogs, 3: Prehistoric Wolf/Dog Hybrids From the Northwestern Plains. *J Arch Sci* 9:125-172.

Wall WJ, Williamson R, Petrone M, Papaioanne D, Parkin BH. 1993. Variation of Short Tandem Repeats Within and Between Populations. Hum Mol Genet 2:1123-1128.

Warren DM. 2000. Paleopathology of Archaic Period Dogs From the North American Southwest. In: Crockford SJ, (editor.) *Dogs Through Time: An Archaeological Perspective.* Oxford: BAR Publishing, BAR International Series 889. pp. 105-114.

Wayne RK. 1993. Molecular Evolution of the Dog Family. Trends Genet 9: 218-224.

Wayne RK, Jenks SM. 1991. Mitochondrial DNA Analysis Implying Extensive Hybridization of the Endangered Red Wolf *Canis lupus*. *Nature* 351: 565-568.

Wayne RK, Gittleman MJL. 1995. The Problematic Red Wolf. *Scientific Am* 273 (1): 36-39.

Wayne RK, Ostrander EA. 1999. Origin, Genetic Diversity and Genome Structure of the Domestic Dog. *BioEssays* 21: 247-257.

Wayne RK, Nash WG, O'Brien SJ. 1987. Chromosomal Evolution of the *Canidae* I. Species With High Diploid Numbers. *Cytogenet Cell Genet* 44: 123-133.

Wayne RK, Geffen E, German DJ, O'Brien SJ. 1989. Molecular and Biochemical Evolution of the Carnivora. In: Gittleman JAL, (editor.) *Carnivore Behavior, Ecology and Evolution.* Ithaca, New York: Cornell University Press: pp. 465-494.

Wayne RK, Van Valkenburg B, Fuller TK, Kat PW. 1990. Allozyme and Morphologic Differences Among Highly Divergent mtDNA Haplotypes of Black-Backed Jackals. *Mol Evol* 8:161-169.

Wayne RK, Lehman N, Allard MW, Honeycutt RL. 1992. Mitochondrial DNA Variability of the Gray Wolf: Genetic Consequences of Population Decline and Habitat Fragmentation. *Conserv Biol* 6 (4): 559-569.

Wayne RK, Geffen E, German DJ, Kopefli KP, Lou LM, Marshall CR. 1997. Molecular Systematic of the *Canidae. Syst Biol* 46: 622-653.

Webber JL. 1990. Information of Human (dC-dA)n (dG-dt)n Polymorphisms. Genomics 7: 388-396.

Weidensaul S. 1999. Tracking America's First Dog. *Smithsonian* 29 (12): 44-57.

Williams RS. 2002. Another Surprise From the Mitochondrial Genome. *N Engl J Med* 347 (8): 609-612.

Wilson EO. 1998. *Consilience: The Unity of Knowledge.* New York: Alfred A. Knopf.

Wilson PJ, Grewal S, Lawford ID, Heal JNM, Granacki AG, Pennock, Theberge DJB, Theberge MT, Voight DR, Waddell W, Chambers RE, Paquet PC, Gonlet G, Cluff D, White BN. 2000. DNA Profile of the Eastern Canadian Wolf and the Red Wolf Provide Evidence for a Common Evolutionary History Independent of the Gray Wolf. *Can J Zool* 78: 2156-2166.

Wilton AN. 2001. *DNA Methods of Assessing Dingo Purity. Symposium on the Dingo.* Royal Zoo Soc New South Wales. pp. 49-56.

Wilton AN. 2003. *Genetic Variations in the Australian Dingo.*
http://www.bioc.unsw.edu.au/anw/dingo.html.

Wilton AN, Steward DJ, Zafiris K. 1999. Microsatellites Variation in the Australian Dingo. *J Heredity* 90 (1): 108-111.

Withrow SJ, MacEwer EG. 1989. *Clinical Veterinary Oncology.* In: Withrow S, Gregory E (editors.) Philadelphia: J.B. Lippineott Co.

Woolpy JH, Ginsburg BE. 1967. Wolf Socialization: A Study of Temperament in a Wild Social Species. *Am Zoologist* 7: 357-363.

Yates BC. 2000. Use of the Mastoid Region of the Crania of Canids to Distinguish Wolves, Dogs and Wolf/Dog Hybrids. In: Crockford SJ, (editor.) *Dogs Through Time: An Archaeological Perspective.* Oxford: BAR Publishing, BAR International Series 889. pp. 269-270.

Yohe II RM, Pauesic MG. 2000. Early Archaic Domestic Dogs From Western Idaho, USA. In: Crockford SJ, (editor.) *Dogs Through Time: An Archaeological Perspective.* Oxford: BAR Publishing, BAR International Series 889. pp. 93-104.

Young SP, Goldman EA. 1944. *The Wolves of North America.* Washington, D.C.: American Wildlife Institute.

Yuzbasiyan-Gurkan V, Blanton SH, Cao, Ferguson P, Li J, Venton PJ, Brewer GJ. 1997. Linkage of a Microsatellite Marker to the Canine Copper Toxicosis Locus in Bedlington Terriers. *Am J Vet Res* 58:23-27.

Zajc I, Mellersh CS, Sampson J. 1997. Variability of Canine Microsatellites Within and Between Different Dog Breeds. *Mammalian Genome* 8: 182-185.

Zajc I, Mellersh CS, Kelly EP, Sampson J. 1994. A New Method of Paternity Testing for Dogs Based on Microsatellites Sequences. *Vet Records* 135: 545-547.

Zeuner FE. 1963. *A History of Domesticated Animals.* New York: Harper & Row.

Zimen E. 1972. *Wolfe and Königspudel: Vergleichende Verhaltensbeobachtungen.* Piper-Verlog, Munich.

Zimen E. 1987. Ontogeny of Approach and Flight Behavior Towards Humans in Wolves, Poodles and Wolf-Poodle Hybrids. In: Frank H, (editor.) *Man and Wolf, Advances, Issues and Problems in Captive Wolf Research.* The Netherlands: Kluwer Academic Publishers. pp. 275-292.

APPENDIX
The Authors' English Setters

CH. Brasswinds in the Nic of Time (Nickolas); CH. Cimarron Sierra Sondancer, CD (Zeke);
CH. Dudes High Lonesome Sondance, CD (Kaleb)

CH. Brasswinds It Had To Be You (Mikah-Mack); Kaleb; CH. Brynnestone Excaliber Kate (Kate);
Piper (black dog of unknown parentage).

The author's English setters. Great dogs past and present.

www.ingramcontent.com/pod-product-compliance
Lightning Source LLC
Chambersburg PA
CBHW061544010526
44113CB00023B/2794